ARCHIVES

LAURA A. MILLAR

ARCHIVES
Principles and Practices

SECOND EDITION

An imprint of the American Library Association

CHICAGO 2017

First Published in the United Kingdom by Facet Publishing, 2017.
This simultaneous U.S. Edition published by ALA Neal-Shuman,
an imprint of the American Library Association, 2017.

ISBN: 978-0-8389-1606-3

Cover image © Clark Duffy/Fotolia

Contents

Figures and tables

Figures

Tables

Foreword to the first edition

Archives and records are important resources for individuals, organizations and the wider community. They provide evidence of, and information about, the actions of individuals, organizations and communities and the environments in which those actions occurred. They extend and corroborate human and corporate memory and play a critical role in maintaining awareness of how the present is shaped by the past. As Laura Millar notes in this book, they are among the tools we can use to help us understand where we came from and where we are going.

Record keeping has a long history. The Gilgamesh epic, originating almost fifty centuries ago, tells how a woman made marks on a wall to record the number of days that Gilgamesh slept. Notched sticks or bones were often used in preliterate societies as a means of recording work done, livestock counted or hunting expeditions successfully concluded. The invention of writing opened the way to more sophisticated methods of recording actions and events, and also to the possibility of communicating information and sending orders and requests by methods other than word of mouth. Letter-writing has been used for correspondence for over four thousand years, and at a very early stage in its development our ancestors discovered that a letter could serve the dual purpose of communicating a message across space and preserving it across time. In early civilizations in Asia and the eastern Mediterranean, the ability to refer back to what had been said and done in the past without having to rely solely on mental recollection supported the development of new methods of government and commerce and systems to monitor the accountability of individuals or workgroups charged by the ruler with particular tasks. Later came the discovery that writing could be used not merely to record but also to create a range of abstract phenomena such as permissions, obligations, commitments and agreements, and to provide evidence of their creation in the event of disputes.

Written records serve these purposes merely by virtue of their persistence – their ability to endure beyond the cessation of the actions they represent – but for at least four millennia people have seen the benefit of setting them aside and organizing their storage in dedicated repositories. As records proliferated, many such repositories were established in the ancient world. From a present-day perspective, these repositories resembled the archival institutions of a later era, and their accumulated holdings can conveniently be described as *archives*. After the end of the Roman empire, however, literacy levels fell and the practice of keeping written records for administrative and accountability purposes declined. In the early middle ages, archives were something of a rarity. They were sometimes seen as treasures with symbolic value, but their chief role was a legal one: as 'muniments' of an organization they served above all to protect its rights and privileges. Royal governments and ecclesiastical corporations preserved their records to serve their own interests, and guarded them against outsiders. In England, by the era of the Reformation, many new forms of record – including minutes of meetings and account books and registers of various kinds – had come into being, but records continued to be kept only for use within the organizations where they were created. By the seventeenth century, the potential value of records for historical research had become apparent, and historians were occasionally able to gain access to organizational repositories, but most such repositories remained closed to all except officers of the parent body.

A change in attitude came during the French Revolution, when a decision was made to preserve records of the *ancien régime* and open them to all users, including those with what we would now describe as cultural interests. The French *Archives Nationales*, founded in 1789, set an example for numerous other institutions; over the next two hundred years, archival services with an increasingly historical remit were established first by national governments and then, in many countries, by local governments, universities and other organizations. Some continental European countries developed a distinction between *archives courantes*, maintained for business purposes, and *archives historiques* with longer-term cultural objectives; but in English-speaking countries the role of archival institutions came to be seen as primarily cultural. Business perspectives were neglected or turned over to a newly-emergent discipline of records management. Some archival institutions began to take an interest in the papers of families and individuals, and during the twentieth century the range of archival institutions expanded to embrace those that collect archives from a variety of persons and organizations as well as those whose sole function is to maintain the historic archives of their parent body.

At the start of the new millennium, much theoretical writing has been influenced by 'records continuum' concepts that eschew binary divisions between business and cultural purposes of record keeping, but in practice continuum thinking has not wholly dislodged the assumption that business needs for records expire in the short or medium term and that the rationale for long-term preservation is essentially cultural. In contrast to the closed archives characteristic of earlier times, and of some totalitarian regimes today, archival institutions in democratic societies normally aim to have all, or at any rate the larger part, of their holdings freely open to all who wish to use them.

The growth of archival institutions over the last two centuries has been paralleled by the growth of an archival profession. There have been archivists almost as long as there have been records, but only relatively recently have they begun to perceive themselves as professionals. It is open to question whether archival work has been fully professionalized, but archivists have certainly moved far in this direction, introducing formal qualifications, codes of ethics and many of the other accompaniments of a profession. Nevertheless, there is ample scope for members of the wider community to become involved in archival work, not only as users but also as champions of archives and as active contributors to the archival mission. Although written primarily for practitioners and students, this book will be relevant to anyone with an interest in archives and records.

Latterly, the discipline has experienced rapid changes, not least as a result of increasing quantities of records and ongoing technological development. Audiovisual and computing technologies have brought new means of creating records, and archivists seeking to preserve such records and make them available to users have found that they require new skills and competencies. The growing bulk of records led twentieth-century archivists to reject the notion that all records could be preserved and attempt to identify criteria for *selecting* records for long-term preservation. Contentious though such attempts must be, they have led many archivists to the idea that the term 'archives' might be confined to records that have gone through a selection process and been judged to have continuing value. Archival services that aim to select records and maintain them indefinitely for future use form the main focus of this book.

However, in the twenty-first century, perceptions of 'archives' have again become fluid. Should the term be restricted to *records* that have been kept because they are believed to have continuing value, or might it have wider connotations? The computer industry has made everyone familiar with the notion of 'archiving' (a word that, until recently, no self-respecting archivist would ever have used); but in doing so it has popularized a belief that 'archives' can encompass almost any collections of materials, especially perhaps digital materials, that have been designated for storage for possible future use. The nascent 'community archives' movement in the UK often emphasizes the keeping of materials that are felt to be meaningful to a present-day community rather than those that can be specifically identified as records of past events.

In fact, archivists have long been aware that the boundaries of archives can sometimes extend beyond records of activities, events and experiences. Millar recounts the tale, famously told in the 1920s by the English archivist Hilary Jenkinson, of the elephant despatched to England with a covering note. The note finds its way to an archival repository; but does the elephant also form part of the archives? Pragmatically, of course, the elephant cannot be housed in the repository, but many items despatched with (or without) covering notes – fabric samples, medals, advertising circulars, posters or magazines, for example – commonly do find their way into archival collections, even though such items might not normally be considered *records*. In practice, archives frequently appear hospitable to anything that has proved capable of being stored in an organization's or individual's filing system. Archives are often said to be 'organic', insofar as they accrue more or less naturally in the course of organizational business or personal life, but in another sense they are shaped by retention and aggregation decisions made by their custodians. Conceptual and physical notions of archives have a more or less uneasy coexistence.

This book offers a discussion of the principles of archives and archival management as well as an examination of many of the practices archivists employ to put those principles into effect. It explores some of the dilemmas archivists face when they recognize that archives are complex and contentious phenomena, and that their own interventions in selecting, arranging, preserving and delivering archives necessarily add further tiers of contentiousness. Unlike most other texts on the keeping of archives, Millar's book does not draw on a single national tradition, but sets out approaches used in many different parts of the English-speaking world. At another level, like all the best writings, it is a personal book; *Archives: principles and practices* reflects its author's understanding of archives derived from her extensive practical experience in Canada and in many other countries. It is to be commended to all who undertake the rewarding work of maintaining archives for the benefit of users today and in the future.

Geoffrey Yeo, University College London
May 2010

Foreword to the second edition

Seven years after Laura Millar's eloquent and wide-ranging book was first published, it is ever more apparent that in future the great majority of records will be created and used in digital form. At present, most record-making environments are hybrid – to varying extents, paper records continue to be created and kept alongside their digital counterparts – but the balance is firmly shifting towards the digital. Organizations are now disposing of their filing cabinets at an unprecedented rate. Even if the wholly paperless office may still prove to be a chimera, the 'less-paper' office is now a visible reality. It has also become clear that archivists will very soon face, if they are not already facing, a digital deluge. The world is creating massive amounts of digital content, and the archivists of the future will encounter quantities of records that exceed anything that archivists have experienced in the past. In this age of digital abundance, human society will still look for evidence of, and information about, actions that have been undertaken, events that have occurred, decisions that have been made, and rights that have been protected, abused or amended. Records and archives will still be needed, and the long-standing archival principles that Millar expounds will be no less valid, but the methods and techniques required to put those principles into practice will often be very different.

In this new and extensively revised second edition, Millar provides greatly expanded coverage of digital concerns. In place of the separate chapter on digital archives that concluded the first edition, discussion of digital issues is now woven into every chapter of the book. Of course, we still have – and will continue to have – the legacy of many centuries of archives created using paper and other analogue media; the skills to manage records created in the past by non-digital means will remain essential, and Millar does not neglect them. But in recasting her book to take account of the fast-moving digital revolution, she offers us an archival manual for the twenty-first century.

Geoffrey Yeo, University College London
March 2017

Acknowledgements

As I said in the first edition, writing a book is a long and arduous process. It turns out revising a book is an even more challenging, and lonelier, experience. It does not seem fair to go back to the well a second time and ask for input from the same people twice; they will just think I was not paying attention the first time. I am very lucky that colleagues, friends and family answered the call as I struggled with what turned out not to be a tweak around the edges but a fundamental rewrite of this book – it is a new book, really – which I suspect is a necessary response to the fundamental changes in information, records and archives in the years since the first edition came out in 2010.

Damian Mitchell at Facet Publishing was that breath of fresh air an author wants in an editor: cheerful, supportive and patient. And I am grateful to the anonymous reviewers who offered comments and suggestions about how I might integrate the discussion of digital records and archives more fully into this second edition. (I suspect that completely rewriting the book resolves any lingering questions there.)

I am grateful to Robin Keirstead and Kelly Stewart for their suggestions about how to balance specificity and detail in the bibliography and for their cheerful support during the race to finish revisions. My ever faithful colleague and friend Heather MacNeil responded with alacrity and good humour to my many questions about new directions in archival description. In Australia, Lise Summers set time aside during my visit to Curtin University in Perth, so that we could share ideas about how the series and function have been interpreted differently in Australia and North America. (Yes, Lise, Canadians define the series *very* broadly. If it looks like a duck, walks like a duck, talks like a duck . . .)

Richard Valpy, always my champion and ally, opened my eyes to the challenges archivists face between doing what they might want to do as dedicated professionals and what they might have to do as officers answerable to sponsor agencies and the public. Geoff Yeo continues to offer unwavering support and remarkable faith as the series editor who convinced me to write the book in the first place.

I am indebted to my students over more than 30 years, including those I taught in a classroom and those I 'adopted' along the way. Whether they like it or not, I think of them as my 'chicks'. I learn more than I teach when I interact with students, many of whom are now colleagues and friends. Their innovative ideas and fresh insights encourage me to keep moving with the times. I particularly thank three of the newest and brightest in this next generation of record-keeping professionals: Drs Donald Force, Elaine Goh and Anthea Seles. By accepting me as cheerleader, den mother and agony aunt during their PhD studies over the last few years, they each let me glean insights from their innovative research into concepts of evidence, the strengths and weaknesses of archival legislation, and the challenges of building 'trustworthy' digital repositories. I have learned much from, and will always cherish, those experiences.

To my long-suffering and uncomplaining husband, yet again I owe a great debt. Brian took over the full spectrum of domestic duties with a smile, kept me plied with tea and made sure hot meals and chilled wine were available as and when, while I locked hands to keyboard to finish this book. We make a great team.

Laura A. Millar
May 2017

Introduction to the second edition

Habit is either the best of servants or the worst of masters.

Nathaniel Emmons (1745–1840)

I began the first edition with a story that bears repeating, which goes as follows. A young woman asked her mother why she always cut the end off her roast before putting it in the oven. 'You have to', her mother replied. 'It's the only way to cook a roast. That's what my mother taught me'. Not satisfied with this explanation, the woman posed the same question to her grandmother. 'Cutting the end off is critical', said the grandmother. 'If you don't, the roast comes out tough and flavourless. That's how my mother did it, and that's the way it is done'. Still unsatisfied, the woman asked her great-grandmother, a matriarch of 90-plus years, if she always cut the end off her roast before cooking it. 'Absolutely', replied the great-grandmother, 'Without fail'. 'But why?' begged the young woman, looking for some logic behind the tradition. Her great-grandmother looked puzzled. 'Well, dear', she finally said, 'I had to. My roasting pan was too small'.

My point then and now is that much of what we do in life comes from habit and tradition. Our parents did it that way, and so do we; our supervisor showed us that method, and we adopted it on as our own; our teacher insisted on that approach, and we have never tried another. Individual and group behaviour – from cooking food to building houses to communicating and documenting ideas and information – are as much a result of the repetition of habits and traditions as the application of theories and principles. We do it that way because 'that's the way it is done'.

From time to time, though, we need to step back and ask why we do something in a particular way, especially if other options are available. Why do we build houses out of wood or brick or stone? Why do some of us prefer Apple Mac computers and some only use PCs? Why do Americans use letter-size paper, while the English use A4 paper? Why do we cut the end off our roast?

Asking why we do something a certain way means examining the theories, principles and history behind our practice. Only then can we decide if our actions suit theory or vice versa. What is the principle on which our practice is grounded? Do theory and reality come together logically? Is the theory unrealistic or the practice outmoded?

The world of archives is infused with a large dollop of academic theory and an equally large dose of traditional practice. Too often one or the other – theory or practice – is over-emphasized. Why do some archivists start arrangement and description with the *fonds*? Why do others emphasize function? If we believe in the philosophy that records follow a life cycle, which ends in the transportation of archives to some form of documentary heaven, how can we argue for an archival role in the protection of electronic records from birth, so that they survive long enough to see the pearly gates? Do we really need to wear white cotton gloves when handling old documents? *Why?* (The answer, by the way, is no. The gloves diminish dexterity, and studies have shown you are more likely to drop the item if you have thick gloves on. If your hands are dirty, wash them. But do not touch photographs, films or negatives with your bare hands; the oils *will* damage the emulsion. You see, no rule applies equally.)

Archivists search, sometimes in vain, for a balance between abstract hypotheses and daily customs, some of which can become increasingly arcane with time. *Archives: principles and practices* seeks to strike a balance between principles and practices. It is as much a 'why-to' book as a 'how-to' book.

To draw a comparison with cooking, this is a book about culinary practice rather than a recipe book. A recipe is a 'how-to' manual for cooking a particular dish, providing a list of ingredients and a set of instructions. If the cook follows the instructions precisely, he or she will end up with a culinary dish that – one hopes – resembles the recipe. A culinary book, on the other hand, focuses not on recipes but on the principles of cooking: the concept of heat transfer; the qualities of different cuts of meat; the chemical reactions that cause beef fibres to soften. Users of culinary books may not find a recipe for the 'perfect' roast, but they will understand the importance of cooking the meat on low heat for hours in order to break down tough fibres.

Another difficulty with recipe books is that they are necessarily specific to particular cultures and regions. Dishes that call for taro root are hard to prepare in Norway, and meals requiring reindeer are challenging to replicate in Papua New Guinea. Culinary books take into account the fact that one cook may have a wood stove, another may use gas and another electricity; they present principles that can be adapted for use in different environments.

Just as there is no one 'right way' to cook; there is no one 'right way' to manage archives. There are too many social, cultural and practical variations in the way records, archives and evidence are created, managed and used to allow one set of procedures, one recipe, to meet the needs of practitioners in different parts of the world.

To address variations in practice while introducing important principles and concepts, the second edition of *Archives: principles and practices* is divided into two parts. Part I addresses the theoretical, conceptual and philosophical issues associated with archives: their creation, management and use. Part II introduces ideas about the strategic, operational and logistical issues associated with archival practice. Where the book provides guidance on many aspects of archival practice, every attempt is made to reconcile specific instructions with the reality that circumstances will vary from one environment to another.

The hope is that you the reader can learn about the principles behind archival practice, balance theories against your own institutional realities, and then identify the best practical actions for your particular circumstances. A business archives equipped with sophisticated information and communications systems needs to develop and deliver systems and services quite unlike those in a remote, poorly resourced community archives. A repository that only acquires historical photographs has different priorities for description and digitization from an institution that collects not only archives but also publications, artefacts and art.

The approach presented here does not eliminate the need to articulate core archival principles. One of the obstacles to the development of consistent archival practice around the world has been an insistence on doing things a certain way because 'we've always done it that way'. Archivists and their institutions can become stuck, and it can be easier to criticize other approaches than to go back and start again. To combat idiosyncrasies, archivists develop standards, which offer a useful bridge between theory and practice. But standards are not laws, and they should not always be accepted as gospel. This book looks for a balance among, first, the theoretical environment, secondly the ideal world of archival standards, and lastly the reality of archival management in practice. My goal is to help bridge the gap between 'we've always done it *this* way' and 'we can never do it *that* way'.

About the book

This book is written primarily for records and archives practitioners, particularly those 'lone arrangers' working in small, often inadequately resourced, institutions who may have inherited an array of archival procedures from their predecessors and need to understand whether those approaches still work and, if not, how to conceptualize new and different models. This book will also be valuable for students of archival management, in universities and colleges, especially the archivist just embarking on a career in archives and still unclear about what the profession exists to do and how she might ply her trade in the working world. I also hope that the book will be useful to anyone interested in or involved with records and archives.

In the ideal world, documentary evidence will be managed effectively from the moment it is created, if not before, within an accountable environment for *record keeping* (a term used throughout the book). In this environment, the best service the archivist as record keeper can provide is not to manage an archival collection after the fact but to ensure the creation and protection of valuable evidence from the beginning.

But reality being what it is, the care of records (mistakenly defined as 'new') and the care of archives (erroneously perceived as 'old') are still considered separate responsibilities in many parts of the world, though the borders are blurring significantly. While the care of current records is essential to effective information management and the creation of authentic and reliable archives, addressing both current records management and archival management in one book is not possible, at least not without providing the most superficial of discussions in a publication that could pass as a doorstop. And simply defining it all as *record keeping* and not discussing custodial archival care sweeps centuries of archival history and practice under the reference room carpet.

Since this is a book about archival principles and practices, then, I have focused my attention on the archival end of the equation: the processes needed to identify materials with evidential value and ensure they are protected and made available for use. But I cannot stop myself from reminding the reader that quality records care is going to be even more important as we struggle with protecting evidence in a mutable digital world.

The 12 chapters in this book are divided as follows.

In Part I, Chapter 1, the concept of archives as documentary evidence is examined, by tracing a path from the communication of an idea, to its capture as information, to the retention of that information as evidence and then to its preservation as archives. The chapter also discusses the importance of content, context and structure to the authenticity and reliability of records and archives. It ends with a comparison of documentary evidence, scientific evidence and physical evidence and with a discussion of the perilous path from data to archives.

Chapter 2 looks at the nature of archives, starting with the ideal scenario in which archives are managed as part of a continuum of care. I then turn to reality, considering how archives might be defined on the basis of what *is* left behind, not on what *should* have been kept. The form of archives, or, more appropriately, the fact that documentary evidence can take many forms, is also considered. I look then at the relationship between archives, art and artefacts and end the chapter with a reminder that archives are only the smallest portion of the residue of our lives. Much that is intangible still has much value, even if not defined as 'archival'.

Chapter 3 highlights significant events in archival history, from the time when archives were only used by records creators to the time when the public began to use archives for historical research. The evolution of life cycle and continuum approaches to archives is outlined, and the impact of postmodernism on archival thinking is addressed. I then connect those historical events to archival theories, explaining the principles of provenance, original order and *respect des fonds*, as well as the concept of a functional, series-based approach to archival management and the notion of a records continuum. I also look at how those theories are being challenged, as archivists debate whether they remain relevant today.

Chapter 4 looks at archives from the perspective of the user. Archives can be sources of history, whether for professional, amateur or family and personal reasons. Archives also serve as tools for accountability, providing evidence to uphold the law or provide proof of infractions. And archives serve as touchstones for memory and identity, finding value as sources for scientific research, social and political studies, popular fiction and film and, ultimately, as a window into the lives of others.

In Chapter 5, I outline different types of archival institution, specifically: institutional archives, hybrid archives, collecting archives, community-based archives, museum archives, integrated institutions, indigenous archives and activist archives. I also address the rise of online repositories and suggest we need to distinguish data or records 'warehouses' from trusted digital repositories; it is the latter that archivists are striving to create in order to manage electronic evidence safely.

In Chapter 6, I look at the fundamental principles of archival service. I believe that archivists must work within a sound ethical framework, especially given that archival work is not a regulated profession. I outline standards of practice I hope archivists will embrace, above and beyond existing codes of ethics. I also comment on the education of the archivist, the role of archival associations and the nature and purpose of records and archives standards.

Chapter 7 ends Part I by looking specifically at the legal and ethical requirements of balancing access with privacy. How does the archivist address copyright and intellectual property requirements? How does the archivist provide equitable access to holdings and still respect the rights not only of records creators but also of those identified in archives, who may wish to remain invisible to the world?

Part II focuses on archival practice, beginning in Chapter 8 with a discussion of the tasks involved in managing the archival institution itself. What is the ideal organizational structure for an archival operation, and how can the archivist identify the right strategic vision for her own institution? What policy framework is needed, and how should the archival institution be administered, from finances to facilities to staff?

In Chapter 9, I review concepts and best practice requirements for archival preservation, emphasizing the need to ensure the security and sustainability of the environment in which archives will be housed. I identify specific archival hazards, such as: acidity, fluctuations in temperature and relative humidity, excessive light levels, pollution, fire and water damage, biological agents such as mould, insects and rodents, and abuse and mishandling. For each hazard I offer suggestions for mitigating the risk. I also offer guidance about the management of different media materials. I consider digitization as a preservation tool, and I offer a short introduction to the challenge of preserving digital archives. The chapter ends with suggestions for developing preservation and emergency plans, both of which are critical tools for ensuring archival holdings are kept safe.

In Chapter 10, the acquisition of archives is examined, starting with a discussion of the two aspects of appraisal: appraisal for acquisition and appraisal for selection. The advantages and limitations of sampling, weeding and culling are considered, along with other appraisal criteria that the archivist should take into account. I explain the different ways archival materials can be acquired, including transfer, donation, loan and purchase; outline the legal and administrative process of accessioning archives; and consider the work involved in deaccessioning archives that the archivist decides do not belong in the institution. The chapter concludes with a brief look at the thorny topic of monetary appraisal.

In Chapter 11, I revisit some of the theories and principles introduced in Chapter 3, including provenance and original order, in order to consider how they work, or do not work, in practice. Two sometimes competing philosophies with a direct impact on arrangement and description – custodial and post-custodial archives management – are examined. I then look at the challenge of controlling language when describing archival materials, which is important to providing quality access and reference. The practicalities of arrangement and description are outlined, followed by a discussion of the ways in which descriptive information might be presented for research use.

In Chapter 12, I look at how archivists can and should make archives available for use, considering not only the role of reference services but also the importance of outreach and engagement. Creating an effective frame-work for reference and access is addressed, along with a discussion of issues associated with providing personal or virtual reference services. The role of digitization as a reference tool is examined, and the importance of documenting reference services is emphasized. I end the chapter by suggest-ing ways in which the archivist can engage with the community, including through online and social media applications, to support research use and to raise awareness of the archives and the archival institution.

The book concludes, as the first edition did, with a brief speculation on where archives and archivists are going as we pursue this new digital frontier. As society begins to embrace the 'internet of things', and our refrigerators and garage doors start to communicate with us while we are on vacation, will the archivist of the future be capturing evidence of spoiled milk in the fridge or the damage wrought (at least where I live, here in western Canada) by black bears digging for breakfast in our garbage cans?

When the first edition was published, digital archives were addressed in a separate chapter. They were treated as something special and different, not directly relevant to 'the rest' of archival practice. How much has changed in a few short years. In this edition, I have integrated discussion of the digital into all chapters, based on my belief that evidence is evidence is evidence, whether it comes in a clay tablet or a digital photograph.

But there is still not enough room to address the care of digital records and archives fully. The content in a digital record may still be archival, but the context in which that record was created and the structure and form it takes are markedly divergent from paper ledgers or black and white photographs. I have neither the room in this book, nor the technical knowledge in my head, to examine in depth the specific technological requirements that govern, or should govern, the care of digital records. Fortunately, many others with greater knowledge than I have written excellent books on digital preservation and electronic records management. I have drawn on these tools for this edition, and I encourage the reader to use these works, which are identified in the resources section at the end of this book, to learn more about the specifics of digital records and archives care.

Additional resources

A book like *Archives: principles and practices* can only provide an overview of the complexities and nuances of archival theory and practice. A paragraph in this book – indeed, sometimes a single sentence – can summarize ideas addressed in entire volumes. The first edition of this book attempted the impossible, by being as comprehensive as possible and identifying all manner of readings that might be of interest. Common sense prevails in the second edition. Now the list of resources follows a minimalist approach. Only a handful of core and recommended readings have been included, almost exclusively book-length works, on the assumption that these books will lead readers to more specific sources. I have also included links to journals, archival agencies and relevant websites, as some of the most useful new research is now easily accessed online, at least for those with a robust internet connection.

Striving for diversity and balance

As noted in the first edition, I have been an archival consultant for over 30 years. I have travelled from my home in British Columbia to countries as far afield as Fiji, Botswana, Hungary, Singapore, France and Brazil. I have seen up close the work of dedicated archivists in national institutions with hundreds of employees and in church archives staffed by octogenarian volunteers. Many of these people are the first line of defence for their society's documentary heritage, and too often they work in severely constrained circumstances. Repositories may come without shelving or desks or doors. Storage vaults may be subject to temperatures that exceed 40°C above or –40°C below. Reference rooms may be occupied by rodents as well as researchers. The 'budget' may be whatever can be eked out of a book sale or a donation box.

That said, I have seen archival practice grow more and more sophisticated over time. Computerized databases are replacing paper finding aids in institutions from the USA to Namibia. Archival institutions from Bangladesh to Iceland have Facebook pages. I am continually amazed and energized by the effort, dedication and sheer determination of archivists to be as engaged with their communities as possible, even if they have had to drape their holdings in tarps to keep out the rain after the window panes have been stolen.

To try to write a book that meets all the needs of all these different practitioners, from the Arctic to the tropics and from major urban centres to remote hamlets, is an exercise in creativity and flexibility. I have tried to make my words as meaningful as possible in all these diverse archival environments. Occasional real-world examples are included, but for the most part I have created fictitious scenarios. There is, at least to my knowledge, no

Cascadia University, no Wickham County Archives and no Cheswick Historical Society. Maureen Lee and James Carstairs are my own inventions. For instance, the examples related to environmental records, particularly in the discussion of arrangement and description in Chapter 11, are a wondrous conflation of reality and fantasy.

For that fictitious case study, I drew on examples from the State Records Office of Western Australia and the Archives of Ontario, Canada, then I tossed in some functional descriptions fabricated out of real examples from the National Archives of Australia's functional thesaurus. Finally, I stirred them all together into a description of archival materials housed in an entirely made-up provincial archives in Canada. I am grateful to the dedication and meticulousness of the archivists in all these real institutions for making their archival resources so readily available on the internet, allowing me to make up new descriptive fictions to my heart's content. And I also send sincere thanks to the very real Provincial Archives of Alberta, which has amazing staff, a beautiful building and probably all sorts of terrific records related to the environment, but which is decidedly *not* the Provincial Archives and Library of Alberta, which remains a figment of my imagination.

Still, imagination has its limits. I am a Canadian and proud to be so. While I use my imagination and experiences to try and place myself in the shoes of an archivist in Kenya or Egypt, inevitably I will fall back on my own cultural experiences, as everyone does. All I can do, as I hope everyone would, is explain my own perspectives and let others translate those explanations into ideas meaningful in their own environment.

The battle between British and American spelling rages on in this book, as it did in the first. I leave it to the editorial dictates of the publisher to 'standardize' language. (Or should that be 'standardise'?) I define archival and technical terms on first use whenever possible, and I have included a glossary at the end of the book for ease of reference. My approach is not to present authoritative statements on archival language, though. I prefer to discuss the various meanings of terms such as archives, *fonds*, function or series, opening the door to deeper evaluation of the underlying concepts.

The word 'archives' is traditionally defined in three ways: the organization dedicated to preserving the documentary heritage of a particular group, such as a national government, a city, a university or a village; the materials acquired, preserved and made available for use; and the building or part of a building in which archival materials are kept – the archival repository itself. I have given preference to 'archives' for the materials and 'institution' for the agency whenever I could, though occasionally I talk about 'facility' or 'repository' to avoid repetition.

Faced with the awkwardness of using 'he or she', or opting for 'they', I have stayed with my choice in the first edition to have one female representative archivist for the book: 'she'. To balance the equation, many (but not all) of the researchers, donors, records creators and other fictitious characters that populate the case studies are addressed in the masculine: 'he'. The intent remains not to presume all archivists are women and all researchers are men; the intent is to help distinguish all the players in a particular scenario.

Whether you are an archival student, a practitioner with years of experience or someone simply intrigued by archives, I hope you find this book a useful starting point for your study of a fascinating and critically important topic. The safe preservation and widespread use of archives is fundamental to accountability, identity and memory in society. Archives join museum artefacts, works of art, oral histories and family and community customs and traditions as the tools we rely on to understand who we are, where we came from and where we are going. They are part of the essence of our individual and collective sense of self, part of the foundations of a civilized society. I hope you enjoy this exploration of the principles and practices of archival work.

PART I
Archival principles

Part I of this book looks at the principles and theories within which archival practice is situated. How do we define archives, and what types of material fall within and outside that definition? How did archival theory and practice develop throughout history, and how do we position our work today within existing theoretical frameworks? Theory notwithstanding, how do people actually use archives? What types of institutions are created to hold archival materials, and what are the similarities or differences between them? Regardless of institution, what are the guiding principles – the golden rule(s) – of effective and ethical archival service? And, especially in a world abounding with cloud computing systems, data security concerns, identity theft and 24-hour news cycles, how can the archivist balance the right of citizens to access evidence with the right of individuals to retain their privacy? These topics are addressed in the following chapters:

Chapter 1: What are archives?
Chapter 2: The nature of archives
Chapter 3: Archival history and theory
Chapter 4: The uses of archives
Chapter 5: Types of archival institution
Chapter 6: The principles of archival service
Chapter 7: Balancing access and privacy.

1
What are archives?

A wise man proportions his belief to the evidence.
David Hume (1711–76) *An Enquiry Concerning Human Understanding*, 1748

The word 'archives' conjures up different images. Some people picture dusty, dry storage rooms where stuffy, brown-bow-tie curators enveloped in ancient cardigans look askance at anyone who speaks above a whisper. Others imagine websites where listeners can download podcasts of radio programmes aired just hours before. Some people think of old parchments, scrolls and leather-bound volumes of medieval treatises; others imagine electronic back-up copies of a corporate report or membership database.

Two centuries ago, the majority of archival materials were two-dimensional, manually created items such as papyrus scrolls, parchment codices, bound ledgers, or black and white photographs. Today, the holdings of archival institutions may include e-mail messages, relational databases, YouTube videos and interactive web pages. Digital technologies have transformed our understanding of the nature of information and communications; what were considered archives a century ago are only the smallest subset of what might be defined as archives today.

Computers and the internet have also bred a growth industry in the dissemination of digital archival information. Governments, corporations, publishers, music producers, writers, performers and artists have all discovered the value of sharing information, including historical records, electronically. Newspapers reprint archived articles in print and online editions. Radio stations post copies of concerts and interviews on their websites. Music producers repackage old recordings, billing them as treasures from the vault. Entire television channels are devoted to broadcasting 'classic' TV shows and movies, and historical documentaries and 'find your ancestor' genealogical shows are among the most popular subset of reality TV on air today. Even local churches record their Sunday sermons and post them on their Facebook pages to serve home-bound parishioners.

As more and more people are exposed to digital information, both old and new, the concept of archives has become more ambiguous. The blanket depiction of archives as brittle old documents used only by scholars has been replaced by another stereotype: that archives comprise any piece of information older than yesterday that might be worth referring to again tomorrow. For those who decide to create an online repository of their favourite recipes or music or newspaper articles and call it their 'archive', the subtleties of language may be of little consequence. But for people whose job is to acquire and preserve documentary evidence and ensure it is available for public use, understanding the concept of archives is critical.

Archives are defined not by their form but by their purpose. A handwritten letter can have archival value, and a data element in a computer's hard drive can have archival value. A collection of all the recordings of Frank Sinatra, or copies of every issue of *National Geographic*, however old, may not have archival value. Why?

A full definition of 'archives', encompassing the three primary ways in which the word may be used, is this:

1. Documentary materials created, received, used and kept by a person, family, organization, government or other public or private entity in the conduct of their daily work and life and preserved because they contain enduring value as evidence of and information about activities and events. 2. The agency or institution responsible for acquiring and preserving archival materials and making those items available for use. 3. The building or other repository housing archival collections.

So the word 'archives' can be used to refer to the materials themselves, to the institution caring for them or to the repository holding those materials. So one could argue, correctly, that 'the archives' archives are in the archives'.

The focus in this chapter is on the first part of the definition: that small portion of all the information, communications, ideas and opinions that people or organizations create and receive as part of their daily life and work, that are captured in recorded form and kept because they have some value beyond the moment. That worth may be not only for the creator or recipient of the 'information, communications, ideas and opinions' but also for others, in the present and future.

In order for something to be preserved for its archival value, then, it must be tangible, whether physical or electronic, visual, aural or written. Archives must exist in some concrete form outside our own minds. There is no way that 'documentary evidence' can be preserved and used if it does not take real form. Further, archives are something other than mere information: archives serve as a form of proof.

To understand how archives come to be, we must start by understanding how data becomes knowledge and knowledge becomes information. Then we can consider how information becomes evidence and evidence becomes archives.

From data to evidence

Only the smallest fraction of knowledge we carry around in our minds ever makes its way outside our heads and into some external form. Human beings gather *data* through our senses. We absorb the experience of a sunset by perceiving the setting sun through our eyes, and we come to know a piece of music by listening to a concert. With each experience, we compile data – from the Latin *datum* or '(thing) given' – putting together sights and sounds in our brains and then mentally organizing that data to make sense of what we have perceived. When we read or listen or watch or smell or taste anything, we are gathering data.

Once we have gathered the data, we interpret those signals and symbols to make sense of them. We turn our data into *knowledge*. We read symbols on a sheet of paper, raw data, and know we are reading a newspaper, in part because we know the alphabet. We read another set of symbols on a computer screen, again raw data, and know we are looking at a balance sheet, in part because we understand that the symbols represent numbers.

We know we are watching a sunset not just because we see an orange ball in the sky but also because we know how to read the clock and see the time of day: it is evening, not morning. We know we are listening to music instead of noise not only because we hear sounds but also because we have taken ourselves to a concert hall, to a place where music is performed. (Admittedly, the distinction between music and noise is sometimes quite blurry, especially as one gets older.)

We take in the knowledge gleaned, from the daily news stories to the company's financial health, and then we can share that knowledge, turning it into *information*. When we call our friends to describe the sunset or chat about the concert, and we listen to their reactions, we are exchanging information. When we e-mail our accountant to query the company's financial statements, and we receive our accountant's explanations, we are exchanging information.

Sometimes, we act on this information. We might decide to buy a recording of the concert or authorize increases in staff pay. Our decisions will be based on our interpretation and analysis of the knowledge we gained from the data we collected.

We might decide that the information should be captured so that we can remember it later. When we take a photograph of the sunset, we are capturing information. If we e-mail our friend to tell him about our night listening to the symphony, we are capturing information about the event and our impressions of it. When we decide to increase staff pay, we capture that information in our personnel and financial records, noting the amount of the increase, the additional taxes to be paid and the justification for the change. We also update our payroll software so that the increased payment can be processed automatically. When we capture this information, we create documentation, which may take the form of a discrete *document*, such as a photograph, memo or e-mail, or it may be a piece of *digital data* (note the different interpretation of the term 'data') that we add to a larger information resource, such as an updated address in an electronic mailing list or a change in pay rates in payroll database.

Information versus evidence

Some of the documentation we create provides us with information, and some provides us with *evidence*. The question to ask when deciding if a piece of information serves as evidence is simple to ask but often hard to answer. Does the information in question substantiate an assertion? Could we use that information later to confirm facts or decisions? Do we need that evidence in order to corroborate our actions? Do we need *proof*?

Documentary evidence, whether a written record or a digital data element, is captured in order to remember something – a piece of information, a decision or an opinion – at a particular moment. The record is not made with the sole purpose of serving history a century from now. But sometime in the near or distant future, that evidence may be brought out to help 'remember' whatever it documents: a date, a face, an event or even an emotion.

The best evidence is not created long after the events in question, when our memories are fallible and subject to after-the-fact reinterpretations of events. Rather, the best evidence is a natural by-product of the activity itself. An authentic photograph of a sunset is taken during that sunset, not the next day. An official memo authorizing a payroll change is issued before the new payment is made, not several months after.

The best evidence also contains enough contextual information to guarantee its authenticity. When we take a picture of a sunset, we have captured information about an event: the setting of the sun. But if we do not provide context about when the picture was taken, where, and by whom, we cannot use that image as evidence of anything more than the fact that the sun sets. It will not serve as proof that our family went to the seaside last August. The 'who, what, where, when and why' that contextualizes documents gives them greater meaning and allows them to serve as evidence.

Part of that contextual information is the relationship of documents or pieces of data one to another within a file, binder, database or e-mail thread. The real evidence of our holiday on the coast is not one photograph of a sunset but an entire album of family photographs, showing us swimming and sightseeing, dining in a restaurant and sailing in a boat, with dates and places and people clearly identified.

Similarly, context is essential to proving that a staff pay increase is legitimate. If our payroll software shows simply that someone is making more income now than he was a month ago but does not tell us when the change was made and who approved it, we cannot prove that the increase was authorized. How do we know someone didn't just break into the computer and change the payroll figures without permission? The real evidence of an increase in staff pay would be formal, written confirmation, safely stored with other personnel records, serving as proof that the head of personnel services authorized the change.

Capturing evidence

When we capture evidence, the resulting product may be a *record* in the traditional sense: a physical or digital item that carries documentary value, such as a letter, contract or photograph. This record purports to be objective. In other words, the record claims to represent actual decisions or opinions or experiences, not fictionalized descriptions.

The strength of static records such as paper documents or printed photographs is their inviolability. Once this type of record exists, the words or numbers or images on the page stay put; changing them is difficult (though admittedly not impossible). A bound ledger, with all the pages intact, is a whole record, which cannot be altered without leaving some obvious evidence of change. An original photographic print that is not faded or torn is complete in itself: a discrete, finished object that cannot be edited after the fact.

But in the digital world, evidence can also be a piece of data: an entry in a database, a message circulated through Twitter or a blog post on a website. (A blog, from 'web log', is a type of online diary, journal or discussion page.)

The raw data we took into our senses – the view of the sunset or the sound of the orchestra – is captured in digital data: a photograph of the sunset stored in our cellular telephone; a recording of the performance saved as an MP3 audio file. (MP3 is a coding format for compressing and storing audio input into a small file, allowing the recorded sounds to be saved and shared easily.)

Unlike paper records, digital data can be altered or deleted in a microsecond. A digital sound recording, unlike a vinyl LP recording, can be manipulated and updated instantaneously. Editing may remove coughs and interruptions and applause but the new version ceases to be an authentic representation of the performance. A digital photograph can be enhanced, with the sunset made brighter or the dog in the background removed, but it is no longer a true representation of the event.

This malleability means that digital evidence is tricky both to authenticate and to preserve. How do we know that a membership database is secure and accessible only to those with proper authority? How do we know that a message sent through Twitter shows the right time and date and so is chronologically accurate? A critical archival task in the digital age is not just to capture and preserve pieces of data but to ensure that, if they are to serve as proof, they are captured with their authenticity intact. Only then can that digital data serve as evidence for as long as needed, whether a week, a year or forever.

From evidence to archives

Only a portion of the information we generate or receive throughout our lives is worth keeping for even a short time, and only a portion of that subset is worth keeping indefinitely. When and how do pieces of evidence become *archives*?

A sales receipt for a container of milk is useful until the milk is home, stored in the refrigerator and consumed by thirsty teenagers. If the milk is sour when the container is opened, the receipt is proof that the milk was purchased from a particular store on a particular day, so that the purchaser can replace it with a fresh container free of charge. Days or weeks after the milk is gone, the receipt has no continuing value.

Receipts for oil changes and engine tune-ups may be useful for as long as the warranty on the car is in effect, which may be four or five years. After the warranty has expired, the owner of the car needs no proof that he abided by the terms of the warranty. Those receipts can be destroyed, unless the car's owner has an abiding interest in the life and history of his vehicle.

Of course, some scrupulous car owners keep all their maintenance documentation until they sell their cars, providing the buyer with a detailed true history of the vehicle. And a devoted car lover might keep a receipt for the very first car he purchased, when he was 18, as a testimonial to that thrilling first taste of adult life. If, 60 years later, that car becomes 'vintage' and is considered a collector's item, all the documentation surrounding its life may have significant long-term value. The records may be seen as archives.

The challenge with this scenario is that the records need to have been created in the first place, and then kept over decades, which demands that the first owner, and all subsequent owners, need to share an abiding (perhaps even obsessive) interest in the story of that vehicle. It takes remarkable prescience to know in 1964 that one's brand-new Chevrolet Corvette will become a collector's item in 2014. Sometimes, the records left behind are valuable not because of the importance of their content but because they survived, intact, against all odds.

Rather than wait and hope that authentic and accurate archives will come into custody someday, many archivists prefer to work with the creators of records and information now: raising awareness of and encouraging the protection of valuable evidence. In governments or corporations, this advisory work often comes as part of a formal records and information management programme, which helps ensure that quality documentary evidence is kept for as long as needed for legal, administrative, financial, historical and other purposes.

In a structured record-keeping environment, archivists help the creators of records and information to define some of their information sources as 'transitory': they have little long-term value and can be destroyed once they are no longer needed. They define other information sources as records or evidence, because they have evidential, administrative or other value that warrants their retention for a certain time. The archivist also determines which evidence has enduring value and should be kept permanently as archives.

Figure 1.1 on the next page summarizes the progression discussed thus far: from data to knowledge, to information, to evidence, and finally to archives.

The qualities of archives

When deciding if something has archival value, it is not enough for the creator of a record, or an archivist, simply to hold up an individual documentary item and say 'this is truly an authentic and original contract between Robert Kessler and William Edelman' or 'this is absolutely a diary written by Adele Chiabaka'. The item in question cannot be confirmed as authentic proof of something just because an archivist has put it into a storage box in her institution. Archival materials derive their value as evidence from a combination of three qualities: content, context and structure.

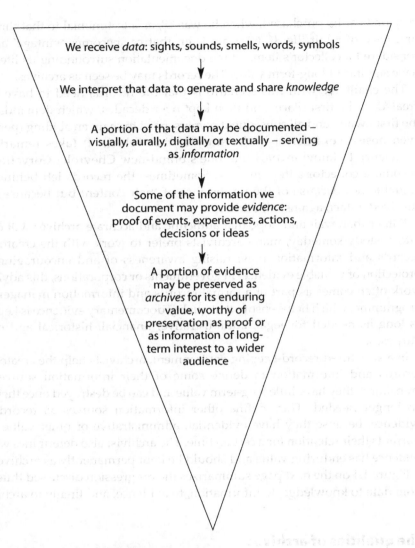

We receive *data*: sights, sounds, smells, words, symbols

↓

We interpret that data to generate and share *knowledge*

↓

A portion of that data may be documented – visually, aurally, digitally or textually – serving as *information*

↓

Some of the information we document may provide *evidence*: proof of events, experiences, actions, decisions or ideas

↓

A portion of evidence may be preserved as *archives* for its enduring value, worthy of preservation as proof or as information of long-term interest to a wider audience

Figure 1.1 *The progression from data to archives*

Content, structure and context

An isolated photograph of a sunset is only information. But a photograph of a sunset contained in an album called 'The Taylor Family Trip to Florida, 1968' – with dates, people and places clearly documented – is evidence. Evidential value increases if there is a clear and authentic relationship between individual items within a larger body of unified records. Consider this example.

A scribbled reminder on a sticky note, or a single entry extracted from a digital calendar, might remind the author to 'meet Mike'. The note captures a piece of information. Someone – we do not know who – intends to meet someone named Mike, at some unknown time and place. The reminder does not prove that the meeting happened, only that it seems to have been planned. The structure of the note is an isolated piece of paper or a few lines taken from a computer database. Was the information captured informally, perhaps in haste? Or was it planned well in advance?

Further, the reminder all by itself does not identify who was going to meet Mike. It could have been a man, woman or child; a colleague, friend, brother or used car salesman. Without any wider context, the content of the message – 'meet Mike' – is vague to the point of being meaningless.

But what if the reminder to 'meet Mike' was found inside the pages of a paper 'day timer' or within a digital calendar, surrounded by information about other appointments and activities? What if the reminder showed the specific date: 8 July 2016? And what if the appointment calendar was maintained by the personal secretary to Donald Trump, who in July 2016 was the Republican candidate for the presidency of the USA?

Now the reminder that says 'meet Mike' contains a great deal more meaning. On 15 August 2016, Mr Trump sent out a message on his Twitter account announcing that Mike Pence, Governor of Indiana, was going to be his running mate in that year's American presidential election. Now that the short *aide memoire* is infused with greater structure and more context, the reader of 'meet Mike' can surmise, though perhaps not yet confirm, that the Mike in question might well have been Mike Pence. The reader can further deduce that the meeting might just relate to the selection of Mr Pence as vice-presidential candidate.

The content of the note has not changed. It still says 'meet Mike'. But now the content is accompanied by structure and context. The structure of the record is now an entry on the 8 July page of the calendar for 2016, allowing the reader to see other appointments and perhaps glean more meaning through other references to Mike. Context comes by the knowledge that the day timer was Donald Trump's, kept during the weeks and months leading up to the presidential election. The context of the 8 July meeting may be illuminated further by accompanying records: phone records showing that Mike Pence and Donald Trump chatted several times; nomination papers showing Mike Pence's name; other tweets from Donald Trump's account about the nomination; minutes of meetings between the two; and so on.

With this contextual information available, other discrete pieces of information may take on more meaning. What if the calendar also included reminders to 'meet Chris', 'meet Jeff' or 'meet Mary'? Would it be reasonable to speculate that those might be meetings with other potential running mates: Chris Christie, Jeff Sessions or Mary Fallin? The location of the notes in the calendar allows that speculation, but other records would be needed to support the hypothesis. At some time in the future, after Donald Trump's tenure as American President has ended, these small pieces of evidence will provide a wealth of information about Trump's decision to select Mike Pence as his running mate.

The principle underlying this ability to clarify content, structure and context is known as the value of the chain of custody: the idea that the integrity of records and archives depends in part on a measure of control not only over their creation but also of their management through time. Knowing who created records, how this person maintained those records, and when and how those records were transferred into a custodial environment such an archival institution helps to explain – and prove or disprove – the integrity of the body of evidence. (The concept of a chain of custody is expanded later, particularly in relation to the archival principle of provenance.)

To summarize, *content* is the text, images, sounds or other information that make up the substance of a piece of evidence. Content is the 'what' in the documentary equation. To preserve content, a piece of evidence must be 'fixed' in space and time. The ink that conveys words must remain on the sheet of paper, and the chemicals that capture an image must remain on the photographic base.

The challenge with electronic records is the difficulty of fixing the content when the very nature of electronic technologies allows us to change that content so easily. Strict controls are needed over who is allowed access to digital data, and details of any changes to digital records need to be preserved, so that the evidence can be preserved over time with its accuracy and authenticity intact. (A digital record is a record that can be stored, transmitted or processed by a computer.[1])

Structure relates to the physical and intellectual characteristics that define how a piece of evidence was created and maintained. Structure provides the 'how' of a document. A page within a bound day timer has a different structure from a loose sticky note found stuck to a blank sheet of paper. A page ripped out of a day timer, sitting by itself in a box of loose papers, has a different structure from an intact day timer. An electronic calendar in a government's official record-keeping system or a tweet stored in a cloud computing system both have different structures from each other. Their location gives more precise meaning to the words 'meet Mike'.

Context is the functional, organizational and personal circumstances surrounding the creation of the documentary evidence. If content is the 'what' and structure the 'how', context is everything else: the 'who', 'where', 'when' and possibly even 'why'. Context identifies who created the information, how that information was used and stored and perhaps even why the information existed in the first place.

Regardless of media, documentary evidence gains its context by being kept as part of a larger, organic, unified body of physical or digital records and data, not as a single item separated from its documentary origins. Context can also relate to how the information was used both before and after it came into archival control. Evidential context changes as the piece of information moves from creator to custodian to user to public.

Content, context and structure do not necessarily provide absolute, unquestionable proof. The only way we could know who really went to 'meet Mike', or who 'Mike' was, would be for us to have been present at the meeting. But until Einstein's theory of a space-time continuum becomes reality and we can transport ourselves backwards in time, we cannot be witnesses to all that has transpired in life. By preserving the content, context and structure of documentary materials, archivists help researchers interpret the evidence and understand historical events more fully.

Static, unique and authentic

Beyond the notion of content, structure and context, archives retain, or ought to retain, three other desirable qualities that help ensure they serve as trustworthy proof. Ideally, anything defined as evidence, be it a handwritten diary or a membership database, should be static, unique and authentic.

Static

When a document is being generated – when meeting minutes are being drafted or an e-mail message is being composed – that document is not considered complete. It is a work in progress. But once the minutes are complete or the e-mail message has been sent, the document becomes a record. That record needs to be secured so that it cannot be changed, intentionally or accidentally. It needs to be *static*, fixed in time and space, or else it cannot easily serve as evidence of the transaction or event it documents.

The committee in charge of a particular activity is responsible for confirming that the minutes of a meeting accurately represent the discussions held and decisions made. So the committee needs to ensure that those minutes are accurate when created and safeguarded ever after. If someone alters the minutes of a meeting after the document has been approved, that document is no longer an authentic record of the meeting. Similarly, if an e-mail is sent but the receiver edits the message later, the e-mail is no longer reliable evidence. The removal of a page from Donald Trump's day timer or the deletion of 'meet Mike' from his digital calendar alters the evidential value of the information.

In order to provide evidence, a record needs to be fixed in time and space: a paper record should be filed securely, and a digital record should be secured within a computer system so that no one can change the contents, which would negate the authenticity of the evidence. Paper records such as written memos or reports or letters are relatively easy to secure. They can be stored away, with controls placed on access, so they cannot be lost or destroyed. Digital records are harder to protect. The joy of computers is that they allow data and information to be manipulated with great ease, but malleability of digital data, which makes it so useful, means it is also extremely difficult to manage and protect. Concepts of originality and uniqueness apply differently in the digital world.

For instance, a membership database is a constant and ever-changing snapshot of the number and nature of the members of an association or group. Tracking memberships in a computer is so much easier than retyping lists or adding and removing address cards in a Rolodex. But in order to rely on the database as evidence, the organization needs to apply policies and procedures to ensure that essential information can be confirmed for a particular time, even if that time is months or years in the past. Was Alfredo a member in 1993 but not in 1994? Did Camelia pay her dues regularly every year? How many members were late with their payments in 2006?

When digital records are deemed archival, steps must be taken to ensure that, while the evidence can still be used and shared and interpreted widely, the original data cannot be tampered with or changed. Still, researchers should be able to take advantage of the fact that the data is in digital form, reordering elements in a database to reach different conclusions based on the outputs of the analysis. The archival challenge is to balance the public's ability to use evidence in creative ways, whatever its form, with the need to ensure the resulting evidence remains inviolable.

Unique

In addition to being static, archives are also considered *unique*. Uniqueness does not derive from each individual piece of paper or data element being unlike any other but from the fact that the evidence – if maintained with its content, context and structure intact – presents a single sequence of facts and information. The minutes of a meeting, stored in the company's official record-keeping system, may not be unique in the purest sense: the three pages in a file folder may very well not be the one and only version in existence. Quite the contrary. The administrative assistant may have printed and filed the 'master' version but also e-mailed copies to each of the dozen members of the committee for their information. Duplicates abound. The uniqueness of the 'official' copy, whether paper or electronic, derives from its content, context and structure: as evidence stored safely within the company's records system, located among other records related to that same meeting.

Still, each copy of the meeting minutes may also be unique in its own context. The committee chair may have annotated her copy with notes to help her prepare for the next meeting. Another committee member may have put the minutes in a digital folder along with a series of e-mails about tasks he has to complete in the next month. As discussed in Chapter 3 and again in Chapter 11, preserving the *order* in which documents are created, used and stored can be central to preserving not just content but also context and structure, infusing archives with the quality of uniqueness.

Authentic

Archives should also be *authentic*. This means that the item in question can be proven to be what it purports to be: that the contract between Robert Kessler and William Edelman is legitimate, or that the diary was written by Adele Chiabaka. Authenticity is demonstrated if it is possible to prove that the person who *appears* to have created, sent or received a piece of evidence actually *did* create, send or receive that piece of evidence. Further, authenticity means being able to prove that the record or data element is exactly the same now as it was when it was first created and then stored for later use.

For paper records, the existence of original signatures, the use of letterhead paper or the addition of official stamps and seals (the hallmark, as it were, of medieval officialdom) are all indicators of the authenticity. Handwriting, for instance, can be analysed to authenticate the authorship of a document. The six remaining signatures purported to be in William Shakespeare's hand have been studied in microscopic detail to confirm his authorship, even though he spelled his name differently each time. Storing records securely and protecting them from unauthorized access also help to ensure authenticity. As noted already, the challenge with digital evidence is ensuring that such an easily changeable piece of information is secured so that it remains stable and authentic over time.

Scientific and physical evidence

In order to place this discussion of documentary evidence in context, it is useful to reflect on differences between documentary evidence and two other forms of evidence found in society: scientific and physical. (As any lawyer knows, a broad range of types of evidence exist, from testimonial to statistical; only scientific and physical evidence are considered here.)

Scientific evidence might take the form of an ice core drilled from a glacier in Antarctica or the cross section of a tree trunk from a forest in British Columbia. The existence of trace gases in ice rings may substantiate or refute hypotheses about weather patterns. Changes in the width or composition of tree rings may help demonstrate fluctuations in temperature or rainfall over centuries.

To make use of these samples as scientific evidence, a researcher must first extract the samples from their natural surroundings, documenting where and when they were gathered, then preserving them so they cannot be destroyed or altered: the ice cores would be frozen, and the tree samples would be kept in a climate-controlled storage room. Then the researcher must devise an experiment to measure or assess a particular substance or quality, after which he compiles and studies the data gathered. The resulting findings can be calculated, recalculated, interpreted and reinterpreted in innumerable ways to prove or disprove particular theories.

The chunk of ice or piece of tree was not created in the course of business, like a report or an e-mail. Neither the ice nor the wood carry documentary value. Although they may be invaluable parts of scientific study, they are not documentary evidence. But by analysing that scientific evidence, the research creates information, such as a statistical table or database of measurements. That new information may be considered documentary evidence, but it is different from the original ice core or cross section, which remains as objective scientific evidence, available for use in a new experiment.

Documentary evidence is also different from physical evidence, a term most familiar in the world of lawyers and courtrooms. Physical evidence includes tyre tracks, footprints, DNA samples or other material items. Like scientific evidence, physical evidence is collected and used to substantiate or rebut assertions or hypotheses. Physical evidence is usually collected in relation to a particular situation, with little expectation that anyone would use the same item for a completely different purpose.

A fingerprint on a wine glass can identify an individual beyond doubt. Footprints can confirm that a certain shoe stepped into a certain flowerbed, an important piece of information when considering whether a suspect did or did not break into a house through the window in the drawing room. Of course, having the physical evidence does not necessarily confirm precisely when the finger left a mark on the glass or when the shoe stepped in the flowerbed. The physical evidence must be interpreted in conjunction with other information in order to demonstrate a linear course of events, which may or may not support a particular theory.

The arguments presented in the courtroom, using the fingerprint or footprint as physical evidence, are captured in written form. These arguments are encapsulated in records, becoming documentary evidence of the action of charging and trying a suspect. But the footprints and fingerprints remain physical, not documentary, evidence. Therefore, they are not 'archival' as defined here, though they are still valuable should the case be reopened in years to come.

The precarious nature of documentary evidence

Identifying something as archival – static, unique and authentic, with its content, context and structure intact – is an art, not a science. The path from data to archives is perilous. Digital records are especially mutable and fragile, but paper and analogue records also need to be protected throughout all stages of record keeping.[2] Even then, regardless of whether records have been kept with their authenticity completely intact, they may still be completely false. Sometimes evidence is wilfully destroyed, fracturing the integrity of content, context and structure. Sometimes records creators are simply bad record keepers, and it is only through luck that some small portion of a larger body of evidence survives. And sometimes authentic records contain outright lies.

The mutability of electronic data

As argued, the mutability of electronic data is one of the great strengths of computerization. Electronic drafts of documents can be rewritten tens or hundreds of times without having to be retyped or reprinted. But for record keepers this flexibility is a tremendous weakness. Every time a paper document is revised, changes are obvious: pencil marks, handwritten notes or the creation of separate versions all provide evidence of alterations. An electronic document can also be edited multiple times, and no one may be able to distinguish between versions, if versions have been kept at all.

In order to preserve an authentic and usable electronic record, the document in question has to be stabilized so that it can serve as proof after the fact. Ideally, then, defining what is archival in a digital environment happens when the record is created, not years later. That way the electronic record can be stored away safely for posterity. But who knows if a piece of information will be valuable in a decade or a century? Or even next week?

Another difficulty with managing electronic records is that they rarely make their context or structure explicit. Recall the note discussed earlier, to 'meet Mike'. In a paper environment, the note would be enhanced by its structure, if it were found within Donald Trump's print-based calendar. Removing the page from the day timer removes the evidential value of the note. Similarly, a digital note that only says 'meet Mike' is meaningless unless it is possible to associate the note with who created it, when and why. If someone saved that message as 'Note to Self', copied that three-word statement onto a USB stick and put the device in a storage box, the archivist would be hard pressed to locate the structural or contextual information needed to make the note meaningful. Electronic files arriving on the doorstep of an archival institution like kittens in a box may seem far-fetched, but in reality it is extremely common for archivists to receive unlabelled CDs, 20-year-old floppy disks and USB sticks full of electronic documents named File 1, File 2, File 3, with little more explanation from the donor than 'this came from my sister's computer'.

A further challenge is capturing and preserving 'the' authentic digital record. Remember the committee minutes. In a paper environment, the master would be filed in the official record-keeping system and everyone would be given a copy. Cumbersome as it was for an organization to manage 10 or 20 copies of a document, it was much easier to identify the official record. In the electronic age, people can e-mail a document to one or a dozen other people, each of whom may download and save the version as her own, resulting in all sorts of potential 'originals'. Knowing who has the official record and that it is secure involves declaring in advance that only the chair retains official committee records and that any other copies are for convenience and should not be considered official. However, if those copies are altered by their owner, they become new records, and whether they are kept or not becomes a matter of company policy.[3]

Authenticity and truthfulness

One may be able to show that a set of records is static, unique and authentic, and therefore it has a high measure of evidential value, but this does not necessarily mean that those records are truthful. Truth is a malleable concept. A document that purports to contain objective facts may only illustrate one person's version of events. Some materials that are considered authentic evidence can be filled with bold-faced lies. While there have been multiple cases of manipulation of evidence, corruption of records and declaration of the legitimacy of 'alternative facts' in the first decades of the 21st century, particularly among governments and politicians, I shall draw on an older example. This example from the Second World War involves a deception by the Allies against the Germans, known as Operation Bodyguard. The name referred to a comment by Winston Churchill that 'in wartime, truth is so precious that she should always be attended by a bodyguard of lies'.

The goal of Operation Bodyguard was to deceive the Germans into thinking that the invasion of Normandy in June 1944 would occur at a place and time other than actually planned. As part of the operation, Allied commanders created official communications that contained false information. From a records perspective, these falsified documents are authentic: they were created by Allied officers at a particular date and time; the information they contain is what the officers intended to communicate; and the records were not altered. The fact that the records were full of lies does not negate their authenticity. Quite the opposite. They are authentic evidence of the Allied effort to lie to the enemy.[4]

Partial evidence

Often, archives hold not just partial truths but, more specifically, partial evidence. One example is the missing 18½ minutes on Tape 342 of the infamous Watergate tapes. Tape 342 was a recording of a conversation between American President Richard Nixon and Chief of Staff H. R. 'Bob' Haldeman, but that tape is missing a large portion of its content. Was the erasure deliberate or an innocent mistake? What was said that we can no longer hear?

Archivists cannot by themselves prevent the wilful destruction or mismanagement of evidence. There will always be someone who wants to hide unwelcome information and destroys records as a means to that end. The role of the archivist is not to fill in the blanks with guesses but to preserve the remaining evidence and, as time and resources allow, try to recapture the missing data with its authenticity intact, while retaining the knowledge that, for some time, that data was missing. In this instance, the American National Archives and Records Administration (NARA) has attempted many times, so far unsuccessfully, to restore the missing audio on Tape 342. Today, NARA holds the tape in a secure, climate-controlled environment and continues to carry out tests to try to resurrect the missing words.[5]

Lost evidence

It is disheartening, to say the least, when those in positions of power manipulate evidence. But it is also lamentable when the creators and users of documentary evidence seem to be, to put it bluntly, simply careless; when they ought to have known better. One such situation involved the Apollo 11 moon landing in 1969, as the American astronaut Neil Armstrong took his, and humanity's, first steps on the moon. Over 600 million people watched the event on television on that July day, the biggest television audience in history to that date. Satellite images of the historic moment were captured not only by NASA stations in the USA but also by tracking antennas in Australia, at the Honeysuckle Creek antenna near Canberra and the Parkes antenna north of Sydney.

Not long after the mission ended, several hundred original slow-scan television recordings created by NASA, along with some telemetry data of the landing and moonwalk, disappeared. Despite years of searching, only a small portion of the original audiovisual evidence has been found. It has been suggested, but not proven, that the data tapes were erased in the early 1980s because NASA procedures at the time were to reuse old data tapes when there was a shortage of unused tape stock, and, it seems, no one bothered to check the content of the tapes to make sure no precious images were lost. But lost they were.

In July 2009, in order to reconstruct images of the original events for the 40th anniversary of the moon landing, NASA ended up copying videotapes and news broadcasts from television stations around the world. Some additional footage from Australia surfaced later and was broadcast for the first time in October 2010, during a ceremony hosted by the Australian Geographic Society to honour astronaut Apollo 11's pilot Buzz Aldrin.

Today, no 'original' NASA recording exists that can by itself provide evidence of the moonwalk from NASA's perspective. Nearly a half-century later, one has to wonder why the technicians involved with recording the moonwalk at the time did not provide better care for recordings right away. Surely someone should have recognized the importance of the event and the evidence? But bureaucracies are strange creatures, and one cannot necessarily count on organizations, especially large and complex entities, to provide adequate records care.[6]

Having explained the nature of archives by examining the relationship between archives and evidence, the next task is to turn the equation on its head. Just because something is evidence does not mean it will end up in archival custody. Equally, just because something ends up in archival custody does not mean it is evidence. But it may still be worth preserving. Why? An archival institution can hold a wondrously diverse collection of materials, as considered in the next chapter.

Notes

1 It is common to use the terms 'electronic records' and 'digital records' interchangeably, as I do throughout this book, and in most cases the distinction is simply semantics. It is important, however, to distinguish between digitized records and born-digital records. Digitized records are copies of original paper or analogue records, produced through the use of scanners or other digital reproduction technologies. 'Born-digital records', which archivists used to refer to as 'machine-readable records', are created in electronic format in the first instance; no conversion from manual to electronic has taken place. Digitization is discussed in more detail in Chapter 9 in relation to preservation and in Chapter 12 in relation to reference and outreach.

2 Archivists use the term 'paper record' to refer to documents such as letters, diaries, maps, architectural drawings and even photographic images on a paper base. The term 'analogue record' refers to records created by capturing a continuous signal in or on the media itself. For instance, the texture on a phonograph record (the grooves) or the fluctuating magnitude of the signal on a video cassette capture the content of information in 'analogue' form. The term derives from the concept that the recording is 'analogous to' or bearing a relationship to the original. Analogue records differ from digital in that digital signals are represented in discrete numbers, 0s and 1s in a binary system, whereas analogue signals are physically attached to a base, such as vinyl or plastic film. The challenge of preserving paper, analogue and digital archives is discussed in Chapter 9.

3 One of the ways organizations try to reduce the confusion of digital duplicates is by establishing shared records systems, such as electronic document management systems, where the official record is stored in one location and anyone who wishes to use it can 'check it out', like a library book. When they take it out and put it back in, the computer tracks that information by capturing metadata, which is defined as a set of data that describes and provides information about other data. (Metadata might include the date the record was created, the name of the person creating it, the name of anyone editing it and the date changes were made, and so on.) The computer system can be programmed to require users to save documents with a different name if any changes have been made. These processes fall within the realm of records management

practice, not archival management practice, and so are beyond the scope of discussion here, but some valuable resources are identified at the end of the book for those seeking an introduction to records management principles.

4   An extensive analysis of the deceptions surrounding D-Day is Anthony Cave Brown's *Bodyguard of Lies: the extraordinary true story behind D-Day*, originally published in 1975 and republished by Lyons Press in 2007. Also relevant is Nicholas Rankin's 2008 work *Churchill's Wizards: the British genius for deception, 1914–1945* (Faber and Faber).

5   The Nixon Presidential Library and Museum, under the administration of the National Archives, maintains information about the tapes on its website (www.nixonlibrary.gov/index.php). This website also includes extensive archival descriptions, links to finding aids and copies of reports and investigations into the analysis of the tapes.

6   NASA's official website, especially the pages devoted to the 40th anniversary of the moonwalk in 2009, includes press releases and other documentation about the search for the missing tapes. While the story is presented from NASA's perspective, the website provides a starting point for learning more about the archival issues associated with the story of the tapes. See www.nasa.gov/mission_pages/apollo/apollo11.html.

2

The nature of archives

Look within. Let neither the peculiar quality of anything nor its value escape thee.

Marcus Aurelius (121–80) *Meditations*, 161–80 AD

Despite my argument that archives are best defined in terms of their qualities as evidence, in reality, I believe that the archivist should not assign a narrow and inflexible definition of archives, or fixate on particular forms or media, when deciding what to keep for posterity. Illuminated medieval manuscripts may have archival value, and so may 19th-century diaries. Electronic versions of a local government's constitution and bylaws, and black and white photographs of the 1933 Chicago World's Fair both provide evidence. So too might a digital membership list for an environmental protest group, a published book littered with handwritten annotations, a *National Geographic* map marked up to show the route of a family holiday, or a medal for service in the 1916 Battle of the Somme.

To determine value based solely on form is not useful. Arguing, for instance, that every e-mail from one person to another should be preserved because it is an e-mail is as useful as saying all 8½" × 11" pieces of paper should be kept permanently because all 8½" × 11" documents are records. The physical base on which information rests should not be a factor in determining evidential value, even though it is a concern when determining preservation strategies. The concept of evidence must be interpreted broadly. A printed document or digital file may not be considered admissible evidence in a court of law, but it may well hold sufficient value as documentary evidence, adding to the richness of an archival collection.

In the ideal world, the archivist receives quality archives with their content, context and structure intact, so their evidential value is easy to assess. But in the real world, the archivist may arrive at the office one day to find a box of old papers or an envelope full of floppy disks on her desk, like those stray kittens on the doorstep. These two scenarios – the ideal and the reality – are discussed below.

Archives as a continuum of care

The 'ideal' archival environment is one in which records come into permanent custody or control through a formalized and sustained information management programme, which defines and distinguishes between information, records and evidence. Formal policies determine whether the organization's official records should be in digital or physical form; which records have legal, administrative, financial or other value; and which materials should be defined as archival. The physical form of the materials only matters inasmuch as the archivist needs to know how to protect films or photographs or data tapes or trophies.

By their very nature, digital records demand a strong and effective continuum of care, which is a core message throughout this book. And one of the essential components of quality care is the management of digital records from the point of creation, capturing content, context and structure from the start. The archivist processing 50-year-old paper archives will look at the titles on the file folders to understand content, context and structure. She will see that one file contains 'Meeting Minutes 1966' and another 'Annual Reports 1967'. The order in which records are stored helps provide that important context.

Digital records do not necessarily end up stored in 'files', so capturing metadata about each digital object is essential to give meaning to the content. As mentioned already, metadata is defined as data or information that describes and contextualizes other data. Metadata explains the context, content and structure of each discrete digital object. (A digital object, put very simply, is the electronic 'item' that needs to be managed.)

Metadata might identify one digital object as a PDF and explain that it consists of the text of a report, while metadata for another digital object might identify it as a photograph that has been stored as a TIFF file as opposed to a JPEG file. Metadata might also explain when the record was created, whether it was altered later and who was responsible for creating it or capturing it in a digital storage system.[1]

When processing digital archives, the archivist has to look at each item in order to decide what it is and whether it is worth keeping, unless a process has been established to ensure that documents with archival value are stored securely, with their metadata intact, and those with no enduring value are removed from record-keeping systems when they are no longer needed. As a result of this requirement to ensure digital records are preserved from the start, particularly in the public sector, archival institutions have shifted their focus from acquiring and preserving historical archives to helping their sponsor agencies to establish and enforce laws and regulations to manage current electronic records effectively.

Archives and what is left behind

Many may consider the creation and management of authentic evidence through a chain of reliable record-keeping actions as the ideal, but it is far from the norm. The preservation of archives is often neither systematic nor guaranteed. By the time the archivist sees some materials, they may have endured years, decades or centuries of documentary strife. Sometimes archival preservation is more by accident than design: the acquisition may consist of a few boxes that survived a fire or some ledgers not forgotten in a cupboard when the company moved offices. Archives may end up in a repository hundreds of years after they were first created, and the journey from creation to preservation might have been fraught with perils of near-Biblical proportions.

One scenario is particularly common in smaller archival institutions, such as a community archives. The local archivist may receive a call one day from a trustee at the local mosque, the treasurer for an artists' guild or the owner of a local business, saying 'please come retrieve this old stuff from my basement, or attic, or loft or storage closet... I have run out of space... I am moving.... I am no longer on the executive committee.' The materials, which may have been created a year or a century ago, may well have been kept in marginal conditions and may arrive in a fragile state. Further, the acquisition may include not just documentary materials but books, magazines, printed maps, copies of magazines, desk ornaments or geological specimens; sometimes the archival institution is seen as a bit of a dumping ground, and the archivist has to sift through reams of castoffs to find the few items with archival value.

Too often, the archivist is not in a position to judge the quality of the materials right away. If her institution's mandate includes preserving the archives of her community, and if the materials purport to be from people or groups in that community, her first task may be to provide a safe haven for the materials. Only later can she sort through the boxes to determine which items are worthy of retention. She cannot say yes or no before she knows what she has in hand. (As discussed in Chapter 10, saying no to a potential acquisition is very hard, but sometimes it is essential to archival success.)

Preserving the Domesday Book

The vagaries of custody are demonstrated in the story of the Domesday Book, England's oldest surviving public record. King William commissioned the Domesday Book, a two-volume survey of all the land held by the King of England and his chief tenants, sometime around 1080. The Domesday Book is a census document: it recorded who owned what land, what the land was worth, what taxes were levied and how many people lived on the land. For many centuries the book served as a record, but it was created and maintained for the king's benefit, not for posterity. He carried it with him from Westminster to Winchester and many other locations as part of his travelling 'office'.

Today, many societies consider census records to be extremely valuable evidence of population numbers, demographics and domestic life. But the evidential value of the Domesday Book was not really appreciated until the end of the 16th century, when people realized that the volumes gave a unique objective account of the nature of towns and villages throughout the country in the 11th century. In the 1740s, the volumes were moved to the Chapter House in Westminster Abbey and in 1859 they were transferred to the Public Record Office (PRO) in Chancery Lane, London, for permanent preservation. In 1996, the volumes were moved to the new PRO offices, now The National Archives in Kew.

While it might have been preferable for the Domesday Book always to have been stored in secure vaults, with adequate fire suppression systems and anti-theft devices, such was not the reality of life in England in the 11th, 17th or 19th centuries. (Indeed, such is not the reality of archival storage in much of the world today.) That these volumes survived at all is something of a miracle, and their value derives in part from the fact that they offer such a rare glimpse into life over nine centuries ago.[2]

When the transitory becomes archival

When the butcher gave our grandmother a receipt for the piece of beef roast she bought for Sunday dinner, our grandmother likely did not feel compelled to keep that receipt permanently. She saw it as transitory, just as we might define a receipt for our coffee at Starbucks as transitory today. If our grandmother *did* keep the receipt, perhaps by accident, it might have ended up as part of an archival collection. Even though its original value as evidence was extinguished as soon as the cooked beef was on the table, it now serves as an interesting example of domestic life from the 1800s. Today, most archivists would protest at keeping any receipts; they are transitory records, superseded by official financial statements, annual reports, summaries of expenditures. But when such ephemeral items survive over a long time, by accident or design, they may be invaluable for unexpected reasons.

One such archival collection – a list of plants and a collection of garden receipts from the 17th century – became a source of evidence for the restoration of the Privy Garden at Hampton Court Palace in England. In 1995, archaeologists, historians, landscape architects and other specialists collab-orated to return the garden to the original design conceived by King William III and his wife, Queen Mary II in 1702. To ensure the restoration was accurate, the team turned to original drawings, maps and plans, lists of plants and other archival materials, including original receipts for the plants purchased by William and Mary. (Well, okay, by their Palace staff. I suspect they did not visit any garden centres themselves.) As it happens, these documents were kept by staff at the time the gardens were constructed, and for some reason they were kept in the Palace's records vaults, 'becoming' archives by virtue of their survival. And now, 300 years later, they have been used as evidence to support the reconstruction of the garden.[3]

An archivist today needs to assess such rare documentary finds not just in terms of the value of comparable evidence today but in relation to their scarcity and value as a window into the past. Is the receipt the only evidence left, precious by its rarity? Do we find a report marked 'draft' but no compar-able document marked 'final', which means the draft version may be the most authoritative? What does an odd piece of paper, such as a sticky note that says 'meet Mike', tell us today, and can we actually use that sticky note as evidence, or is its content, context and structure so obliterated that we can make no sense of it whatever?

The forms of archives

While the physical form of archives is not the first question to consider when assessing their evidential value, it is natural to think of archives as consisting of traditional documentary materials: diaries, letters, reports, photographs or ledgers. To counteract this misapprehension about the form of archives, it is instructive to consider those materials that sit on the border between 'archives' and 'other' but that might still have archival value.

Publications

Published items, whether in digital or paper form, may not seem at first glance to be archival. Often printed materials are categorized, rather vaguely, as 'special collections', 'rare books and special collections', 'ephemera', 'grey literature', 'fugitive literature' and so on. To determine the archival value of these published materials, the archivist first needs to consider their uniqueness within the context and structure of the larger body of archives.

By themselves, books, magazines, journals or newspapers are generally not considered archival. They are not documents created and used in the course of daily life and work and kept because they provide evidence. They are deliberate creations, intended for dissemination, produced primarily with an eye to their use by others. They are not 'innocent by-products' of people's lives and work.

But copies of an author's published novel may provide evidence that the publication existed. The book itself is the cumulative evidence of the writing and editing process, which may be documented separately in the author's manuscripts, page proofs, editorial notes and communications with the editor. Thus one can easily argue that the novel has evidential value. More than likely, the book would remain with the author's archives, though in some institutions, such as university special collections departments, the actual copy may end up stored in another location to facilitate preservation and use.

Sometimes a publication written by someone other than the creator of the archives has archival value. For instance, Isaac Newton's annotated copy of Elias Ashmole's *Theatrum chemicum Britannicum* (1652), housed at Penn Libraries at the University of Pennsylvania, contains several additions and notations in Newton's own hand. The notes serve as evidence that Newton had read and considered Ashmole's study of alchemy (the transmutation of metals into gold, a field of study closely linked with investigations into spirituality and astrology). Newton's handwritten notes in a book written by someone else provide enough evidence to argue that Newton – one of the most influential scientists in history – was aware of and perhaps influenced by Ashmole and others interested in the less-than-scientific practice of alchemy. The book, though a published work, becomes archival evidence by virtue of Newton's annotations.[4]

Ephemera can also find a legitimate place within collections of archival materials, if the items provide evidence or information that enhances an understanding of other archival materials. Ephemera are those bits and pieces of transitory documentation created for an immediate purpose and then considered obsolete, such as tickets, flyers, pamphlets and posters. The digital equivalent of ephemera, such as a tweet or a Facebook post, may also carry evidential value, though its preservation opens up a complex web of technological and administrative requirements. By themselves, these fleeting, transitory items provide little more than confirmation of an event or occasion or evidence of a random communication. But in a wider context they can serve as evidence.

A printed poster, for instance, may confirm that a musical concert was planned for a particular day and place, but the poster alone does not provide evidence that anyone actually showed up to hear the music. Woodstock, the music festival held at a dairy farm in Bethel, New York, in 1969, was epitomized by the saying, 'If you can remember it, you weren't there.' A poster for the concert is an interesting piece of ephemera, but as a discrete item its evidential value is marginal at best. The poster becomes fairly solid proof of attendance, however, if it resides in the archives of a now-aging hippie, accompanied by photographs of him dancing in the mud and a copy of a documentary film made of the event, which includes clips of him being interviewed at the farm. As part of this larger body of records, the poster becomes infinitely more meaningful. It substantiates the grey-haired hippie's claim, 'I was there . . . even though I don't remember it very well.'

Photographs

Photographs – from tintypes, stereographs or Polaroid prints in the physical realm to JPEGs or TIFF files in the digital – are commonly useful as much more than pure evidence. Images can depict costumes and hairstyles or illustrate architectural features and changes in modes of transportation. More than many other archives, photographic materials highlight the distinctions between then and now.

But the context in which photographs were originally taken is still critically important. Knowing who took the photographs, when and why, is essential to understanding not just the content of the image but also the meaning behind the event depicted. Photographs of a parade float, a train in a station, a group of soldiers sitting in a trench or people walking on a beach tell us what parades, train stations, soldiers and beaches looked like.

But what if the float is in the first gay pride parade, down Christopher Street to Central Park in New York in June 1970? What if the train in the station was used to move Japanese Canadians to internment camps in the Second World War? What if the soldiers were members of the Australian and New Zealand Army Corps at the start of the 1915 Gallipoli Campaign? What if the people on the beach are Syrian refugees in 2015, making landfall in Greece? Seeing the content but not knowing the context prevents us from truly understanding the image. We need to know the who, what, where, when and why of the images to allow them to serve as proof. When assessing them, therefore, the archivist needs to consider their evidential value as well as their usefulness as information.

Audiovisual materials

What about commercial films, musical recordings or home movies? The last is generally easy to assess: an 8 mm film of a family at Christmas in the 1960s is tangible and engaging evidence of their life a half-century ago. A movie recording a safari in Kenya in 1982, a CD of an orchestra's performance in France in 1976, and a YouTube recording of a speech given by a noted economist at an international conference in 2012 all bring to life static documents such as letters and postcards, concert brochures or the printed text of a speech. While the preservation of such audiovisual materials can be challenging, their evidential value often warrants the effort and expense.

But the value of other audiovisual materials may be less obvious. Consider a training video used for new recruits in the army reserves or a DVD of a cooking demonstration. Did the video arrive as part of the archives of an army reserve unit? In that case it would be core evidence of the steps taken to train new recruits. Or was it found in a box of discards from the local library, with no contextual information to demonstrate a link to the community? In that case, its evidential value is non-existent. Did the DVD feature the noted chef whose papers are now part of the archives' holdings, or was it a commercial production found among a box of books and magazines offered to the archives by someone cleaning out their basement? The former offers evidential value; the latter does not.

Maps and plans

Architectural drawings, maps, renderings and other cartographic or diagrammatic materials can also provide documentary evidence. Fire insurance plans are among the most popular materials in many municipal and city archives, providing evidence not only of the location of a building but also of its size and shape, the construction materials employed and the various uses of the building over time: restaurant, laundry, residence and so on. Copies of published road maps, atlases or tourist maps may have less value. Their archival worth may increase if they are part of the archives of a tourist agency or cartographic publisher, or if someone has traced onto the map the journey the orchestra took on its tour, which can be linked to photographs to verify the route taken.

Digital information sources

Apart from digital records that often have evidential value, such as electronic spreadsheets, photographs, word-processed documents and so on, other more ephemeral digital content needs to be considered, including websites and web pages, Twitter messages, blog posts and Facebook messages. Again the archivist faces the question of evidence. Was a critical government decision announced on Twitter, in which case the tweet is proof of that decision, with archival value? Is the website the organization's primary tool for communicating news, in which case each unique iteration of the website could serve as evidence of the organization's activities? Are the photographs on Facebook copies only, and are the original digital images safely stored elsewhere?[5]

Archives and art

It can be difficult to decide the place of fine art, such as oil paintings, watercolours, sketches or sculptures, in an archival institution. Art can serve as documentary evidence, especially when the items were produced before photography became common. Sketches of soldiers on a battlefield, paintings of English country villages or portraits of Dutch burghers can provide the only visual evidence of a long-ago place, person or time.

But art can also carry aesthetic value, which elevates the job of appraisal into another realm. Aesthetic value and the notion of artistic beauty are important considerations, but they are not what motivates archival preservation in the first instance. The best archival decisions about art do not focus on territoriality (this object belongs in my institution even though I do not have the resources to care for it) or on questions of monetary value or prestige (this object raises the cultural standing of my institution). The best decisions focus on what evidential value exists and what is best for the item.

Today, when digital copies of art can be made so easily, keeping an original piece of art simply for the pleasure of owning it, when it carries little documentary value and especially if storage conditions are not optimal, is unwise. Of course, the archivist may have little choice but to keep the piece, if the item has value but there is no other appropriate facility available.

Archives and artefacts

Another boundary emerges when the archivist is presented with three-dimensional objects. Archival collections often contain artefacts, just as museum collections contain archives. To forestall territorial disputes, the archivist should work with her colleagues in museums and galleries to share information and co-ordinate actions. The intellectual and historical links between archives and artefacts should be maintained even if the items themselves find a home elsewhere.

Artefacts as evidence
Classic examples of artefacts in archival collections are trophies, medals and plaques. These items were not created in the course of daily life and kept as documentary evidence. Rather, they were deliberately manufactured to commemorate an achievement or memorialize an event. But these artefacts may help explain aspects of the life of a person or the work of a group. They can serve as evidence.

A trophy may be engraved with nothing more than 'John Carlson – first place'. Considered in relation to associated archival materials, the trophy may flesh out the story of John Carlson: a steamfitter who not only competed with his provincial tennis team, receiving first place honours in 1948, but was also president of the local tennis association for 25 years. If the trophy is removed before the link is made between object and context, both the archival collection and the artefact lose meaning.

Looking at the artefact out of context, the museum visitor may not learn anything more about John Carlson than that he was an otherwise anonymous person who received first place in some event. Similarly, the researcher studying John Carlson's archives without knowing about the trophy is denied an opportunity to look beyond documentary facts and engage with tangible, physical objects that help bring to life the story of this champion tennis player. Regardless of where an artefact ultimately resides, the archivist has a particular responsibility to maintain the intellectual links among all items that arrive at the door of the repository, even if some ultimately reside in another facility, such as a museum, a gallery, a library or – as in the example below – a zoo.

Hilary Jenkinson's elephant
In 1922, English archivist Sir Hilary Jenkinson published his famous archival treatise, *A Manual of Archival Administration*. In his book, Jenkinson, who worked at the PRO in London, struggled with the place of three-dimensional objects in his definition of 'document'. Jenkinson had been presented with a range of unusual items in his archival career, including human hair, whips, penny pieces and 'a packet of strange powder destined to cure cancer'. When searching for a principle on which to base practical decisions of arrangement and description, Jenkinson resolved that such items must be considered part of the document, since they had been received in the archives as part of that archival unit.

Taking his argument to an extreme that even he referred to as a *reductio ad absurdum*, Jenkinson presented a hypothetical scenario involving an elephant sent home to the secretary of state in England from the Viceroy of a faraway colony. The elephant had been accompanied by a 'suitable covering-note or label'. The question Jenkinson asked was this: 'Is the elephant attached to the label or the label to the elephant?' Jenkinson wiggled out of the dilemma by suggesting that the matter was in fact administrative, not archival. Logically, the elephant would have been sent to the zoo long before the note made its way into archival custody. The archivist should never have to deal with matters of pachydermal storage.[6]

But Jenkinson did not solve the *archival* problem. Archivists are frequently faced with acquisitions that include all manner of three-dimensional materials, from uniforms to bowling balls to football helmets to baby boots (bronzed or otherwise). Whether or not an archivist decides to add these items to the institution's holdings becomes a matter of policy not theory. Are other institutions in the region, such as a museum, gallery or library, better suited to receiving and retaining those items? What is the argument for keeping the objects in the archives? Perhaps they are worth keeping; they provide evidence not available elsewhere, they will be useful in exhibits or their acquisition may allow the archivist to expand her institution's scope and mandate.

The archivist needs to develop and implement sound and well thought-out acquisition policies and procedures, which should form the basis for answering the question of whether or not to keep the object. The museum curator, gallery manager or librarian should ask the same questions when faced with archival materials. They should not simply split out the different media materials, pack up that which does not fit their particular definition of archives, publications or artefacts, and pass the box on somewhere else without documenting the existence, origins and inter-relationship of the different materials.

Keeping Jenkinson's elephant, had it arrived in the archival institution instead of finding a home in the zoo, would benefit neither the elephant nor the archives. Separating items is often essential to managing them. As long as the contextual information is retained, even across institutions, potential users will be able to reconstruct the totality of the materials intellectually, if not always physically. If, however, archives and artefacts are so intertwined that separating one from the other would erase any ability to understand either, then the relationship between them must be maintained.

Archives and the intangible

Before closing this chapter, it is important to emphasize that archives are, as the South African archivist Verne Harris has said, only the smallest 'sliver of a sliver of a sliver' of the data and information societies create, use and share.[7] The vast majority of society's communications, information and ideas are never documented. We may only recall a sunset or a musical performance in our memories. We may end a negotiation about a pay increase with a handshake, not a written agreement. We may never photograph our workplace or keep our voice mail messages. The absence of records does not mean that the information, ideas or events never existed, but only that there is no residual documentary evidence of them.

Many forms of communication and memory making do not even result in what might be defined as documentary evidence. Folk tales and songs, etchings on cave walls, rituals, family stories and other cultural creations are used to shape memories into narratives, transferring information and knowledge from the individual to the collective. A traditional song performed in an aboriginal community in Canada, a religious service in Greece or a Māori haka or war dance in New Zealand all have cultural meaning within those communities. These songs, services and performances are more ethereal than archives but often of equal or greater social value. Sometimes a decision is taken to make a record of the experience: to capture a song or service or dance on film, perhaps. But capturing the event is not the same as experiencing it. And in some cultures, experiencing the event, whether in person or through a recording, is a privilege limited to only certain members of the group.

The challenge for the archivist when deciding what comes into archival care is to consider not just the legal and administrative conditions that define the materials as documentary evidence but also the cultural qualities that infuse them with wider social value. Archives are tangible expressions of fact and act that provide documentary evidence; some of what a society considers part of its memory may not fit within those documentary boundaries.

But this does not mean those intangibles are not worth keeping, just that they are different from archives, just as artefacts and art and publications are different. Every institution has to clarify the boundaries around its collection, or else the poor archivist will be chasing nebulous pieces of information with the archival equivalent of butterfly nets.

The Canadian philosopher Marshall McLuhan argued in the 1960s that 'the medium is the message'. One could argue that the archivist approaches her work the other way around: looking for the message that comes from the totality of archives and then deciding if a particular documentary source, regardless of its medium, provides enough evidence to warrant retention. It is inappropriate to split up archival holdings simply because some items take one physical form while others take another. But practical decisions must also be made. Sometimes it is best to send the elephant to the zoo.

———————

Having looked at the idea of archives as evidence and then considered how different media materials may or may not form part of an archival collection, the next task is to provide a brief overview of developments in archival history and then to introduce major archival theories and principles. Inevitably, those theories have been challenged, and new and alternate approaches to archives must also be considered. The complex intersections between archival history and archival theory are tackled in the next chapter.

Notes

1   A PDF (portable document format) is a format for storing digital documents so that they can be opened and used independently of any particular piece of software. A TIFF (tagged information file format) is one format for storing digital graphics. Another format is called JPEG (Joint Photographic Experts Group; or JPG), after the organization that created the standard. The differences between the two are important for digital preservation: a TIFF file is not compressed, so the actual digital data in a TIFF-formatted object can retain its original quality. A JPEG file, on the other hand, is usually compressed to save space in a digital storage system, so the object might lose some quality each time it is opened and saved.

2   Dozens of works have been published on the Domesday Book. For information on the custodial history and current status of the Domesday Book, and to access information from the book online, go to the website of The National Archives (www.nationalarchives.gov.uk) and search for 'Domesday Book'.

3   A short but informative analysis of the restoration of the gardens is Mavis Batey's *The Story of the Privy Garden at Hampton Court*, Barn Elms Publishing, 2006.

4   Information about this particular book can be found at http://franklin.library.upenn.edu/record.html?id=FRANKLIN_2374826. A fascinating discussion of the ways in which annotations, bookplates and even the bent corners of pages can provide contextual information about historical publications is given in Laura Aydelotte's 'Isaac Newton's books', posted on the Provenance Online Project website (https://provenanceonlineproject.wordpress.com/2016/09/20/isaac-newtons-books/) on 20 September 2016.

5   Many social media applications are governed by ownership and copyright laws that conflict with the rights of the people whose content is housed on those sites,

a fact not well appreciated by many who rely on social media to store their family photographs. Treating a Facebook page as a safe storage repository is a recipe for archival disaster. In such cases the archivist can provide a valuable service by offering guidance to researchers, users and the public about how to store digital records archives for posterity.

6 See Jenkinson, H. (1922) *A Manual of Archival Administration, Including the Problems of War Archives and Archive Making*, Clarendon Press, 6–7.

7 See Harris, V. (2002) 'The Archival Sliver: power, memory, and archives in South Africa', *Archival Science*, **2**, 63–86.

3

Archival history and theory

No theory is good except on condition that one uses it to go beyond.
André Gide (1869–1951) *Journals*, 5 August 1931

While the concept of archives as evidence is considered a central component of archival theory and practice today, it was not always thus. Across the centuries, the reasons archives were valued and ways in which they were preserved varied according to local custom or inclination. No doubt, future generations will define archives and evidence differently; such is the nature of a discipline that manages the products of information and communications. As information and communications change, society's sense of the worth of documentary products must also change. I have no ability to predict the future, but I believe strongly that we can learn from the past. So in this chapter I offer an extremely brief overview of the history of archival development, summarizing ideas captured in countless archival texts. Then I introduce central archival theories and principles and place them within that historical framework. I end the chapter by considering how archival theories and principles are being challenged today.[1]

Trends in archival history

We have had archives – documentary evidence – since before we have had records as we define them today. Pictographs have evidential value, as do stone stele, clay tablets and totem poles, if one can read the visual or symbolic content and capture the meaning. With such a long past, tracing the evolution of archival milestones over several centuries can only offer a whisper of the deep and complex history of the materials themselves and the people who manage them. But this overview, concise as it must be, will help orient the reader to the changing perception of the role and use of archives in different times and places.

Archives for church and crown

For millennia, archives were considered the sole property of the agency that created them, be it church, state or sovereign. Whether on papyrus, leather or bone, early records were preserved for their owner and most assuredly not for the public. The discovery of hundreds and thousands of clay tablets from as early as the 2nd millennium BC in archaeological sites in Syria, Egypt and Turkey provide clear evidence of the desire by ancient societies to create and preserve records, whether for short-term use or later reference.

But at a time when few people had the technology to create documents or the capacity to read them, those records that were made were largely under the control of a select group of bureaucrats, scribes or clerics. He who controlled the information (and it was almost always a 'he') held the reins of power. The arrangement, storage and use of those records were based on what worked best for that organization, not for anyone else, whether then or in the future.

Still, libraries had long been in existence, including the famous Library of Alexandria, a centre of scholarship built in Egypt in the 3rd century BC and destroyed several times over the next 800 years. Coincidentally or not, it was in the 3rd century that paper became more widely used, and by the 10th century paper mills had become commonplace in such dispersed locations as Egypt, Ethiopia and China. Increased access to paper and ink and a slow but consistent growth in literacy led to more people creating and using records.

Monarchs and religious leaders were still the primary records creators, but philosophers, historians and scholars were also creating their own documentary outputs, leading to a call for more places to store and use records and histories. Libraries, town halls, scriptoria, temples, treasuries or portable storage chests became 'archival repositories'. But it was not until well into the 17th and 18th centuries that, in some corners of the world at least, people outside the halls of power gained greater access to records.

Archives for the people

The turmoil of the French Revolution in the late 1790s prompted a new vision for archives in Europe. After the First Republic defeated and executed King Louis XIV, its leaders set about restructuring all aspects of French society. Among the sweeping changes, this government declared that an autonomous, new Archives Nationales would be established, removed from direct political influence. This hands-off approach to archival management was not entirely successful. After all, the new government was itself responsible for the destruction of archives from the old regime, in part to buttress its version of history. But real change had taken place: greater public access to government records was a circumstance not imagined only decades before.

As the European public made more use of archives, historical research flourished. While historians had been drawing on some form of record from the time of the Greek historians Herodotus (484–425 BC) and Thucydides (460–400 BC), it was only in the early 19th century that archives became a pre-eminent source of history. Scholars such as German historian and educator Leopold von Ranke (1795–1886) demanded 'authenticity' in historical analyses, requiring that scholars make greater use of original documentary materials. An academic interest in primary sources led to heightened pressure on governments, churches and other institutions to increase public access to their archives; many complied, if reluctantly.

At the same time, particularly in the new nations of the USA and Canada, both of which had a great interest in their origins but few authentic documentary sources in hand, scholars and citizens pushed for the preservation of not only official records but also personal papers. National and university libraries expanded their collecting focus; historical societies, museums and community archives were established. Many governments formalized the care of their own archives, establishing repositories to house their older records. Soon, a division began to emerge, between institutions solely responsible for their sponsor agency archives and institutions dedicated to collecting archives from other sources.

Archives as collections

The result was a fork in the road for archives. A government archives in Vienna might care primarily if not exclusively for the archives of that government. A university library in London or Boston might acquire and preserve archives from many different sources but have nothing to do with the university's records. Problems began to arise when creating agencies that, one might argue today, ought to have cared for their own institutional archives, turned that responsibility over to another organization, sometimes haphazardly.

While collecting institutions were happy to receive documents not wanted by the creating agency, the chain of custody was, in effect, broken. Not only was there a risk that governments and organizations would lose sight of the responsibility to manage the evidence of their actions and decisions, but there was a greater risk that the public's perception of the value of archives would turn away from evidence and accountability toward history and scholarship.

This collecting orientation reached full flower in Canada, where the national archival institution, established in 1872, started life with a mission to acquire, actively and vigorously, anything that helped tell Canada's story. One must remember that the country itself was only created through Confederation five years before, in 1867. There were not a lot of 'original' archives sitting around in offices waiting to be collected. And there was no national museum, library or art gallery that might acquire other materials on behalf of the nation. This situation prompted the government to appoint a Dominion Archivist, who began his work not by collecting official records but instead by copying historical documents in French and British archives. He (and his successors) also collected artefacts, art, war memorabilia and any manner of historical object.

This all-embracing approach broadened the perception of the nature of archives and the purpose of archival institutions. By the middle of the 20th century, a principle (some say a theory) evolved in Canada, and was later adopted elsewhere, called 'total archives'. A total archives approach justified the duty of an archival institution (most often a publicly funded institution) to acquire and preserve all types of archives and other historical resources, in all forms and media, copies or originals, from any creating agency whose activities had a bearing on the history of the jurisdiction: be it nation, state or city.

This approach was not accepted without question. For instance, Americans, who saw the value of segregating public and private initiatives and believed firmly in individual and local responsibility, preferred to separate state archival institutions and private-sector historical societies. In England, public and private were divided at the national level with the creation of the British Library (within the British Museum) in 1753 and the establishment of the PRO in 1838. But local government archives across England tended to adopt a broad remit, caring for both local authority archives and community papers. In all cases, an important principle was being redefined: archives as evidence for the king were being replaced by archives as collections for history.

The archivist as custodian

The ground shifted again in the 1950s and 1960s. The bureaucracy and administration required to fight two world wars had generated massive volumes of government records around the world. At the same time, the blossoming of information technologies such as photocopiers and typewriters led to the creation and duplication of ever more documents. The storage rooms of governments in Europe, North America and elsewhere began to burst with records, leaving those responsible for their care reeling under the weight.

The American archivist Theodore R. Schellenberg, author of several treatises on archival management including the manual *Modern Archives* in 1956, was one of many who acknowledged that 20th-century archives needed to be managed more systematically. Schellenberg and others introduced a 'life cycle' approach, in which records care was divided into three phases: active, semi-active and inactive.

In the active or current phase, records would be created and used to support the administrative requirements of the creating agency. In the semi-active or semi-current phase, records with continuing administrative value would be retained for ongoing reference by the organization, ideally in some separate storage location to save space and money. Those records with no further value could be destroyed as soon as they were considered obsolete. Finally, in the inactive or non-current phase, those records with enduring value would be sent to a separate archival facility, ideally but not always within the organization itself, and any remaining obsolete records would be eliminated.

Because the institution receiving the archives sat at the end of this life cycle, the archivist rarely played a direct role in managing those records while they were actively used. The archivist's job was to decide what small percentage of records was worth keeping, either by reviewing all records in the storage rooms before any were destroyed or by defining sets of records with obvious continuing value and requiring their transfer to archival care. (The dreaded 'selective retention' appraisal criterion – 'we can't decide now if these records will be useful later so we will send them to the archives and let the archivist decide sometime down the road' – took firm hold at this time.)

Another consequence of this life cycle approach was that people began to perceive of records as new and archives as old. Two disciplines emerged, particularly in North America, to provide services at these two ends of the cycle. The archivist, seen as historian and scholar, was responsible for preserving the stuff of history, the old stuff. The records manager, perceived as technician and administrator, was responsible for managing records to improve efficiency and effectiveness in the office, the new stuff. They did not have much to do with each other, these two professions, defining their scope of responsibilities very differently.

The archivist as record keeper

In Australia, a different approach to records and archives management emerged. Interestingly, the Australian attitude was a direct consequence of the same 20th-century conditions that led to the definition of a life cycle. The wars and the technology boom affected Australia as well, but the difficulties of managing a massively growing body of records and archives were exacerbated by the fact that the Commonwealth government (established in 1901 as a federation of six existing colonies) was in a state of relentless organizational flux by the early decades of the 20th century. Government departments were restructured with painful regularity, and the records associated with different government functions were moved so often, with every bureaucratic change, that it was increasingly difficult to track their administrative chain of custody, never mind their actual location at a given time. Severe space shortages compounded the problem.

In 1944, the federal government's first archives officer, Ian Maclean, made the pivotal decision to prioritize current records care over historical archives management. Like Canada and the USA, Australia was a new country, and Maclean and his colleagues – including an important figure, Peter Scott, one of Maclean's colleagues at the Commonwealth Archives Office (CAO) in the 1950s and 1960s – were not bound by the pressure to manage centuries of medieval documents, like their counterparts in Europe. New approaches were possible.

In 1966, Scott and his CAO colleagues devised what they called the 'series system' of archival management. In this system, the focus would be on capturing information about records, sometimes even before the materials came into archival care, rather than waiting for boxes of archives to land in a storage depot. *Control* was emphasized over *custody*. To support this more dynamic approach, record keepers would focus on defining government functions and then identifying the different agencies responsible for those functions over time. They would then identify the 'series' of records that documented those functions. The three discrete pieces of information – function, agent and series – would be captured in separate descriptive tools and linked together to show *who* was doing *what* and *when*, and to identify which records were created to provide evidence of those functions.

The details of the series system (and its evolution into a functional approach to archival management, to macro-appraisal, and ultimately to the concept of a records continuum) are addressed later. For now, the important point is to mark this historical milestone. While the life cycle left the archivist at the end of a chain of duties, on the periphery of records care until archives were in *custody*, the series system allowed the archivist to identify and define records of value even when those materials were still in the office of the creating agency, so the archivist could gain *control* even before she had custody.

At the same time, though, a growing number of institutions continued to focus on collecting 'old' archives from their communities to support history and scholarship. Two different perceptions of the nature and scope of archives emerged, one focused on evidence and proof and one on historical information or antiquarian treasure.

The impact of postmodernism

Another shift in perceptions about archives occurred with the rise of postmodernism in the 1980s and 1990s. The philosophy of postmodernism was seen as a reaction to the certainty and authority associated with modernist perspectives, which themselves were a shift away from the belief in reason and rationalism that were hallmarks of the Enlightenment. Postmodernism emphasized differences instead of similarities, conflict instead of consensus and doubt instead of truth. The concept, which began in the world of architecture, rejected the notion of unity and harmony between form and function, positing instead that all constructions were subjective, whether they were physical or intellectual. An office building was not just a place to work but a political statement; a book was defined not by what the author intended but also by what the reader(s) interpreted.

Archivists began exploring postmodernism as early as 1966, with the publication of philosopher and historian Michel Foucault's *The Order of Things*, an examination of the nature and origins of the human sciences, and his companion piece *The Archaeology of Knowledge* (1969), which questioned the idea of authenticity and truth in communications. But it was Jacques Derrida's book *Archive Fever: a Freudian impression* (published in French in 1995 and in English in 1996) that directly challenged the notion that records and archives could be objective sources of evidence.

Drawing on the writings of Derrida and others, postmodern archival thinkers questioned the idea that archives could be innocent by-products of life and work, as had been assumed by Jenkinson, Schellenberg and others. They also argued that archival materials did not tell only one 'story' but could be interpreted in different ways depending on the audience. Postmodernists claimed that all texts were conscious creations and that archivists played an active role in selecting materials for preservation and therefore in deciding how evidence and history were shaped.

The benefit of postmodernism for the protection of archives as evidence was that archivists were given the freedom to interact with records and archives well before they came into custody. Since the postmodern archivist was not objective, direct involvement in records care would not diminish this non-existent objectivity. Postmodernism encouraged archivists to shed their role as guardians or gate keepers, instead placing the archivist in the position of steward, a person whose job was to manage a fluid documentary resource on behalf of everyone in society and not impede the path for those seeking documentary truth(s) in archival holdings. Many embraced this more direct role, seeing archival management as a mechanism for supporting social justice, by helping to protect the archives not just of the agents of power but also of the marginalized in society.

But still, postmodernists argued, the archivist had to remember that archives could not really serve as objective 'evidence' since there was, really, no one truth to tell. The drawback to postmodernism, then, was the danger that archivists would feel either paralyzed – unable to make a decision because there were too many variables – or excessively empowered – moving beyond 'objectively' managing the records that society created to actively helping to create records in the first place.

In recent years, the postmodern interpretation of archival service has taken a new twist. There is a growing call among archivists, historians and the public to become even more engaged with archival care in order to 'decolonize' the archive. The argument for decolonization is that traditional approaches to archives and history (even postmodern approaches) have been patriarchal and imperial, driven by the elite in society and not representative of the concerns of minorities or the marginalized. Those who advocate decolonization believe that archivists have to redress this wrong, for instance by de-emphasizing histories based on government archives; placing more value on non-traditional sources of information such as oral histories, aboriginal stories and community rituals; or questioning the right of scholars or archivists to participate in archival or historical work if those people are not themselves part of the community represented in the archives.

A brief discourse on archival theories

As can be seen from the above short history, the archival landscape has changed over thousands of years, from archives for the king, to archives as history; from whether archives are best cared for in custody or controlled from a distance; from the belief that archives serve as evidence to the suggestion that archives are only biased representations and partial truths.

As history has changed, so too have the theories and methodologies used to manage the archival record. So the next task is to consider archival theories in more depth, then to position them in relation to current events in the first decades of the 21st century. As already demonstrated, many archival principles have been challenged more than once over time.

Formalizing idiosyncratic practice

A German named Jacob von Rammingen (1510–82) is credited for writing the first two manuals on archival practice in 1540. Baldassare Bonifacio (1585–1659) wrote his own manual in Italian in 1632. But it is fair to suggest that up to the 19th century, archivists around the world still approached their job each in his own way, depending on the needs of the bureaucracy or the demands of the 'boss', whether monarch, religious leader or head of government. When archives were only used within an agency itself, methodologies could be whatever each organization wanted them to be.

As more and more institutions opened to the public in the 18th and 19th centuries, though, one can only imagine the chaos in the reading room, as idiosyncratic approaches in different repositories defeated the logic of the researcher. In 1841, in an attempt to standardize practice (at least in his own institution), the French historian, librarian and archivist Natalis de Wailly (1805–86) wrote a ministerial report for the Royal Archives in France, calling for two significant changes in archival practice:

- Archivists should not intermingle the archives of different creating agencies but instead keep them together, according to what de Wailly referred to as their 'provenance'.
- The archives of each creating agency should be kept in the original order in which the materials were created and used by that creating agency; they should not be organized by an artificial criterion such as name, place or topic.

De Wailly's two principles came together in an overarching philosophy that became known as *respect des fonds*, an approach that became firmly entrenched in European archival thinking in the 19th century. In their 1898 *Manual for the Arrangement and Description of Archives*, Dutch archivists Samuel Muller, Johan Feith and Robert Fruin expanded on de Wailly's vision, though they gave preference to the term *archief* instead of Wailly's *fonds d'archives*. The English archivist Hilary Jenkinson built on this concept again in his 1922 *Manual of Archive Administration*, stating that the archivist should manage archives as an 'organic whole' and not combine them with the archives of any other office.

Today, the concepts of provenance, original order and *respect des fonds* are seen by many as cornerstones of archival practice, though nothing is forever, and other archivists have challenged these concepts as artificial and limiting. Before critiquing these concepts and introducing alternative approaches (largely derived from the Australian focus on series and functions) we first have to provide some definitions and interpretation for provenance, original order and *respect des fonds*.

Provenance

In the archival context, provenance is defined as the origin or source of something, or as the person, agency or office of origin that created, acquired, used and retained a body of records in the course of their work or life. Archivists emphasize the importance of respecting the individual, family or organization that created or received the items that make up a unit of archival materials.

In order to preserve the provenance of groups of archival material, the archivist does not put together archival materials from different creators nor reorganize groups of archives by subject, chronology, geographic division or other criteria. To do so would be to destroy the context in which the archival record came to be, diminishing the role of the creator and the relationships that person or agency had with other people or groups.

Illustrating provenance

Archival provenance focuses on the history or biography of the creator. Who created and used the records before they made their way into archival custody? A fictitious example illustrates this interpretation.

A city archives in Wellington, New Zealand, acquires the personal papers of a prolific, award-winning commercial photographer, Maureen Lee. Among the more than 30 large storage boxes transferred as part of the donation are textual records, sound recordings, more than 10,000 photographic prints and even more photographic negatives. In her career, Lee photographed politicians, sports figures, media celebrities and other well known public figures, but she also photographed urban streetscapes and buildings in the city.

The archival institution has also acquired personal papers and government records related to many of the figures documented in Lee's photographs, as well as archives about the city itself. Among those holdings are the archives of local architects who built many of the buildings Lee photographed, as well as official government records related to urban planning and development at the time Lee was active.

Despite the connections between Lee's work and other archival materials, the archivist does not move Lee's photographs of a politician out of her archives and put them with other archives by or about that politician. Nor does the archivist move Lee's photographs of a building and place them with the architect's designs for that building or with the government's planning records for that city block. Instead, the archivist retains the integrity of the Lee archives, keeping all the photographer's records together as one unit. The archivist relies on archival description to lead researchers to information about all the people, subjects and places documented in Lee's archives. The different media materials may end up stored separately to support preservation, but description, not physical rearrangement by subject or place, allows the user to bring the materials together intellectually by linking Lee's archives with the subjects, people, dates and places represented in them.

Other meanings of provenance

Archivists do not have sole possession of the term provenance. Both 'provenance' and 'provenience' are used in archaeology, museology and librarianship. Archaeologists use the term 'provenience' to document the geographical and physical environment in which an object was found. To capture the provenience, the archaeologist identifies precisely where the object was found and indicates the position of one object in relation to others in the same site. The archaeologist also explains the nature and condition of the physical setting in which the object was found: the type of dirt, the depth in the ground or the existence of any other natural or artificial elements. All this information is used to contextualize the object, supporting speculations about its origins and history.

In museums, art galleries and libraries, the concept of provenance relates to the 'pedigree' of the object, as documented in a chronological history. Unlike archives, which may stay indefinitely in the custody of the person or organization responsible for their creation, artefacts and publications do not always remain in the same hands over time. Works of art, pieces of furniture and first editions are typically created in order to be sold, traded or given away, sometimes dozens or hundreds of times. Information about their origins and physical movements help confirm that objects are in fact what they claim to be. Provenance is captured to show a progression in ownership and use and thus is comparable to the archival notion of a chain of custody, which archivists document in a 'custodial history' note in descriptions, as illustrated in Chapter 11.

Original order

Closely tied to the principle of provenance is the concept of original order, defined as the order and organization in which records were created, used, maintained and stored by the creator or office of origin. Original order is usually interpreted as the sequence established by the *creator* of the records, as shown in the last remaining order of archives before their transfer into archival custody. Sometimes, though, original order may be perceived as the order in which archives were most likely used and managed at a particular time, an interpretation often used when the archives arrive in garbage bags or shoe boxes with no 'order' at all.

Perhaps Maureen Lee used an alpha-numeric filing system for her photographic prints and negatives, identifying them according to the year an image was taken, the name of the client and a sequential number and code. For example, photographic negatives taken as part of a project for a Mr Alfred Zahler might have been coded as 1961-Zahler-1neg, 1961-Zahler-2neg, 1961-Zahler-3neg and so on. Photographic positives might have been coded as 1961-Zahler-1pos, 1961-Zahler-2pos and so on. Photographs taken for the Condon City Council in 1987 were coded as 1987-Condon-1neg, 1987-Condon-1pos, etc. Lee might have stored her correspondence, photographic release forms and other documents in separate folders, labelled 1961-Zahler or 1987-Condon, linking the different evidence together with this coding system.

In this scheme, the subject of the photographic images was not considered as part of the filing system. Lee did not separate the images taken for Mr Zahler and put them with images taken for the Condon City Council because the content or background was the same. She did not combine all the photographs commissioned by Condon City Council over 20 years, even if she had numerous such commissions. Each was a separate project and she preferred to manage them separately. Part of the story of Lee's professional work is reflected in how she organized the products of that work. Original order retains the *structure* of the archives in order to illuminate not just the *content* of an archival collection but also the *context* of how the materials came to be.

Applying original order also offers a practical advantage. Retaining existing filing systems saves the archivist from having to decide on and apply a new and artificial structure. Of course, original order can be problematic for the researcher, who often tends to think more about subjects and dates than creating agencies, so the archivist needs to apply methods and tools to mitigate the difficulties of access, such as creating finding aids and indexes.

Respect des fonds

Archivists combine the principles of provenance and original order into the overarching principle of *respect des fonds*. Defined fully, *respect des fonds* is an overarching concept, of which provenance and original order are parts, that means that in order to protect the integrity of archives, all archives from one particular creator or source (provenance) must be kept together as a unified whole, not separated into artificial groups or intermingled with archives from another source, and that all archives within that unified whole should be preserved in the order in which they were made and used (original order).

To repeat de Wailly's vision, *respect des fonds* is the principle that archives from different creating agencies should not be intermingled, and that the original order in which materials were created and used should be respected. By protecting the external integrity of archives (provenance) and their internal integrity (original order), the archivist supports the protection of the content, structure and context of archives, allowing them to serve as authentic and reliable documentary evidence.

The content of Maureen Lee's archives is what is in the boxes of documents, including Lee's photographs of landscapes, celebrities, buildings and her own family. The structure of her archives is defined by how the materials came to be created and how Lee filed, managed and used them, including how she applied her own particular coding system. The context of Lee's archives is found in the events of Maureen Lee's life and career. Who is she? What is the nature of her photographic work? What is the story of her personal life? In order to preserve the evidence of Maureen Lee, the archivist adheres to *respect des fonds*: protecting the integrity of the archives as a unified whole, and maintaining the structure and order in which the archives were created and used.

The second example illustrates the value applying the principle of *respect des fonds* to protect archives as evidence. Imagine that a government archivist acquires a body of records related to the work of the government's Emergency Response Department. This department deals with emergencies such as hurricanes, fires and floods. Among the documents she receives are records related to a major hurricane in 2015, including logs documenting emergency response actions taken during and after the hurricane; digital photographs of first responders in action; e-mails and text messages between government offices and partner agencies during the crisis; and debrief reports assessing the department's performance throughout the emergency. The archivist also receives archives from the government's Public Awareness and Community Outreach Department, including press releases, communications logs, photographs and performance reports related to departmental activities during the same 2015 hurricane.

Both departments work closely together, and they may both have been in the same place at the same time during the hurricane. But their functions and activities are different, and the records they generate relate to their own responsibilities: emergency response for one and public awareness for the other. In keeping with the fundamental principle of *respect des fonds*, the archivist would preserve the provenance and original order of the archives by retaining the records according to the filing systems used by each creating department. She would then prepare descriptive tools that explain the role and scope of these different government agencies, along with indexes that might include specific search terms for the particular hurricane, to facilitate access to archives about that particular event.

What if the archivist took those archives apart and filed everything to do with that hurricane together by the subject of hurricanes? What if she took all the photographs of hurricane damage from the Emergency Response Department and put them together with all photographs from the Public Awareness and Community Outreach Department, or with photographs donated by private citizens who experienced the hurricane, just because they were all photographs? What if she brought together all records from different government departments and organized them by year, regardless of which department created or used them?

Disassembling archives and reorganizing them by subject or medium is a violation of the core principles of provenance and original order. The archivist may have eased the research path for particular researchers, but she has destroyed the evidence of how agencies responded to particular emergencies, including the hurricane in 2015, by erasing the context and structure of the records. She has also imposed an artificial order on the assumption that her chosen content-focused arrangement, be it subject or form or date, is the one and only logical approach. She has not allowed the archives to remain unaltered by-products of actions and transactions.

The concept of the fonds

The end result of this combination of principles – provenance + original order = *respect des fonds* – has been articulated by archivists in the concept of the *fonds*. A *fonds*, sometimes called a group, is conceived as a unified body of archives with one discernible provenance, maintained with its structural order intact. The definition of the *fonds* is

> the whole body of documents, regardless of form or medium, created or
> accumulated by a particular individual, family, corporate body or other agency
> as part of life and work and retained because those materials have ongoing
> archival value as evidence of those functions and activities.

In the example of Maureen Lee above, provenance and original order would be respected if Lee's archives are kept together as one unit, in the order in which she created and used them. They may be identified as the Maureen Lee *fonds*. The archives of the Condon City Council might be identified as the Condon City Council *fonds* (or archives or records). The archives of Alfred Zahler would be the Alfred Zahler *fonds*.

A trickier question is whether the archives of the Emergency Response Department or the Public Awareness and Community Outreach Department are each separate *fonds*. Some archivists argue it is more logical to focus instead, as the Australian series system does (again as discussed in depth in Chapter 11), by defining the different functions carried out by agents within the government, which result in series of records. Ultimately, as discussed later, the difficulty with the *fonds* is not so much the idea of keeping archives together according to provenance; that approach makes good sense. The difficulty is twofold: the archivist is in danger of assuming that the archives she has in hand represent the whole body of archives created, accumulated and used by a particular individual, family or agency; and in order to define that whole body of archives, the archivist needs to wait until materials come into her custody before she participates in their care.

For now, let me just restate the general principle of the *fonds*, which is, in theory, that applying the principles of provenance and original order traditionally results in the creation of a conceptual and physical 'container' for the archival materials of a particular creator. Therefore:

one creating agency + one body of archives in custody = one *fonds*.

As will be discussed in depth in Chapter 11, the concept of *respect des fonds* has been widely adopted by archivists in many parts of the world, though the term *fonds* itself has sometimes found less favour, in part because it carries little meaning to a research public used to terms such as 'papers', 'archives', 'collections' or 'records'. Still, other archivists have not embraced the concept of the *fonds*, instead pursuing a different path.

The concept of a records continuum

As explained earlier, Australian archivists developed the series system, focusing on functions, agents and series instead of on whole bodies of archives in custody, in order to deal with continuous organizational change. The 'series system' was later expanded into a broader theory of 'post-custodialism', an idea that became better known outside Australia when the

Canadian archivist Terry Cook visited Australia in 1993 and subsequently published a landmark article outlining what he believed was a 'revolution' in information management in a postmodern age.[2]

Embracing this post-custodial approach, as he called it, Cook rejected the idea that archives would only exist physically in one place and that series of records could have only one creator. Cook said that records could live anywhere and have multiple creators. He claimed that approaching records care in a more dynamic fashion did not involve abandoning archival principles but instead strengthened the archivist's resolve to be a guardian of evidence, wherever that evidence may be.

In the 1990s, Frank Upward, an Australian archivist and academic at Monash University, worked with colleagues Sue McKemmish and Livia Iacovino to develop what they called 'the records continuum model'. Markedly divergent from the North American life cycle model (which was increasingly out of favour in many corners), this continuum model built on the series system and the theory of post-custodialism to conceive of records care as a holistic process, not a linear chain of events. The authors suggested that it is not reasonable, and perhaps not possible, to define one distinct and closed *fonds*, as records are continually changing in their form, use and value over time.

The continuum model outlines four dimensions of records-related activities that can take place at a particular place and time: records are created, captured, organized and pluralized, as explained briefly below:

- *Create*: an action, transaction or event is documented. In other words, a record or piece of evidence is made.
- *Capture*: this piece of evidence is kept and stored for immediate or longer term protection in a personal or corporate record-keeping environment; descriptive information such as metadata is added to allow the evidence to be found and understood again by the creator. In other words, the record or other piece of evidence (a digital database, photograph or report) is stored in the personal or office records system.
- *Organize*: the evidence is contextualized with more information, such as descriptive elements, so that it can continue to be accessed and used over time. In other words, the record or piece of information is arranged, described and contextualized.
- *Pluralize*: the evidence becomes part of an archival or record-keeping system, becoming part of the holdings of a larger archival system, such as the archives within a national or state institution. In other words, the record or piece of evidence, with its descriptive information included, is added to the collection of an archival institution or incorporated into an

online archival resource so that it forms part of the documentary memory of society.

Building on these four records-related activities, the continuum model then identifies related record-keeping interactions, defining *who* is doing *what*, and *why*, to manage records at different stages. The four intersections relate to *transactionality*: the work taken to manage a record (*what* action takes place); *evidentiality*: the purpose of the record (*why* the record exists); *record keeping*: the nature of the record (*what* documentary product is generated); and *identity*: the people taking the actions to manage a record (*who* is responsible for the record-keeping work). The *when* is depicted by the concentric circles on the model: the circle closest to the centre represents the time the earliest activities take place, when the record is in the hands of the individual who created it or within his or her office; the next circle reflects work performed later in the record-keeping process, when the record is set aside for longer term preservation; and the third and fourth circles reflect even later stages of the process, when the record is made available for wider use, as defined more precisely below:[3]

- *Transactionality* is the interaction between the four activities and the action taken. *Create* is a single transaction: the creation of a document. *Capture* is a larger activity: the management of a group of records by a group such as a department. *Organize* happens at a broader level: records are managed as a function within the organization. *Pluralize* takes place when records are managed for the purpose of serving the wider society.
- *Evidentiality* is the interaction between the four activities and the purpose of the record. When a document is created it is a *trace*, but when it is captured it becomes *evidence*. When it is organized it serves as *corporate* or *individual memory*, and when it is pluralized it serves as *collective memory*.
- *Record keeping* is the interaction between the four activities and the record itself. The activity of create results in a *document*, which may or may not be *archival*. The activity of capture results in a *record*. The activity of organize results in an *archive* for the organization. The activity of pluralize results in *archives* for society.
- *Identity* is the intersection between the four activities and the people doing the work. The *actor* or individual creates records to document his or her activities. The capture of those records is done by a *unit* or group of people in an office. The *organization* as a whole organizes those records for its own purposes. The *institution* pluralizes those archives for the benefit of society.

It can be difficult to absorb all the nuances of the records continuum model. The really important change in thinking lies not in the details but in the vision behind the model. The records continuum model recognizes that waiting to manage records when they are 'old' is not logical or effective and provides a dynamic description of the actions taken, people or groups involved, evidence produced and reasons for actions taken, at each stage of the record-keeping process. Unlike the approach taken to provide custodial care of existing *fonds*, the continuum model also creates a mechanism for protecting records from the time of creation. Many who favour the continuum approach tend to refer to those involved with records and archives care as record keepers (or recordkeepers in Australian parlance), rather than distinguish between two distinct professions: 'records manager' and 'archivist'.

Focusing on functions

Archivists have also drawn from the series system and the records continuum model to suggest that rather than focusing first on who made or used archives, the emphasis should be on what work was being performed and what records were generated, then linking those two elements to who carried out that work over time. Some archivists interpret this function-oriented approach as 'functional provenance'. By linking provenance and functions more closely together, the archivist can maintain intellectual control over the archives in her custody or control even as departments and offices change names, locations or mandates. The functional approach can be applied to arrangement, description, appraisal and even records management (or record keeping), as discussed in Chapter 11. And as discussed in Chapter 10, functional appraisal, also referred to as macro-appraisal, focuses on an appraisal not of extant archives but instead on the functions and activities performed within an organization, in order to decide which records should be kept.

Challenging archival theories

Provenance, original order and *respect des fonds* are accepted theories in much of the archival community around the world. The concept of a records continuum and a focus on functions is increasingly popular in other circles. Many archivists love to debate whether one is right and the other wrong. In a book like this, which emphasizes the importance of looking for a balance, it is not appropriate to dismiss one or the other approach out of hand. But neither approach is free of problems. Looking at some of the strengths and weaknesses of these theories and principles helps us assess each approach fairly. The different issues below highlight some of the weaknesses with the different approaches.

The absence of a 'whole'

It is impossible to think that an archival institution will ever have in its possession the 'whole' of the documents of any individual, family or corporate body. Records are destroyed, lost or transferred even before they come into archival custody. Even once she has archives in hand, the archivist appraises them, keeping some records and destroying others. Inevitably, the archivist manages residue, not entirety. If there is no whole, then using the term *fonds* as it has been defined by many archivists, particularly in standards for archival description, implies a totality that does not exist. (Descriptive standards are addressed in depth in Chapter 11.)

Consider this example. The Hudson's Bay Company, originally based in England, was at the heart of the exploration, development and settlement of Canada from the time the company was founded in 1670. Today, more than 3000 linear metres of Hudson's Bay Company archives are kept as part of its corporate archival collection at the Provincial Archives of Manitoba, in the heart of the Canadian prairies. But not all records of the Hudson's Bay Company are in the provincial archives. Official company records such as currency notes, indentures, account books, ledgers and balance sheets have found their way into the collections of other provincial, city and community institutions across Canada. In order to adhere to Canada's archival descriptive standard, *Rules for Archival Description*, many of these disparate units of Hudson's Bay Company records, some no more than a few pages long, have been given the same title: the 'Hudson's Bay Company *fonds*'.

If the *fonds* is intended to be an organic whole, how can several repositories each claim to have the Hudson's Bay Company *fonds* in their possession? How can one ledger book or a five-page letter be a *fonds*? In this instance, the term *fonds* has simply been applied as a convenience, but the real story behind these materials has not been highlighted. How did the bits and pieces not in the Provincial Archives of Manitoba end up separated from the company's central records system? When were they discovered and deposited into archival institutions in cities or towns thousands of miles away from the company's headquarters? How do they fit with comparable archives housed in the Winnipeg repository?

One solution to this problem is not to use the term *fonds*, and I for one do not much like it, not because the word itself is not appropriate but because it has been so badly misapplied. *Fonds* is really meant to refer to the archives of one creating agency that exist together in one place (archival institution or other) not *all* of the records of that creating agency. One could continue to use the word *fonds* as long as the researcher understood that the archives in question did not represent the whole of the archives of any one creator. But still, using the term means focusing all descriptive work on the materials in hand. The inter-relationships between different bits and pieces – the items or units or *fonds* in repositories across the country – are not emphasized. When descriptions find their way into archival databases, the researcher can search for Hudson's Bay Company and find 10, 15 or 20 different *fonds* and make his way through the descriptions to find what he wants.

But equally important to many researchers and archivists is the story behind how those materials came to be in those different institutions. So another answer is to document as fully as possible the custodial history of the records, which is the story of their existence before they came into archival hands. Documenting the story of the archives should be a core descriptive task; the information helps demonstrate the chain of custody – as provenance does for art and artefacts – or at least helps to explain where, when and how the links in that chain became disconnected over time. Custodial history also holds the archivist to account as she must document in an archival description her own decisions for acquiring, appraising and managing the materials over time.[4]

The importance of items

What if all that arrives are a handful of items? When managing individual items or small units of materials, the archivist needs to focus even more attention not just on provenance but, again, on custodial history. For instance, an archivist may discover in her holdings a two-page fishing licence. The document relates closely to the archival institution's maritime theme, and it is a rare find. But it comes devoid of any contextual information or custodial history. If the archivist focuses on the *fonds* so strictly that she decides that the two sheets of paper do not represent a whole body of archives, then why should she keep the material in the first place?

In reality, those two pieces of paper can provide a lot of evidence and information. Say that the document identifies the issuer of the licence (the government of Spain), the recipient (the fishing vessel *Estrella*) and the date of the licence (1865). A signature suggests that Alonzo Bolivar was the man who purchased the licence. To contextualize this isolated item, the archivist would need to research the process whereby the Spanish government issued fishing licences, to understand how this licence came to be.

She might learn that two copies of a licence would have been produced: one kept in the government records system and one given to the applicant. She might discover that the government's copy of all licences from the 1800s are still intact in the national archives, so the licence in her hand very likely was the copy given to Alonzo Bolivar, who evidently owned or operated the *Estrella*. She might then try to locate historical information about Bolivar and discover a news report from 1867 showing the sinking of the *Estrella* in a December storm, with all hands lost. The report might list all the members of the crew, including Captain Bolivar, whose remains are buried in the local churchyard. A check of the parish registers might identify his relatives and, from there, his descendants, some of whom still live in the town. It may turn out that they have photographs, diaries, letters about Great-Great Uncle Alonzo, and perhaps they would be delighted to donate these materials to the archives and see this evidence of their long-lost relative.

In this case, the search for the *fonds* is pointless. But the search for the *story* can lead to more acquisitions, greater community connections and a richer documentary heritage. The time involved in such research is not inconsiderable, but the archivist who forfeits this journey simply because she is focused on finding a custodial whole risks missing out on an important component of community archival service.

The overlap between archives and collections

Another complication with the *fonds*-oriented approach is the need to distinguish between organic accumulations of archives and what archivists might refer to as artificial collections, which are groups of materials brought together deliberately according to some unifying characteristic. A shoebox full of old postcards, several binders of resource material on the history of logging or a collection of autographs pasted into an album might all be considered artificial collections.

Someone may have found a box of blank postcards at a garage sale and discovered that the vast majority of the cards depicted his home county in decades past. He may have delivered the box to the County Archives, and the archivist may choose to keep all the images as a postcard collection. The postcards come with no provenance and no original order, and one could easily argue that they are not archival, in that they do not provide authentic evidence of actions or transactions; they have lost their context and structure. But they still provide valuable historical information, and they could be a useful addition to the institution's holdings.

Alternately, a collection of documentary materials might form part of the archives of the person who put those materials together in the first place. For instance, a historian may have photocopied articles and book chapters related to logging in order to write a history of the forest industry in her state. She put these copies together in binders as a reference collection, and eventually the binders came to the archives as part of the historian's *fonds*. Despite the fact that they are photocopies, the materials may offer valuable evidence about the historian's sources. Her handwritten notes and comments on the pages may help explain how she came to some of her conclusions. The archivist would examine the reference collection in relation to the historian's other archives and determine if the resources should be preserved as evidence.

Archival orphans

What if there is absolutely no indication of the creator or owner of an item? What if the archivist found a photograph of a little girl deep in a box of backlogged holdings? The photograph appears to have been taken sometime in the late 19th century, based on the girl's appearance and dress, but no other information is available, and there is absolutely no evidence that this little girl even had a connection with the community.

In the absence of any contextual information, the photograph only provides information about the style of dress in the late 19th century, and perhaps about the nature of portrait photography at the time. If, in the future, more information is unearthed that contextualizes the photograph, its status in the institution might change accordingly. But for the moment, the photograph comes with no provenance and so has lost its archival resonance.

Ultimately, because the archival institution exists to acquire, preserve and make available archives as evidence, it may be difficult to justify the expenditure of resources on single items with no evidential value. The archivist may be able to rationalize the effort involved in contextualizing the fishing licences discussed earlier, but she may not have the time and resources to go on a scavenger hunt to identify a little girl lost, especially if the archivist has a backlog of thousands of identified photographs waiting to be described.

Does the archivist process the image as archival, even though it is anonymous? Does she destroy the image? Does she put it in an information file and consider it a reference tool, like a news clipping or an extra copy of a brochure? The archivist's decision affects the perceived value of the item. Keeping it assigns a value it might not deserve. Destroying it removes any chance that the little girl might be identified someday. Putting it in a reference file might be something of a cop out: the image is kept, but with no information about content or context. It is then handled and dirtied and damaged, which reduces its physical stability and diminishes its lifespan. Sometimes, hard decisions have to be made, and orphans have to be removed from the doorstep.

Multiple provenance

As Cook and others argued, there can be 'serial' provenance: this is the essence of the series system and the functional approach. Different agencies can have responsibility for activities, and their records, in a linear fashion over time, one office taking over from another to carry out the same functions. But what about 'multiple' provenance? What happens when responsibilities cannot be delineated clearly? Archives can contain not just serial but multiple provenance(s). Further, the archives may be reorganized many times between creation and custody; where is the 'original order' among several possible options? Family archives present a strong case that provenance and original order can be complex.

Imagine that Carl Cameron, patriarch of the Cameron family, left his personal papers with his daughter Adele on his death. Adele may have rearranged his papers, added or removed items and perhaps incorporated her own archives into the collection. The provenance now shifts from the individual, the father, to serial, the father then the daughter. The original order Carl offered is gone, replaced by Adele's order. If Adele passes her papers on to a son or niece or nephew, and they also arrange, rearrange, add and remove materials, the provenance expands and original order is again recast. The provenance is now serial and multiple, and the order is very far from 'original'. How does the archivist define the body of archives in her care? Is it a *fonds*? If so, whose *fonds* is it? What is the provenance? Cameron the elder? Cameron the daughter? Cameron the family?

The archives themselves have changed innumerable times. The archivist needs to consider whether her job is to document the materials or the story behind them. The full story is not just how they were created and used in the first place, or how they appeared when they arrived in the archives. The real story is how they were kept, and changed, from start to finish. The archivist may not know anything about this story, though, when the materials first arrive, so she has to be vigilant about learning as much as possible about the history of the records, not just the history of the creators and users, before she makes assumptions about the 'real' ownership or order of the materials.

Societal provenance

Some archivists have expanded this concept of serial and multiple provenance to articulate a notion of societal provenance, based on the idea that archives can move through time and space. They can be created by one person, used by another, interpreted by another and reused by another, both in or outside archival custody. Societal provenance focuses not on the creator as an agent with power or authority but also on the other players who are engaged with or influenced by the activities that led to the creation and use of the archives in hand.

Consider this example. A government department responsible for environmental management might be defined as the creator of a series of archives related to managing permissions for gas exploration. The archivist following the theoretical definition of provenance would define the government department and the creating agency and would interpret the original order in relation to how the records were created and used by that department. But what about the farming communities or aboriginal families whose land was being used for exploration? They and their land are the *subjects* of the records in question. In traditional archival theory these individuals or groups might be identified in archival descriptions, along with subjects or dates or events. But are those people actually *co-creators* of the records?

Perhaps the files contain extensive correspondence between a farmer and the government's exploration team or between an aboriginal chief and the head of the department. A narrow definition of provenance does not give space to those who did not 'create or accumulate and use' the archives as part of daily business, even though those people or groups created records that form part of the *fonds*. The assumption most archivists would make is that those other players would have kept their own records, and the provenance of those materials would be in relation to those other groups, not the government. The archivist needs to think outside the box of both these approaches and consider what evidence she is really trying to protect. Evidence of the action? Proof of its impact? Something else? The archivist needs to be careful not to let archival theories, or the tools created to support them, suppress the opportunity to represent clearly all those engaged with the functions reflected in the archives.

Original order and the last resting place

The challenge of multiple provenance, and the related question of the 'final' original order, is well illustrated in the following example, which demonstrates the need for the archivist to look closely at how records actually came to be, and how they came to be where they are when she receives them, not at how they *ought* to have been created, managed and used.

In 1903 a pair of explorers, journalist Leonidas Hubbard Jr and lawyer Dillon Wallace, along with Métis guide George Elson and several packers, set off on an expedition into northern Labrador, referred to at the time as one of the last 'blank spots' on the Canadian map. Sadly, the expedition was not successful: Hubbard ended up dying of exposure while Wallace and Elson barely made it out of the bush alive.

Hubbard's widow, Mina, was upset not only at the loss of her husband but also at Wallace's public implications that the expedition's failure was Hubbard's doing. To prove the journey was possible, she hired George Elson to help her retrace the expedition. For some reason, Wallace also decided to repeat the expedition, and in 1905 a race ensued, which ended when Mina and her party reached the intended destination six weeks before Wallace, demonstrating that the original expedition could have been a success.

Among the stories told of the two expeditions was a rumour that there might have been an intimate relationship between Mina and George Elson during the trip. The historian James West Davidson and physician John Rugge, who documented the tale in their book *Great Heart: the history of a Labrador adventure*, confessed they could find no 'outright declaration' of an affair, but they did note that George Elson had kept a diary in which he wrote rather enigmatic entries about what it would be like to be married to a white woman and stating that he did not necessarily want Mina to be 'only a friend'. Each time George came close to writing something revealing, however, he would instead write 'see separate entry' or 'see other book'.

In their archival research, Davidson and Rugge could not find any 'other book'. What they did find, in the back of George's surviving journal, were a number of ragged edges close to the binding, showing that several pages at the end of the book had been cut out. Turning to Mina's diary, the authors found an entry where she debates about asking George to sign an agreement not to write anything about the trip without her consent. She added, 'I almost think I had. There would be no questioning about the thing then.' The authors presumed that the 'thing' might have related to George's feelings for Mina, whether requited or not.

As the authors pointed out, it was not the words in the documents themselves that led them to suspect some sort of imagined or real relationship between George and Mina. Rather, it was the fact that George's diary, the one with the missing pages, was found in Mina's personal archives. A diary created by one person, George, was among the personal papers of another person, Mina. That unusual location begged for historical interpretation. In this case, the authors concluded that the appearance of the diary with Mina's papers, along with her diary entry about whether or not George should be allowed to write anything about the trip, provided a fairly reasonable basis for suggesting that there may have been some intimacy, or at the very least an overt and therefore potentially embarrassing desire for intimacy, at least on George's part.

If the archivist who found George's diary with Mina's papers had followed a narrow interpretation of provenance, she might have decided that since the diary was written by George, not Mina, the provenance was George, and the diary was in the 'wrong place'. If she focused instead on original order, she might have accepted that the diary was in Mina's custody but not asked how it came to be there. If *respect des fonds* had been abandoned and the different archival materials separated and processed as individual items, their contextual links would have been entirely eradicated. Any chance of understanding the story between George and Mina would have been lost.

The loss of context can happen even if archives are kept together. What if the archivist microfilmed George's journal but did not add a note in the archival description explaining that several pages from the end of the journal were missing? Users might end up thinking that the microfilmed copy represented the document in its entirety. Photocopying or digitizing documents can also obscure structural information that helps illuminate not just the content but the context of the archives. In this case, context and structure, with a diary in the custody of someone other than its author and with missing pages suggesting some content has been removed, demand that the archivist interpret provenance and original order broadly in order to respect the history behind the archives.[5]

Making order out of chaos

A final comment needs to be made about original order. What happens when there is no original order? Is *that* the original order? Perhaps the archivist has been presented with several boxes of personal papers, manuscripts and research materials created by a deceased poet, who had no family or close friends to help sort through his personal effects. The papers were taken from cupboards, filing cabinets and storage shelves, packed into used wine boxes and brought to the archival institution by the local moving company hired to clean up the author's home. The chance that the guys packing the boxes paid any attention to 'original order' is remote, at best.

The archivist may search in vain for some logic to the order, and she may define an accidental order as intentional. Was the copy of *Cosmopolitan* magazine stored next to the notes for a poem because the author was seeking inspiration from a *Cosmo* article? Or were the magazine and the notes tossed into the box by the packers, who cared about getting the job done, not about preserving documentary evidence of authorial intent? The pages in a manuscript could be upside down and sideways because the author was diligently sorting sections of the work to move words and phrases from place to place, or it could be that the poet, or the movers, dropped the papers on the floor and picked them up higgledy piggledy.

In the absence of any signs of original intent, the archivist has little recourse but to create an artificial order, building on any original order she can discern and retaining (but not overemphasizing) linkages between materials. The archivist cannot turn back time and restore archives to a hypothetical 'original order', but she can save time by not agonizing over how best to apply archival theories when the best course of action is to put the materials together in some sensible fashion and move on to the next task on her desk.

Theoretical functions and real records

The functional approach to archival management (introduced earlier and examined in more detail in Chapter 11) does not get off scot-free when considering challenges to archival theories. In governments and business, functions and agents can be defined very precisely. The work of government is often clearly articulated in legal or policy instruments. Large organizations develop corporate mandates, hierarchical structures and strategic plans that define precisely what they intend to do, and when and why. Thus it is relatively easy to create a standardized definition for business activities that take place within a jurisdiction: managers in organizations can agree among themselves the tasks encompassed in functions like accounting, communications, engineering, health care, international relations or governing.

Although everyone starts the process with different perceptions (especially, perhaps, about governing), a little brain power helps the group discern between 'demonstrating' (which they might define as instructing others in, or explaining or illustrating operations, methods or products) and 'protesting' (which they might define as openly expressing objection or dissent).

In attempting to codify functions, many managers of archival institutions are working with their governments (and the functional approach is largely a public-sector effort at this stage) to develop authority lists of preferred terms. Archivists are choosing between environmental management and natural resources care, for instance, or between community services and welfare. One can only imagine the politics associated with this process, even in a highly structured and bureaucratic environment.

But how can the archivist define functions in the private sector, such as in community-based organizations or in groups of loosely affiliated individuals? Will it be possible to create a thesaurus of terms that is representative of so many activities in life that are not structured? For instance, the archivist will be challenged to codify functions and agents responsible for work performed in 'flat' or co-operative organizations, where hierarchies have been replaced by flexible and dynamic working groups. The archivist is going to have a hard time delineating accountability and record-keeping responsibility if the organization itself refuses to be pinned down.

Identifying functions for personal activities is even harder. One might be able to define shipping or arts development or fishing or taxation pretty precisely. But can one put definitional boundaries around loving or hating or anticipating or experiencing? Are these functions? Or are they qualities of being? If the archivist acquires the archives of a housewife and mother, does the archivist assign a function for 'mothering'? Does that one word help the archivist define who that woman really was? Much of what explains us as humans, and which finds its way into the archival evidence we leave behind, cannot be codified. The effort to create functional thesauri for public and corporate record keeping is useful, but those who think it will be possible to create standardized language to define with pinpoint precision all of the 'functions' in their particular universe are cautioned to take a reality check.

Functional approaches to record keeping can be equally limited when addressing societal provenance. If the orientation of a functional approach is toward identifying agents with authority and record-keeping responsibility and then linking those agents with the functions they performed and with the resulting records, where do the other people involved with the functions fit in? Secondary parties to an activity – the subjects affected by but perhaps not responsible for actions and decisions – would not be identified as co-creators. Right or wrong? Such questions are a matter of lively debate in the archival community.

Finally, the relationship between the theory of functions and the reality of the archives themselves must be considered. The post-custodial approach allows the record-keeping professional to work more closely with decision makers in the creating agency to 'make and keep good records' (a powerful and fitting expression first coined by national and state archival agencies in Australia). But there will always be a difference between what an accountable agent *should* do and what they *actually* do. No matter how well the record keeper protects the records that result from a function, she cannot guarantee that functions will be documented in the first place. (Government e-mails go missing all the time, it seems, especially these days.)

The archivist needs to be aware of that gap between theory and reality, even if she cannot bridge it. The absence of information is information. What if a government department announces a significant shift in policy but no records can be found in the series representing that function to provide evidence of the rationale? What if a government official is accused of sharing secrets with a hostile foreign power but the records showing he was in a meeting with his foreign counterpart cannot be found? How will the archivist – or anyone – know about this gap between the expectation that records should exist and the reality that they do not?

If the archivist defines functions too prescriptively and then assumes (wherein lies the danger) that the right records will naturally fall into place, she is only managing what is, not what ought to be. No matter how close the archivist is to the beginning of the story, she cannot make records come into being. While many archivists in government circles are considering the need for 'duty to document' legislation that requires agencies to create records of key decisions, such requirements do not yet exist. The archivist can try to improve accountability by urging agencies to make and keep good records, but success may only come through legislative change and political will. And that archival role circles us back to the beginning of this chapter. Is the archivist an objective custodian, responsible for managing that which is in hand, which was the case for centuries? Or is the archivist an active (and activist?) participant in the creation of records, subjectively imposing an archival imperative on how governments or organizations, or even individuals, choose to manage the evidence of their actions, transactions and decisions, even, in the extreme, requiring that people make records when many would choose otherwise?

———

Concepts such as provenance, the *fonds*, the series system, the continuum, post-custodialism and a functional approach provide valuable frameworks for archival practice. It is important to understand these theories and principles, which can influence all aspects of archival practice. But theories go only so far. Even though the primary focus of the archival mission may be to preserve evidence, and even though that evidence may be best managed by respecting archival theories, what effect does all this attention to matters of principle have on the public? In the end, archives exist to be *used*. The next step, then, in our exploration of archival principles is to look at archival materials from the perspective of the user. Who might use archives? Why? These questions are considered in the next chapter.

Notes

1   It is important to acknowledge that this review focuses on western record-keeping traditions, in part because the theories and methodologies most often discussed (or argued about) by archivists today derive from European, English, North American and Australasian approaches. This orientation, while necessary to contextualizing current archival practice, does not mean that archival customs in other parts of the world do not have value.

2   See Cook, T. (1994) 'Electronic Records, Paper Minds: the revolution in information management in the post-custodial and post-modern era', *Archives & Manuscripts*, **2**, November, 300–28.

3   The illustration for the records continuum model has not been reproduced here, but readers can see the image and read more about the model in Frank Upward's two articles outlining the records continuum: Upward, F. (1996) 'Structuring the Records Continuum, Part One: postcustodial principles and properties', *Archives & Manuscripts*, **24** (2), 268–85, and Upward, F. (1997) 'Structuring the Records Continuum, Part Two: structuration theory and recordkeeping', *Archives and Manuscripts*, **25** (1), May, 10–35.

4   For an insightful look at the story of the Hudson's Bay Company archives, see Simmons, D. (2007) *Keepers of the Record: the history of the Hudson's Bay Company archives*, McGill-Queen's University Press.

5   Davidson, J. W. and Rugge, J. (1996) *Great Heart: the history of a Labrador adventure*, McGill-Queen's University Press. See particularly the epilogue, 337–61.

4

The uses of archives

To be ignorant of what occurred before you were born is to remain always a child. For what is the worth of human life, unless it is woven into the life of our ancestors by the records of history?

Marcus Tullius Cicero (106–43 BC) *Orator*, 46 BC

Why should societies keep archives at all? Who cares about preserving the documentary remains of anyone's life or work or keeping the evidence of government or corporate decisions? Why do we bother recording our activities and experiences at the time they happen, and why should anyone bother committing the resources needed to keep those accounts for the indefinite future?

Archives are not just 'neat old stuff'. As discussed already, archivists today define archival materials first and foremost as sources of documentary evidence. Archives prove rights, confirm obligations, verify events and substantiate claims. They help us remember the past, and they safeguard us against inaccurate recollections or intentional deceit. A written contract reminds two parties of their agreements, but it also prevents one or the other party from avoiding their obligations, because the document exists as proof of the original accord. A photograph of the family at sunset on the beach helps us remember a wonderful holiday, but it also serves as proof that we were on that trip at that specific time. One of the first steps in deciding whether or not to keep archives, then, is to consider their potential value as evidence, which allows the archivist to ensure that, at the very least, she has captured those archives that can be used as proof.

But in order to make a thoughtful decision about whether or not to keep any group of archival materials, it is important to remember that archives are ultimately kept in order to be used, by anyone for any reason. Researchers, scholars and average citizens refer to archives to find proof; to gather research data; to illustrate, illuminate or explain. Archives are tools that people use to look beyond the present moment and understand the wider context of a family, community or society. Like George Mallory who said he wanted to climb Mount Everest 'because it's there', anyone can use archives for any reason, as long as the archives 'are there'. The contract may be evidence today; a century from now it may be a valuable illustration of how contracts were executed 100 years before. The photograph may be proof of a holiday, but in decades to come it might show evidence of erosion on the beach, or the manner of dress at a particular time and so on. In this chapter, I consider some of the myriad ways in which archival materials might be used.

Archives as sources of history

One of the largest and most conventional groups of archival users are historians. This category includes both those deemed to be professional, who make a living studying the past, and those whose historical interest is a personal vocation, not a means of employment. The textbooks, documentaries, local histories, family chronicles, magazine stories and other productions by these users are the means by which many other people learn about the past.

Archives and the discipline of history

As discussed earlier, historians have turned to original sources of evidence from the days of the Greek historians Herodotus and Thucydides. When Leopold von Ranke argued that the job of history was 'to show what actually happened', his colleagues realized the only way to show what happened was to draw on archival materials. Today, historians rely on all manner of archival sources from personal diaries to government reports to interpret the past. To these researchers there would be no history without archives. Every time new archival collections are made available or existing holdings are described in more detail, historians have the opportunity to re-examine past events through a new lens.

The challenge for historians, aside from their own responsibility to be as unbiased and objective as possible, is to be able to access and use new archival discoveries. Many archival institutions have the right to establish their own conditions of access, which can hinder the job of interpreting the past. The role of Pope Pius XII during the Holocaust and the Second World War, for example, has long been a source of controversy. Histories written in the 1970s and 1980s drew on resources available at the time, including Vatican archives. In recent years scholars have suggested that the story is more complex and they have pressed the Vatican to release relevant records. To date, the Vatican has kept the records of Pius XII's papacy closed, even though there is an unwritten policy within the Vatican to release records 75 years after the start of a papacy; if this had been honoured Pope Pius XII's archives would have been opened in 2014. As long as there is a chance to view, and *review*, documentary evidence, historians will have the opportunity and responsibility to reassess their conclusions about the past.[1]

Archives, genealogy and family history

On a more personal level, people with time and resources to spare are often driven to learn about their family's past. Genealogy is one of the fastest growing leisure activities in North America and Europe, as shown by the tremendous growth of commercial enterprises such as Ancestry, the online family history tool that provides access to billions of historical records. The more than 2 million paid subscribers to Ancestry (who left the company with revenues of more than US$700 million in 2015) can search for ancestors online and create and share family trees. This genealogical research would not be possible if individuals, or companies like Ancestry, could not access and use, or digitize, records such as passenger lists, military service files, baptismal records, inscriptions of grave stones and so on, all of which live in archival repositories.

While for many genealogy is a pleasurable hobby, family history can also be a fraught search for lost truths. Adoption data, medical histories or records of war or natural disasters often reveal the stories of family members who disappeared or were never known in the first place. For instance, the records of foster care homes or institutions in Australia are crucial to helping the children of Aboriginal and Torres Strait Islanders, known as the Stolen Generations, uncover the story of their removal from their aboriginal home and their transfer to state custody, a process that took place from the start of the 20th century to the 1960s and 1970s.

The same situation occurred in Canada from the 1960s to the 1980s in a practice called the 'Sixties Scoop', where aboriginal children were taken from their families and put up for adoption or placed in foster homes. The archives of governments, schools and children's welfare organizations have proved critical to helping these children, now adults, discover their origins. That type of information is not just of passing genealogical interest. Such evidence could be essential to understanding the origins of a person's medical conditions, their place and date of birth and other personal information:

evidence that might be taken for granted by those not raised in foster care or adopted at birth.

Archives as tools for accountability

Therefore archives are not just sources of traditional or family history but can also be critical to supporting accountability, protecting individual and collective rights and ensuring those in positions of power meet their assigned responsibilities. Archives help societies uphold the rule of law, a fundamental concept of democracy originally enshrined in western culture in the Magna Carta in 1215. The rule of law decrees that no one person has the right to act outside the boundaries of society's rules of conduct. In keeping with the rule of law, a single person or specific group does not carry authority over others as a consequence of some perceived divine right or as a result of the exercise of totalitarian power. Rather, a person's rights come through the law and are upheld in part through the creation, preservation and use of evidence, which can be used as proof to support legitimate claims and refute unsubstantiated declarations.

Archives, truth and reconciliation

The Sixties Scoop mentioned above took place in Canada from the 1960s to 1980s, but the history of aboriginal child care has a much longer and even more disturbing history, which Canadians are addressing through a process of truth and reconciliation. This truth and reconciliation process, in turn, depends on archives.

Between the 1870s and the late 20th century, over 150,000 aboriginal children (including First Nations, Métis and Inuit) were placed in residential schools across Canada. Many of these schools were funded by the government and administered by churches. Today, many people believe that the removal of these children from their homes and families had significant negative consequences, including the loss of native languages and cultures, along with reported instances of physical, psychological and sexual abuse and neglect.

In June 2008, the Prime Minister of Canada delivered a formal apology on behalf of the Canadian government, and the government established an Indian Residential Schools Truth and Reconciliation Commission to 'document the truth' about the history of the residential schools experience. This Commission presented its report in May 2015, arguing in its findings that Canadian archival institutions should be supported in their efforts to ensure that they can support the 'inalienable right' of aboriginal people to 'know the truth' of the residential school experience.

As articulated in the Commission's report, archival materials are at the heart of the desire to document truth. Former students at residential schools, along with their families, communities and others affected by the residential school experience, have shared their stories through interviews and written statements, records that are now being housed in a national research centre in Winnipeg, Manitoba. Other archival sources, including school records, photographs, inspectors' reports and personal papers, are also being copied, with the copies preserved in the research centre so that they may be available to the public. Educational institutions are also being urged to draw on the stories of residential school attendees, and the evidence found in archives, to raise awareness among children and adults today of this period in Canadian history.[2]

Archives and the evidence of repression

Records that serve accountability today may have been created in the first place for highly objectionable reasons. For instance, the East German Ministry for State Security, or Stasi – a secret security service that monitored the activities of hundreds of thousands of alleged 'enemies' of the state from its creation in 1950 to its ultimate dissolution in 1990 – compiled a vast assemblage of files documenting its investigations. The records were used to substantiate claims of anti-government action, which resulted in the execution of many supposed dissidents, often without any formal right to protest their innocence.

When the reunification of Germany started in 1990, the Stasi began to shred files in an attempt to destroy the evidence, but protestors halted the process and even rescued bags of shredded documents. A government agency, the Office of the Federal Commissioner Preserving the Records of the Ministry for State Security of the German Democratic Republic, was established to oversee the care of these records. After much public debate, it was decided that the records would be made available for use; individuals would be given the right to see their own files and make copies of documents, and the media would be allowed to review files as long as no personal information was disclosed.

For decades now, a team of hundreds of archivists and technicians has been using sophisticated computer technology to resurrect the content of some 45 million pages of shredded documents. In this case, the preservation of these archives, even those shreds that 20 or 30 years ago would have been beyond rescuing, has allowed German citizens and others to exercise their right to understand their individual and collective past and perhaps seek some recognition, if not actual redress.[3]

Archives, human rights and justice

In Cambodia in the 1970s, the repressive Khmer Rouge regime, led by the dictator Pol Pot, reportedly killed millions of citizens, in part to root out counter-revolutionary activities. Detailed records were kept of all people arrested, interrogated and assassinated, including arrest forms, photographs of arrested and executed prisoners, handwritten confessions or summaries of activities, notes on torture methods used and execution schedule and orders. When the Vietnamese invaded Cambodia in 1979, they took the Khmer Rouge off guard, and these administrative records of incarceration, torture and death were left behind, almost entirely intact.

While the records were created as part of a shockingly criminal, hostile, evil regime, they have subsequently been used to establish accountability for the crimes committed. The overwhelming body of documentary evidence, and the fact that it was found at the place in which it was created and used, allowed scholars, lawyers and humanitarians to draw on this archival resource to refute any attempts by Khmer Rouge representatives to claim innocence of the deaths that took place during their regime.[4]

Archives as touchstones for memory and identity

These less-than-uplifting stories of archives demonstrate the legal and administrative value of documentary evidence, particularly to combat, or at least to provide irrefutable evidence of, oppression, hostility and tyranny. But archives can also communicate facts and information that help to preserve individual and collective memories, position ourselves more clearly in our historical framework and understand more fully who we are, where we came from and, perhaps, where we are going in our societies.

A wedding photograph taken in 2010 reminds a young couple of their happy day, but decades hence it may be the emotional centrepiece of a 50th anniversary party, and even later it might illustrate how brides and grooms dressed for weddings at one time. A sound recording of a speech given at an academic conference may be evidence of the words and ideas of a noted scholar, but listening to that recording years later may give a young man a chance to hear the voice of his long-gone grandfather.

Like scientific or physical evidence, the fact that documentary evidence may have been created for one purpose does not mean it cannot be used for another purpose. Recall the ice cores or footprints discussed in Chapter 1. Ice does not form in Antarctica in order for scientists to measure it 20,000 years later. A burglar does not leave his shoeprint in the flowerbed in order for police to find the print and prove the shoe was his. (Quite the contrary, one suspects.) A contract, e-mail or report is not created in order to provide historians with something to study a century from now. That document was created to record a decision or a transaction: to confirm mutual obligations (a contract), schedule a luncheon meeting (an e-mail) or assess a new marketing strategy (a report).

The diaries of fishermen or farmers from a century ago, created in the first place to keep track of daily activities or to capture personal reflections, are being used today to study changes in fish stocks or in crop productivity. Ships' logs, created in the first instance to document the movement of a particular vessel from one side of the ocean to another, can provide evidence of changing weather patterns. Maps created to mark off areas of settlement in the 18th century might be used today to prove a person's claim to a certain parcel of land. A home movie made in 1956 may have documented a family trip to a seaside village; a half-century later it might be used to illustrate changes in population density along the coast. Some other examples of expected and unexpected uses of archival materials are illustrated below.

Archives and science

As Canadian archival educator Tom Nesmith articulates so well in his discussion of the 'archival turn' in history, medical researchers in recent years have drawn heavily on documentary resources to research a range of scientific questions, such as, for example, associations between fetal and childhood trauma and later negative health conditions. In this case, scientists studying famine in the Netherlands during the winter of 1944–45 relied heavily on medical records held in Dutch archival repositories, including the City of Amsterdam, to identify people born during those years. The researchers were then able to use other records to identify health problems and, ultimately, to make a strong link between an exposure to famine and later incidences of cardiovascular disease, diabetes, cancer and obesity.[5]

Archives and social awareness

Scientists interested in current social, environmental or other issues turn to archives to provide longitudinal data about particular events. Consider the question of climate change. Scholars wishing to gather convincing evidence of changes in the environment look to records of droughts, famines, snow falls, ice cover, spring flowering dates and the timing of autumn harvests. These records might come from farmers' journals, ships' logs, gamekeepers' diaries, newspaper stories, explorers' diaries or artists' sketches of mountain glaciers.

Similarly, social scientists may turn to archives to identify historical changes in public health conditions, such as the rise or fall of ghettos or the quality of life for people on the margins of society. By drawing on impartial historical sources, researchers are able to present accurate accounts of changes over time, which can be more persuasive than editorials in raising public awareness of social conditions.[6]

Archives in fiction and film

Many authors use archives as part of their research for works of fiction, from historical novels to adventure stories to children's tales. A. S. Byatt, Julian Barnes, Umberto Eco, P. D. James, Geraldine Brooks and E. L. Doctorow have all based their fictional accounts on archival evidence. The Scottish novelist Sara Sheridan, who draws on archival materials as source material for her historical novels, has been quoted as saying that 'without archives many stories of real people would be lost, and along with those stories, vital clues that allow us to reflect and interpret our lives today'.

Archives also play a central role in film, from historical documentaries to mainstream stories. American Ken Burns, among the best known documentary filmmakers, draws heavily on archives for his stories of the American Civil War or the Roosevelt family, the evolution of baseball or jazz music or the history of prohibition in the USA. Hollywood films from *Gandhi* to *Lawrence of Arabia* to *Schindler's List* all drew on historical events, as did films such as *12 Years a Slave* or *The King's Speech*, which were based directly on archival sources (though one must accept that liberties are taken with facts in the interests of entertainment).

Archives as a window

Archives can also be used more generally to expose people to the experiences, emotions and opinions of people long gone, helping to engage with history and remind them of the lives, happenings and hardships of their forebears decades or generations back. One well known example is the diary of Anne Frank, a Jewish girl in Amsterdam during the Second World War who went into hiding with her family as the Nazis advanced into the Netherlands.

While in hiding, Anne kept a diary, full of factual information about the war as well as personal opinions and stories of everyday life, as much as her life was 'everyday'. In 1944, Anne and her family were arrested, and some months later she died of typhus in the Bergen-Belsen concentration camp. Her father, Otto, who survived the war, discovered Anne's diary on his return to the house in Amsterdam, and he arranged to have it published in 1947.

Anne's journal is famous today not because Anne was well known at the time. In 1942 she was just another young girl in Amsterdam. Her diary is perhaps most notable simply because it survived while she did not. The diary has become an iconic piece of Holocaust literature, a glimpse into the ordinary moments of a teenage girl's life amid the extraordinary circumstances of a world war.

In honour of the international significance of the diary, housed in the Netherlands Institute for War Documentation in Amsterdam, it was added to the UNESCO (United Nations Educational, Scientific, and Cultural Organization) Memory of the World Register in 2009. The act of keeping Anne's diary safe and making it available for public use has been an important step in creating empathy for the life of Jewish people during the Second World War. The diary has also served as a vehicle for creating a sense of identity for Jewish people, and Dutch society as a whole, by acknowledging and documenting a disastrous time in history, rather than ignoring a tragic past.[7]

So far we have considered the nature of archives as evidence, studied the disparate materials that may cross the threshold of an archival institution, looked briefly at archival history, considered how archival theories and methodologies have developed and are interpreted today and explored the reasons archives may be useful to society. The next task is to outline the different types of archival institution one might find in different societies. The next chapter provides an overview of a variety of 'typical' archival institutions, recognizing that, in the real world, the borders between 'types' may be quite blurry.

Notes

1   While the archives have not been made available as of early 2017, the historian Mark Riebling was able to use Vatican archives already open for use, along with archives in German repositories, to provide a new perspective on the

controversy, recounted in his 2015 history *Church of Spies: the Pope's secret war against Hitler*, Basic Books.

2   Copies of the final report and call to action by the Truth and Reconciliation Commission can be found on the official website (www.trc.ca/websites/trcinstitution/index.php?p=890). It should be noted that in Canada the terms 'aboriginal' and 'native' are used to refer very generally to indigenous Canadians. The more specific terms – 'First Nations', 'Métis' and 'Inuit' – have much more precise meanings: First Nations people are defined as members of formally established aboriginal groups, governed by their own band councils or other oversight bodies. Métis people are traditionally defined as persons of mixed Native American and French Canadian ancestry, while the Inuit are the aboriginal people of Canada's far north.

3   The English-language website for the official agency working to reconstruct the Stasi files – the Federal Commissioner for the Records of the State Security Service of the Former German Democratic Republic – can be found at www.bstu.bund.de/EN/Home/home_node.html;jsessionid= 9F71FA82DD5DD46970786D0B67758CF3.2_cid329. Australian lawyer and writer Anne Funder's 2003 award-winning analysis, *Stasiland: stories from behind the Berlin Wall*, Granta, draws on the archives themselves and on interviews with victims of and members of the Stasi to explore the manoeuvrings of, and consequences of, the system of repression. In 1997, British historian Timothy Garton Ash wrote about his experiences as a graduate student in Berlin in *The File: a personal history*, Random House. Garton Ash fell under the watchful eye of the Stasi when he moved to Berlin in the late 1970s to research Nazi history. In his book, Garton Ash compares the government's files with his own personal diary, finding vast discrepancies between his accounts of his activities and the 'official' evidence of his time in East Germany, another acknowledgement of the archival tenet that archives may be authentic but that they may not, in fact, tell the 'truth'.

4   Several accounts of the discovery and use of the Khmer Rouge records have been produced, including Dawne Adam (1998) 'The Tuol Sleng Archives and the Cambodian Genocide', *Archivaria*, **45**, Spring, 5–26; Michelle Caswell (2010) 'Khmer Rouge Archives: accountability, truth, and memory in Cambodia', *Archival Science*, **10** (1), March, 25–44; and Caswell's recent book-length study published in 2014, *Archiving the Unspeakable: silence, memory, and the photographic record in Cambodia*, University of Wisconsin Press. In January 2017, the Documentation Center of Cambodia (DC-Cam) announced its intention to launch an interactive multimedia website later to make publicly available documents related to the Khmer Rouge regime. The website (www.thekhmerrougehistory. com) was not yet operational when this book went to press, but more

information about the Documentation Center's work can be found at
www.dccam.org/.

5   See Nesmith, T. (2015) 'Toward the Archival Stage in the History of Knowledge',
    Archivaria, **80**, Fall, 119–45.

6   One of many such organizations that relies on archives for historical study is the
    American Society for Environmental History, founded in 1977, which fosters
    scholarship in the study of environmental history, publishes the peer-reviewed
    journal *Environmental History* and promotes the use of archival resources in
    historical research. See the organization's website, especially
    http://aseh.net/teaching-research/archives, which outlines different archival
    sources valuable to the study of environmental history.

7   In January 2016, the copyright of the diary expired in keeping with European
    Union copyright laws. A copyright challenge ensued between the foundation
    that distributes royalties from the book and scholars wishing to publish the diary
    online. In the end, an Amsterdam court ruled that the original text of the journal
    could be reproduced for research purposes, and so an online version published
    in 2016 was deemed not to have violated intellectual property restrictions.

5

Types of archival institution

Wise and prudent men have long known that in a changing world worthy
institutions can be conserved only by adjusting them to the changing time.

Franklin D. Roosevelt (1882–1945) Address at the Democratic
State Convention, Syracuse, New York, 29 September 1936

Today, archival institutions can be found in virtually every corner of the
world, from governments, universities, corporations and clubs to historical
societies, religious organizations, political groups and co-operatives. There
are over 1000 self-proclaimed archival institutions in Canada, thousands in
the USA and countless more around the globe. These institutions have been
established to serve the needs of their society, and they are governed by the
laws, cultures and priorities of that society.

Too often, archivists attempt to categorize archival institutions in relation
to administrative placement rather than scope of service. For example,
archivists might distinguish between church archives, government archives
and university archives. But this approach does not account for the fact that
one government archives might only manage the records of that government,
while another government archives might also acquire private papers, or that
one university archives cares only for its institutional records while another
university archives has a broad responsibility for acquiring and preserving
manuscripts and special collections. Ultimately, archival institutions will
always represent whatever their society decides they should represent.
Therefore, a more useful way to understand the different 'types' of institution
that might exist in different societies is to focus on the services they might
provide rather than on the adjective attached to the name: *church* archives
versus *special collections* department versus *business* archives.

A distinction can be made at the start between those institutions that manage only the archives of the sponsor agency itself and those that acquire and manage non-sponsor archives (private and personal papers, the archives of other corporations or associations and so on). In practice these two services often merge and overlap; rarely can an archival institution claim it focuses on one duty to the exclusion of the other. (And it is critical that the archivist in any institution remembers to protect her own organizational records too. Even if her community archives is primarily involved with collecting and preserving records from the community, the archivist must provide effective care for her archival institution's own operational records.)

An overview of several different types of archival institution is presented below, including institutional, hybrid, collecting, community-based and museum archives; integrated institutions; and indigenous and activist archives. Online repositories and trusted digital repositories are also discussed. In each case a short description of the qualities and scope of service of such an institution is followed by illustrations of agencies that might be considered reasonable examples of each type.

Institutional archives

If one adheres to the argument that archives are all about evidence and that caring for archives from the point of creation is the ideal management scenario, then institutional archives are, in theory, the purest form of archival facility. Modelling their administrative structures on the approach taken when archival collections were treasures meant for king or crown, these institutions devote the bulk of their resources and energies to the preservation of the corporate record. Unlike their medieval and early modern predecessors, though, most institutional archives today are open for some form of public use, although that public may be limited to citizens, shareholders or stakeholders, and some of the holdings may not be made available even to those groups.

The National Archives in the UK, the Bundesarchiv in Germany and government archives in India, Pakistan, Cambodia and Northern Ireland are examples of public repositories with a primary focus on institutional archives care. The National Archives of Australia (NAA), on the other hand, is primarily responsible for the archives of the Australian government but also acquires personal papers of selected individuals, such as governors-general or prime ministers. But the NAA's mandate is not so broad that it could be defined as 'hybrid', as discussed below.

Businesses, churches and banks often focus solely or primarily on their organizational archives, not on the acquisition of private papers. But even these institutional archives may collect materials created by individuals or groups outside their formal boundaries, blurring the lines between what one might consider an 'institutional' and 'hybrid' operation.

The post-custodial, continuum approach to archival management is most easily applied in institutional archives. As an official member of the creating agency, the archivist can participate actively in guiding how records and archives are managed: setting policies for quality records creation and care, providing training and guidance to staff and monitoring and auditing records systems to ensure compliance with standards and requirements. The institutional archives that adopts a continuum model to records care is often seen as the most viable structure for effective records management, especially in the management of electronic records, since – theoretically – accountable and efficient records practices can be designed into office practice from the start.

Hybrid archives

Hybrid archives actively collect both sponsor and non-sponsor archives. (The term 'hybrid' has also been used to refer to archival collections that include both physical and digital resources, but that is not the intended use of the term here.) Often, hybrid archives began as institutional repositories but expanded their focus over time to include the acquisition of non-institutional archives.

National and state archives in small or economically challenged countries, for instance, sometimes take on responsibility for the preservation of non-government materials in the absence of a university or a national library. There may simply not be enough money available to justify establishing more than one institution for years to come. Other hybrid institutions may begin by acquiring non-sponsor archives and only later take on institutional records responsibilities, so the archivist has to play a serious game of catch-up to achieve strong and sustainable records control.

Some few institutions are established with dual vision from the beginning, but it is more common for institutions to find themselves more or less responsible for one or another duty as dictated by the interests and priorities of the time. Examples of government archival repositories that include private archives in their collections can be found in the Bahamas, Belize, Tunisia and Canada (which has recently transformed itself into an integrated institution, discussed below).

Universities are ideal locations for the establishment of hybrid archival institutions, although sometimes the responsibility ends up being divided among various separate agencies within the umbrella of the university. For instance, Cambridge University Archives, which is part of the Cambridge

University Library, holds official university materials dating back to the 13th century, including accounts, letters patent, matriculations and degree records, royal letters and mandates, records of the university senate and councils, and minutes and papers related to faculty boards, degree committees and other university bodies.

Cambridge University Archives does not manage the archives of individual colleges but holds an extensive collection of manuscripts of international importance, including the papers of Sir Isaac Newton and Charles Darwin; military records related to the English Civil War, the Napoleonic Wars and the Crimean War; and four major collections of business archives, including the records of the trading company Jardine, Matheson & Co., which is reputedly the largest single collection of 19th- and 20th-century company papers related to business activities in Asia and the Far East.

Many religious archives are also hybrid institutions. The Vatican Secret Archives, mentioned earlier, preserves the historical archives of the Holy See and acts as the Central Archive for all official records created by the Vatican. The holdings of the Vatican Secret Archives are divided into several categories, including records related to the offices of the Curia, the archives of papal delegations and the archives of councils, religious orders, monasteries and abbeys. While the Archives primarily concerns itself with the official Vatican record, it also collects the archives of families or individuals of significance to the Vatican, including noble families linked to the Pontifical State, people associated with the Papal Court and other individuals of note. This practice of collecting private archives in the Vatican Secret Archives began in the late 19th century, when noble families connected to the Vatican agreed to donate or sell their archives, sometimes to avert personal economic disaster.[1]

In England, York Minster Archives collects historical archives related to the Christian Church and to Yorkshire history and also manages the official archives of the Minster itself. The holdings of the Archives date from c. AD 1000 to the present day and include the archives of the Dean and Chapter of York (the governing body for the Minster) and non-sponsor records related to the Yorkshire area, including manuscripts created by deans and bishops, politicians, antiquaries and historians, booksellers, baronets and scientists.

The Norfolk Record Office, the primary archival repository for the county of Norfolk, England, is also a hybrid institution: it collects and preserves a wide variety of records, including local government archives; archives pertaining to manors in the area and to local groups, businesses and individuals; local county council archives; and religious records related to the Diocese of Norwich.

Collecting archives

Another type of archival institution focuses exclusively on collecting archival materials for research use. For example, while some universities establish hybrid institutions to care for both institutional and private archives, others assign that work to entirely distinct organizational units. The university archives may serve a purely institutional purpose and the special collections department may focus on the acquisition of non-institutional materials for research use.

One example of this division of responsibility is at Oxford University in the UK. The university archives is a 'pure' institutional archival repository, focusing solely on the preservation and management of the university's official records, while the Bodleian Library serves as the primary collecting institution for the university. The Bodleian, arguably one of the most important research repositories in the world, first opened to researchers in 1602 and is today the second largest library in the UK after the British Library.[2]

Another collections-oriented institution is the Library of Congress, in Washington, DC, which was established by an Act of Congress in 1800. The institution was originally intended to serve as a reference facility for members of Congress, but when the library was destroyed by British troops in 1814, former American President Thomas Jefferson offered to donate his personal collection as a replacement for the lost books. Jefferson had an eclectic assortment of publications, and he argued that the library should expand its scope to include books on philosophy, literature and science. His donation opened the door to the active acquisition of all manner of books and manuscripts, and today the Library of Congress, which employs over 3000 staff, holds more than 160 million items. In 2016 the Library received nearly 1.8 million on-site visitors and recorded 92.8 million visits and more than 454 million views on its web pages.

A Canadian example of a collecting institution is the Canadian Centre for Architecture (CCA), founded in Montreal in 1979, which has become one of the world's largest research collections devoted to the study of architecture. The CCA holds thousands of prints, drawings and photographs as well as a large collection of archival materials from different creators, including architects, designers, urban planners and others.

In the USA, the Huntington Library in California, founded in 1919 by wealthy businessman Henry E. Huntington, collects a wide range of archival and published sources from the Middle Ages to the 21st century on such diverse topics as the English Renaissance, medieval manuscripts, British and American history and literature and the American Southwest.

Community archives

Another type of institution is the community-based, local or regional facility. Sometimes perceived as collections oriented and sometimes as institutional or hybrid, the community-based archival institution is distinguished more by its local character than its acquisition orientation. The scope and responsibilities of these types of archival institution – often established by or associated with historical societies, special interest groups, associations, municipalities or local government authorities – are almost entirely guided by the cultural, social and political priorities of the jurisdiction they represent.

In the USA, for example, local historical societies usually collect private materials related to the state or region, while state-run archival facilities manage the government records and archives. Examples include the San Diego Historical Society in California, which actively collects archives and artefacts related to the history of San Diego and environs, and the Connecticut Historical Society, which maintains a research library and archival collection as well as developing museum exhibits and programmes. (Some institutions might fall into the category of museum archives, discussed below, which can sometimes be considered a type of community repository.)

As mentioned already, local governments, or local authorities, in the UK tend to establish archival repositories to preserve the records of the local government, but many are really hybrid institutions, as illustrated above. In the UK, the term 'community-based archives' often refers not to local government repositories but to archival holdings managed by non-profit and non-governmental community groups, which are independent of government and might even exist to challenge government. Examples of this definition of a community archives might include Auchencairn History Society in Scotland, which is more of a web-based information resource, which makes available digital copies of archival materials, rather than a bricks and mortar facility.[3]

The concept of community-based archives is not only interpreted as geographical. Ethnic and special interest groups may establish archives to preserve archives related to their lives and experiences. Thematic archives, such as the archives of opera, hockey, surfing, rock and roll or slavery, are established by and serve the needs of community groups. Often, such groups establish archival repositories because they feel their interests or priorities are not being addressed by mainstream institutions such as government archives, and some community institutions might also fit into the category of 'activist archives' discussed below.

Museum archives

While a museum archives might easily be categorized as a type of collecting institution or type of community archives, in fact museum archives often blend the functions of institutional archives, collecting archives and community or local archives. A museum archives might perform several functions, including:

- managing and preserving the official archives of the museum institution
- acquiring the personal papers of curators, directors, trustees, staff or others involved with the work of the museum
- collecting archives and historical materials related to the museum's mandate
- acquiring archives from or related to the creators or owners of objects held by the museum (such as artists' papers collected by an art gallery).

While many museum archives are structured around the needs of a particular geographic community, others focus more on a larger theme or vision. Art galleries, natural history or science museums, or historic sites and interpretive centres define their 'community' based on their mandate and collecting focus, not necessarily on their physical boundaries.

The Museum of Modern Art Archives was established in 1989 in New York; it is a research facility that supports the curatorial and historical work of the museum, which in turn focuses on the preservation and display of modern and contemporary art. The institution defines its acquisition scope broadly, preserving its own institutional archives and acquiring archives in all media that support research and education into modern and contemporary art, including the business or personal papers of artists, architects, designers, dealers, critics, scholars, art historians, arts organizations and other galleries.

On a smaller scale, the Museum of Scottish Lighthouses in Aberdeenshire, Scotland, collects archives, artefacts and memorabilia related to the history of lighthouses across Scotland. Archival holdings include an original royal charter allowing Trinity House (the general lighthouse authority for England) to control navigation around the English coast; a Christmas card showing a Norwegian lighthouse; and a magic lantern and collection of slides created by Alistar Hislop, the keeper of Ailsa Craig lighthouse off the Firth of Clyde in the early and mid-20th century. Theoretically, this museum could also acquire archives related to lighthouses around Scotland, which raises the question of overlapping acquisition mandates, as discussed in Chapter 10.

Integrated institutions

In an age when the boundaries between information and evidence are blurring, resource allocators, particularly in the public sector, see benefits to converging 'information' services within an integrated agency. Consequently, many governments are actively merging libraries, museums and archives, sometimes under the umbrella term 'memory institutions'.

In 2003, the UK PRO merged with the Historical Manuscripts Commission to become The National Archives. In 2006 the Office of Public Sector Information and Her Majesty's Stationery Office were also merged into the Archives. The restructuring was not just an administrative change. It was a statement of the government's intention to position this new information-oriented institution as a leader in the management of information policy, with a direct responsibility for establishing best practice standards in information and records management across the UK government.

Another example is the amalgamation of the National Library of Canada and National Archives of Canada into Library and Archives Canada in 2004. The original national archives, first established in 1872, followed the 'total archives' approach, as discussed in Chapter 3. This approach led the national archival institution to acquire all types of archives, in all media and from all sources, both government and private. But the national library, established in 1953, also started with a mandate to collect private manuscripts and media materials. For many years the two institutions worked closely together and even shared the same building, but they were considered administratively separate although they were carrying out duplicate and sometimes overlapping operations. To reduce this overlap and streamline operations, the two institutions were merged into Library and Archives Canada in 2004 with the following mandate:

- to preserve the documentary heritage of Canada for the benefit of present and future generations
- to be a source of enduring knowledge accessible to all, contributing to the cultural, social and economic advancement of Canada as a free and democratic society
- to facilitate in Canada co-operation among communities involved in the acquisition, preservation and diffusion of knowledge
- to serve as the continuing memory of the Government of Canada and its institutions.

The impetus for the merger at Library and Archives Canada may have been largely administrative, to reduce the duplication of services and save money.

But it may also have been philosophical, based on a belief that information is information. The end result seems to have been that, after some disruptions in the early 2000s, Library and Archives Canada is now a relatively happy marriage of two existing institutions, whether or not the union began with a shotgun.

In other cases, integration may be a term used for a practical convenience, as different cultural agencies are brought together under one roof to present a united public front, but behind the scenes each maintains its own principles and practices. For instance, in the American state of Alaska, the state library, state archives and state museum were all moved into one building in June 2016, with the opening of the Andrew P. Kashevaroff State Library, Archives and Museum in the state capitol, Juneau. The building itself was constructed to meet the highest standards for preservation of all the materials, artefacts, publications and archives.

While integrated physically into one institution and administered by one branch of government (the Division of Libraries, Archives, and Museums), and sharing high-quality preservation and storage facilities, each unit continues to maintain its own systems and approaches for such tasks as acquisition (or collecting), description (or cataloguing) and access (or interpretation). The division aspires to create shared access tools, but each group within the larger agency has to consider what is gained and what is lost by adapting existing practices to suit other disciplinary approaches. How, for instance, might the units share descriptive information if they follow different standards for description and cataloguing? The future will decide how far this effort at integration will go.

Indigenous archives

While indigenous or aboriginal archival materials may find a home in mainstream institutions such as government archives or museums, indigenous people are increasingly choosing to preserve their own heritage in institutions of their own devising. Thus a newer type of institution in many countries, particularly in Canada, could be defined as an indigenous archives. But because indigenous culture so often reaches well beyond the boundaries of written documents or publications, the holdings of an aboriginal-run centre may include not just archives or books but also artefacts such as animal bones, hunting tools or clothing; film footage or sound recordings of songs, stories, celebrations or other events; artworks depicting historical moments or locations; or sacred and ceremonial objects. Many indigenous archives are integrated institutions, serving not just as repositories of documents but also as libraries, museums, cultural centres, interpretive centres and locations for ceremonial activities.

The archivist working with indigenous collections, whether within an indigenous institution or in another kind of repository, needs to remember that not all materials of value to that particular community can or should be defined or managed by archival principles alone (or at all). The archival definition of 'documentary evidence' is valid, but so too are different definitions of information and evidence, reflecting other values defined by the indigenous community in keeping with its own culture.

Activist archives

Another increasingly prominent type of archival institution is the activist archives. Activist archives first began to appear as postmodernism gained ground, as an effort to counter perceived 'truths' in mainstream institutions. Many were driven by a desire to protect archives as evidence for social justice and to combat autocracies and tyrannical governments (whether actual or perceived). Thus I have conceived of an 'activist archives' as an institution that does not just acquire archives and make them available for research use but that does so to promote a particular political or social agenda.

One can argue (and many postmodern thinkers have) that all archival institutions are political creatures because they represent the biases and prefer- ences of the people and agencies that establish and manage them. It is useful, however, to consider purely activist archives as a separate category of institu- tion, since many of the decisions and actions taken by these institutions – what they collect, who may use their holdings and how they operate – are based on a clear and overt political vision. They do not deny their orientation and intent.

An example of an activist archives is the South African History Archive (SAHA), dedicated to documenting and providing access to archival holdings that relate to and support the protection and advancement of human rights in South Africa. SAHA was originally established by anti-apartheid activists in the 1980s and was closely aligned with political groups such as the United Democratic Front, the Congress of South African Trade Unions and the African National Congress. However, over the years SAHA seems to have moved away from direct political alignment, committing itself to collecting materials as widely as possible, in order to document South African history and current events and thereby to support democracy, justice and accountability.

In 2015, SAHA launched a new initiative, the Right to Truth Project, intended to make the archives of the South African Truth and Reconciliation Commission more accessible. The first project in this new initiative is to process recently released Section 29 records, which relate to closed hearings held under the Truth and Reconciliation Commission as part of Section 29 of South Africa's Promotion of National Unity and Reconciliation Act (1995). Thus one can see that SAHA has transformed itself over time, but it has retained its autonomy.

What happens, though, when an effort to document (and gain support for) a political movement is so successful that the 'activist' institution joins the mainstream? Consider the example of the ONE National Gay and Lesbian Archives in California. The collection itself began in 1942 when Jim Kepner, a journalist, author and leader in the gay rights movement, began collecting material related to gay, lesbian, bisexual, transgendered and queer individuals and issues. In 1971, Kepner named his collection, then still housed in his Los Angeles apartment, the Western Gay Archives. As the collection grew in size and scope, it was moved from place to place. Finally, in 2010, it found a home on the campus of the University of Southern California (USC), and today the ONE Archives is a formal part of the USC Libraries system.

Created as the result of immediate concerns and one-time events, in this case to challenge existing perceptions about the rights of members of the lesbian, gay, bisexual, trans and queer community, these archives would perhaps not find another secure home without the efforts of a dedicated activist such as Kepner. One might ask now, though, whether the ONE Archives can still be perceived as an 'activist' archives or whether it is now part of the mainstream archival community, in part by virtue of its administrative and physical location within a formal university archival system. If a precious but at-risk collection of anti-establishment archives finds a safe home within an established agency, is that defined as success through sustainability, or defeat through diminished autonomy? There is a question ripe for philosophical debate.

Online repositories

As discussed in Chapter 3, activist approaches to archives are growing as notions of decolonization take hold. To combat what they feel is excessive control over information, many archivists engaged with archival activism are seeking alternative methods to bring documentary evidence more fully into public view. One of the options is to obtain copies of archival materials and make them available through online repositories. The theoretical question is whether such repositories of documentary materials – whether created for political purposes or not – are really repositories or institutions. Or are they simply digital collections of copies, which suggests they are libraries more than archives?

One of the most prominent digital archival repositories is the San Francisco-based Internet Archive, founded by computer engineer and entrepreneur Brewster Kahle in 1996. The Internet Archive is now the digital home to over 15 petabytes of data, including web pages and digital copies of books, magazines, textual materials, television and radio programmes, software, movies and music. Another internet giant, Google, also aspires (as the company puts it) to 'bring all the world's information to people seeking answers', by creating databases of web pages, scholarly citations and art works.[4] Whether these online repositories hold authentic and original archival material, and whether the documentary materials stored in those computer servers are preserved with their content, context and structure intact, are matters of speculation.

Trusted digital repositories

Archivists have sought to guarantee the authenticity and security of virtual (versus physical) archival evidence by establishing strict criteria for online storage, creating the concept of a 'trusted digital repository'. When the average person hears the phrase 'digital repository', they might imagine an actual storage device: a special computer server with particular properties to store anything digital. In reality, the concept of a trusted digital repository is much more complex.

A trusted digital repository is not a thing; it is a concept. It is the outcome of a combination of people, policies, procedures and technologies, all of which work together according to standards and best practice requirements, to ensure that digital objects – any items to be preserved in digital form – can be captured and preserved with their authenticity as evidence protected and their content, context and structure intact. The trusted digital repository also allows researchers and the public to access and use those digital objects without compromising the authenticity and integrity of the materials.

Establishing a trusted digital repository is similar to establishing a safe and secure archival environment for traditional paper or analogue archives. The goal is to create an environment that ensures the items in care are safe from loss or damage; that no one can destroy or alter originals; and that privacy and security are protected. As digital preservation expert Adrian Brown has put it, the task the archivist faces is to construct a digital repository that people *can trust*, so it may be more useful to talk about trust*worthy* repositories instead of trust*ed* repositories.[5]

While the number of actual trusted digital repositories in operation in early 2017 is still low, it is possible to discern three distinct approaches to the creation of such a repository. The first approach is to create a centralized repository created and maintained by the creator of the records. This digital repository would be comparable to an institutional archival facility that manages the physical archives of its sponsor agency, such as a digital repository for the protection of national or state government records in electronic form.

The main strength of a centralized approach is that the agency can maintain control over the management of electronic records from creation through acquisition, preservation and use. The major weakness is that if the sponsor organization cannot provide sufficient and sustained resources to maintain the repository over the long term, the records will be at risk. A digital repository is not a time-limited project, any more than the acquisition and preservation of physical archives is a one-time effort.

The second type of digital repository might be a decentralized or third-party-managed repository, created with the purpose of receiving and preserving the archives of different creating agencies or individuals. The agency responsible for running the digital repository would be a contracted service provider. The strength of such an approach is that it can provide a safe location that can be used by smaller archival agencies that do not have the resources to establish their own digital repositories. The major weaknesses relate to long-term maintenance and quality control. What if the service provider goes out of business? What if the supplier does not provide services that meet acceptable standards? There is a grave risk of failure if sustainability is not built into the model.

A third type of digital repository is a networked repository. In this case, several archival institutions combine resources to create a shared repository for the management of electronic records acquired by each institution. In this model, one institution, such as a state or provincial archives, might provide the technology and infrastructure, while others, such as community or museum archives, would pay a fee for storing their digital holdings in the repository. This form of co-operative service is seen by many archivists as a logical direction for electronic archival care in the future. Cost sharing and collaboration can reduce expenses for each institution and increase the chance of sustainability through collaboration. A major drawback, though, is co-ordinating the efforts of traditionally independent organizations. What happens if some partners decide to leave? Will the co-operative model be sustainable with two partners instead of ten? Archivists are just starting to consider these different options for digital archives management.

As shown here, the range of archival institutions can vary dramatically. No single approach is absolutely right in every instance. In one jurisdiction, people may completely support the preservation of public and private archives by central governments, trusting its public servants to do the best job they can for everyone in the society. In another jurisdiction, the level of trust in government may be so low that private archival institutions or 'shadow' archival work – activist archives concerned with social justice – are established, as people try to thwart agents of authority they do not believe are acting in their best interests by obtaining copies of otherwise secret records and making them publicly available. Not every nation-state defines 'democracy' the same way, and not all of those in positions of power respect the idea of the rule of law.

Regardless of organizational frameworks, the institution acquiring and preserving archives on behalf of its society has a moral, if not legal, responsibility to operate in an accountable and effective manner for the benefit of all stakeholders, however those groups are defined. The archivist as a practitioner also has a responsibility to provide the best possible professional service, irrespective of the type of institution in which she works. The responsibilities of archival service are outlined in the next chapter.

Notes

1   The word 'secret' in this case does not mean 'restricted' or 'confidential'; it derives from the Latin *secretum* or 'private' and refers more to 'personal' than 'secret' as we understand those words today. In fact, the Vatican archives were opened to the public by Pope Leo XIII in 1881 although, as noted in Chapter 4, access to some holdings continues to be restricted.

2   The New Bodleian Library building, which had been opened by King George VI in 1946, was closed in 2011 for renovations, opening again in 2015 as the home of the university's special collections under the new name 'the Weston Library'.

3   The website for the Auchencairn History Society is at www.auchencairn.org.uk/index.php/community-council-communityarchive-85.

4   The Internet Archive's website is at https://archive.org/index.php. Google's corporate philosophy is described online at https://www.google.ca/intl/en/about/company/philosophy/.

5   Brown, A. (2013) *Practical Digital Preservation: a how-to guide for organizations of any size*, Facet; see especially pages 82–3. This book and other resources on digital records care and preservation are identified in the resources section.

6

The principles of archival service

When a man assumes a public trust, he should consider himself as public property.

> Thomas Jefferson (1743–1826) quoted in B.L. Rayner, *Life of Jefferson*, 1834

While the nature of a particular *archival institution* will influence the nature and scope of its holdings and operations, the central principle of accountable and trustworthy *archival service* must be to make certain that archives are captured and protected with their evidential value intact, and then to ensure that those archives are made available as fully as possible, so that they may benefit the widest possible constituency. If archives are collected but stored away in the basement of the repository and never cleaned of dust, insects or mould, then they have not been protected for posterity. If they are acquired and preserved but never made available to anyone but the person who collected them, then they do not support a society's quest for evidence, information and knowledge.

The act of acquiring and preserving archives is a service that must be performed in an accountable and structured fashion, with respect not only for the documentary evidence itself but also for the individuals and groups who created that evidence and for the people who may wish to access that evidence now and in the future. To understand the nature of archival service, it is necessary to outline the core duties and skills of the archivist and then to examine a central challenge the archivist faces: balancing the rights of some to access and use archival materials for any manner of research with the rights of others to ensure their own personal information is protected from illegitimate use. This chapter looks at the principles that guide the work of the archivist in providing archival services to society. Chapter 7 is devoted to a discussion of the specific challenge of balancing access and privacy.

Archival obligations

Irrespective of the scope of the archival institution, the archivist working in that institution, or the archivist working as an independent consultant for a number of clients, has a responsibility to perform certain core duties. Her ultimate goal is to support the effective care of archival materials, so that they are preserved and managed as authentic and reliable documentary evidence and then available for the widest possible use. How does she do that?

Adopting an ethical framework

There are no official controls on archival employment; as discussed later in this chapter, archival service is not a formal, regulated profession. Anyone who can demonstrate a capacity for and interest in archival work may find employment as an archivist, depending, of course, on the nature of the job in question. A government archivist position may require extensive education and experience, but a part-time job in a community archives may be filled by someone with local history experience who has taken some community college courses on archival management. Still, all archivists want to provide the best possible archival service, and the associations that support archival work have helped that effort by developing codes of ethics and practice, which they encourage their members to recognize and respect.

The International Council on Archives (ICA), the international association representing archival institutions and professionals around the world, published an international code of ethics in 1996. Similar codes are in place at the national level in countries such as Australia, Austria, Canada, the Netherlands, New Zealand, Spain, Switzerland, the UK and the USA. I believe that it is time these various codes of ethics were revised, particularly to address the challenges of digital records and perhaps to break down the divide between records management and archives management, a divide that will not serve modern records and archives care well in the future. Instead of describing the requirements of specific codes of ethics, I have opted to write about the optimal ethical framework in which archivists work, recognizing that not every aspiration identified here can be achieved in reality. My suggestions touch on issues that I believe all archivists, whether they work in institutions or serve as independent consultants, ought to consider.

Respect for the integrity of the records

The archivist will protect the integrity of the archives in her care, doing everything possible to maintain their value as documentary evidence. This includes providing a safe and stable environment for the receipt, storage and handling of archival holdings, regardless of form and medium, and striving to protect the content, context and structure of archives during any work to arrange, describe, preserve or provide access to holdings. This principle also means that the archivist should take all steps to gain legal, administrative, physical and intellectual control over all the materials in her care as quickly, effectively and comprehensively as possible. Archives that sit in storage closets, unidentified and unorganized, are worse than a backlog. They are a breach of the trust that donors place in archival institutions and archivists: to receive, manage *and make available* valuable archival resources. If the archivist cannot guarantee that materials will be safer in her care than they were before they were transferred into custody, she should think carefully about whether to accept them in the first place.

Impartiality and transparency

The archivist will maintain impartiality and transparency in all her duties. This means that she will appraise, acquire and manage archival material on behalf of her institution in an unbiased fashion, in order to preserve the best evidence possible, and she will be transparent about her actions and decisions, so that others can understand the rationale for any actions taken, from acquisition to arrangement, description, digitization and access. While one can acknowledge the postmodern argument that all actions taken by anyone in society are inherently subjective, on an individual level the archivist needs to act on the basis of institutional need and priorities, not personal inclinations. This means, for instance, that the archivist should not accept acquisitions that violate the legitimate claims of other agencies, nor should she choose to keep some items in an acquisition because she finds them of personal interest or discard other items because she does not accept the perspective they present. The archivist also needs to remember that she is responsible not just for managing archives today but also for developing and maintaining the infrastructure needed to protect them and provide access to them five, ten or 20 years from now. Whether the archivist works for one institution or is a consultant with several clients, she should always act in the best interests of each agency, and she should always document fully all actions taken and decisions made to leave a clear record for the future.

Professional competency

The archivist will perform her duties competently, without impairment.

Whenever possible, she will adhere to best practice standards for all aspects of records and archives management, with the goal of providing the best possible care for archival holdings. She will remain knowledgeable about current archival practice and will actively seek to learn new theories and methodologies, through formal studies or informal learning opportunities. When she does not feel competent to take an action, she should seek help and advice rather than carry on and hope for the best. Regardless of whether or not archival work is formally recognized as a profession, archival materials should always receive the best possible care, which means not just understanding principles and theories but also being able to adapt them to the realities of the immediate situation. The archivist will not choose one course of action over another because she believes one is theoretically 'better' than another or because she has a vested interest in following a particular approach; she must always focus on what is going to serve the records best in the long term. The best archivist will keep her mind active, her knowledge current and her skills sharp, remaining open to changes in theories, principles and practices.

Respect for human rights

The archivist will respect fundamental human rights at all times, refusing to participate in or support practices that violate or diminish anyone's basic rights. For instance, the archivist will provide balanced and impartial public service, without judging the nature and purpose of anyone's interest in archives. She will respect the privacy not only of the people whose records are in her care but also of the researchers using those records. She will make decisions about acquisition, appraisal and archival management based first and foremost on protecting the archives as evidence, to ensure they remain tools for accountability and transparency. The archivist will also remember that she must respect the rights of people in the future, not just the present. For instance, when considering an acquisition, the archivist may see fit to accept reasonable restrictions on access, but she should avoid imposing excessive or inappropriate controls that suit one individual today but will not be beneficial to society in the future. This responsibility to respect the rights of everyone in society extends beyond donors and researchers to include the archivist's dealings with colleagues and the wider public. The archivist is an ambassador for a profession premised on the principle that archives are tools for accountability, identity and memory and on the belief that a wise society learns about itself by using archives in the widest and most creative ways possible. The archivist will represent these professional ideals best by remaining open, respectful, supportive and non-judgemental about the diversity of human interests, opinions and beliefs.

Respect for the rule of law

Whenever possible, the archivist will respect the principles of the rule of law, which is the idea that societies should be guided not by the arbitrary decisions of individuals or groups but by commonly agreed principles of fairness, morality and justice. In practice, this respect for the rule of law is applied when the archivist upholds the laws and policies applicable to her institution, as well as to local, state or national laws. The principle also urges the archivist to respect relevant professional codes of ethics or guidelines issued by archival or other associations. The archivist's goal should be to adhere to the highest standards of legally acceptable professional conduct in the protection of documentary evidence, in order to maintain the spirit of archival service as a mechanism for protecting evidence to support accountability, foster identity and preserve memory. The challenge, of course, is what the archivist does if she believes that actual laws, policies or ethical standards are not in keeping with the spirit of the rule of law or the vision of accountability and transparency in society. For instance, a government may pass a law allowing public officials to destroy records, even though they contain valuable evidence of critical actions and decisions. The archivist then has to consider whether she can or should protest against the law, which she may believe violates her responsibility to protect records as evidence. She may choose to use her position to try to change the laws, in which case she has to consider the consequences for her career. She could receive a reprimand, at best, or even be expelled from her post. In such cases, the archivist in an institutional setting may need to garner support from allies, such as the leaders in her professional association, to lobby for changes or to raise public awareness, as she may not be at liberty to speak out herself. As discussed later, archival associations can play an important role in advocacy, holding agencies, particularly government and public-sector organizations, accountable for their record-keeping practices and speaking out against violations of the rule of law when individual archivists cannot.

Respect for her own well-being

The archivist must retain her own integrity and protect her own well-being as a professional and member of society. When representing the archival institution, the archivist needs to set purely individual interests aside and focus on her role as steward and custodian. But she also has an obligation to society: as a professional, citizen and human being. If, for instance, a senior official in her government declares that the archivist must destroy a box of archives that present his services in a negative light, she has to consider not just her (now precarious) job prospects but also her obligations to the public. Can she stand up for her principles and refuse to destroy the records? What will be the cost to her if she protests, or the cost to society if she complies? Again, the ability to draw on colleagues in her wider professional association to help lobby for action can be a great benefit in such situations. A little public scrutiny can do wonders for resolving an otherwise intractable problem. Ultimately, archivists are human beings, like everyone else, and must and should act in keeping with their own conscience.

The archivist who adopts an ethical framework based on key principles such as those articulated above does so because she sees her duty as serving as a trusted custodian – a steward – of society's documentary memory. The best archivist takes a very long view of her work. She needs to be comfortable with the fact that even if something she acquires and processes today cannot be released to researchers for another 50 years, eventually those materials will tell a truth that might help shape her society for the better.

The role(s) of the archivist

The different roles of the archivist – custodian or record keeper, records manager or archives administrator – have already been mentioned in this book. How the archivist's duties are defined will depend on her particular job description. She cannot help her sponsor agency manage current records if her job is to care for literary papers, and she cannot acquire the records of the local union if her mandate does not extend to private archives acquisition. Regardless, the archivist can and should play an inclusive, supporting role in the management of society's documentary evidence. In the ideal world the archivist will not just be a manager of historical archives or an administrator of modern records. She will also bring to her job a belief that her larger responsibility is as auditor, protector, historian and advocate.

Auditor

As auditor, the archivist's responsibility is not just to manage the day-to-day care of archives but also to advise on and oversee the development of records and archives policies and legislation; the establishment of records-related standards, systems and infrastructures; and the creation of processes for preserving a well-rounded and accessible documentary record of society. If she is not given this authority formally, she can still press the case for improved records care, whether in a staff presentation, a board meeting or a coffee break with the boss.

Protector

As protector, the archivist arranges and describes the materials in her care; implements adequate preservation mechanisms; develops emergency response programmes; and protects the content, structure and context of archives. She also advises her sponsor agency of the importance of caring for records in all media, even if some of those materials are not in her care at the moment.

Historian

As a historian of the record, the archivist documents the organizational, administrative, technological and personal histories that give archives their meaning. She uses her skills and knowledge to contextualize archives, which may include capturing information about current activities within the organization, even if no records about those activities have come into her care, so that she leaves behind a rich documentary framework for the next archivist, who may be responsible for managing the agency's archives a decade from now.

Advocate

As an advocate, the archivist encourages society at large to value records and archives as evidence, as information and as tools that support individual and collective memory. She speaks up at staff meetings to remind her colleagues of the link between archives and accountability, identity and memory. She develops 'elevator speeches' and case studies to show how records and archives are important, in case she gets five minutes with the president of the organization. She plays an active and supportive role with her professional associations, so that she can add her voice to collective calls for improved records and archives care.

The archivist as consultant

Increasingly, archivists are serving as consultants, working for many clients, not just one institution. An archival consultant may provide electronic records management advice to a municipal government, develop a strategic plan for a religious archives, teach arrangement and description to a group of archival volunteers and develop a handbook on digital preservation for a local historical society.

The benefits or drawbacks of consulting work, and the economic realities that are driving many archivists to take on itinerant or temporary positions instead of permanent jobs, are beyond the scope of discussion here. But it is important to note that the archival consultant is and ought to be bound by the same ethical framework set out above, so that she can perform her duties with integrity, objectivity, transparency and balance regardless of her client.

The consulting archivist must meet one more condition, however. Even more than the archivist in an institution, an archival consultant has a deep responsibility to protect the confidentiality of her clients, because she may have many of them, not just one. While it is often useful to draw on previous experiences when undertaking a new consulting task, the archival consultant must remember that each client has unique needs. It is not appropriate simply to copy a report produced for one client and cut and paste it for another client; the archivist needs to put in the effort and energy required to do a proper job each time, even though after five or ten or 20 clients she will start to see patterns, which will make her work easier. Cut-and-paste consulting casts a negative light on everyone in the profession; even though the advice provided may need to be the same in each case, the message must be delivered in keeping with that particular client's real needs and priorities.

Similarly, while the archival consultant may find it appropriate to draw on previous experience when offering guidance to a new client, she must always avoid indiscretion in her conversations with clients and colleagues. The disclosure of confidential information about a client is just as inappropriate for an archivist as it is for a doctor or lawyer.

The education of the archivist

Increasingly, archivists develop their knowledge, skills and abilities by pursuing a formal education in records and archives management through a university or college. Around the world, more and more graduate and undergraduate archival studies programmes have emerged, offering training and education in a range of information, records and archives topics.

The nature of the courses can vary dramatically in different jurisdictions. Paleography (the study of writing systems) and diplomatics (the act of authenticating ancient documents) may be part of the core curriculum in Europe, where archivists work regularly with ancient and medieval texts.

Such courses may be optional at best in the USA or Australia. Some archival programmes emphasize preservation and reprography; others accentuate historical research and scholarship; others focus on the management of digital records. The care of artefacts or intangible cultural materials such as songs or dances, or the preservation of art or publications, may be seen as outside the scope of archival studies in some jurisdictions, but in others those tasks may be central to integrated and holistic archival education.

In today's world of instant communications and globalization, it is much easier for archivists from different parts of the world to exchange ideas about archival theories and practices. This 'cross-fertilization' has been a great boon to archival education, allowing instructors to highlight the cultural and social realities of archival practice from Africa to Asia and from Australia to the South Pacific. The ability to introduce different cultural perspectives also challenges archival students (and practising archivists and archival educators) to rethink their own perspectives (biases?) on archival concepts and traditions. Archival educators need to think creatively about the skills, knowledge and abilities needed not just in their own jurisdiction but in the global world of evidence management, before choosing priorities for their own constituency.

Despite inevitable variations in education around the world, most formal programmes in records and archives management will address subjects such as the following:

- theories and principles related to information, evidence, records and archives
- professional responsibilities, including professional ethics
- administrative responsibilities, including the importance of legal and administrative frameworks, strategic and operational plans, facilities and financial systems and effective mechanisms for oversight and quality control
- the creation and management of authentic and reliable evidence, regardless of medium or form
- the effective management of evidence (whether through a 'life cycle' or as part of a 'continuum of care' or both)
- the selection and acquisition of evidence with enduring value
- the capture, preservation, arrangement and description of evidence, whether physical, analogue or digital
- the requirements for making evidence available and supporting research and reference use
- the tasks involved with engaging the wider public with both the documentary resources and the institution caring for them.

It is easy to suggest that everyone working in an archival institution ought to start with pre-appointment education, just as doctors begin with medical studies and lawyers with a formal education in law, but such educational requirements are almost impossible to enforce in the archival world. Archival institutions are established by groups for their own reasons, and those groups will engage the services of an archivist to meet their particular archival needs. An archivist in a national government will have a very different remit from an archivist in a local museum. Some archivists may be professionally trained and work full time; others may be para-professionals with technical training. Still others may be dedicated volunteers. Each scenario may be appropriate for those particular needs. To support that diversity, it is incumbent on the wider archival community not to get so consumed with credentials that it limits the ability of institutions, especially low-resource institutions, to survive.

The role of professional associations

One of the tasks of professional associations can be to lobby for improved status for their members, while, one hopes, recognizing the reality that archival service is remarkable in its diversity. International, national, state and regional records and archives associations can also speak out about the value of archives to society, lobby in favour of improved record-keeping practices and protest decisions that negatively affect the condition of archives, archival institutions and archivists.

Archivists joining their professional associations will benefit from membership services such as easier access to publications, online resources and job aids; the opportunity to attend annual conferences, meetings and workshops; and the rising tide of increased public awareness of archival service through the power of a collective voice. At the same time, archival associations, like any professional body, need to be held to account by the membership. Associations need to demonstrate the effective use of member dues; keep their overhead costs low; target expenditures on agreed priorities; and consult members before taking a position on controversial matters.

As records and evidence become more pivotal, and more precarious, in a digital society, there is a growing need for someone to speak out on behalf of the record, not only on behalf of the archivist or the institution. Archival associations cannot always take political stands that reach beyond professional borders, but individual archivists may also not be able to speak out without risking their jobs. There have been growing calls for the creation of advocacy groups driven by the wider public, not the archival profession, to argue for effective records care and against actions that violate the protection of evidence as a tool for supporting the rule of law.

The place of standards

One task that professional associations have done well in recent years is to identify the need for, and push for the development of, best practice standards for records and archives care. National and international agencies such as the International Organization for Standards (ISO), the ICA and other groups have developed standards for all manner of records and archives service. For instance, the ISO has issued a range of standards related to records management, digital preservation and metadata management. The ICA and national archival groups have developed standards for different components of records and archives work, many of which are discussed in later chapters in the book.

The purpose of standards is to impose consistency and control. Before archivists developed specific standards for description 30 or so years ago, the researcher might come into one archival institution and face a series of card catalogues along a wall, each holding cards with three-line descriptions of hundreds of feet of records. He might go to the next institution and be presented with an item-level list of everything in a dozen boxes but no contextual information to explain how the archives came to be or who created the records. Now the researcher expects to see some consistency in descriptive information, letting him know the who, what, where, when and why of the archives.

To perform her duties effectively, the archivist needs to know that different standards exist and apply them as reasonably as possible, in keeping with her specific responsibilities. Those standards most applicable to the topics central to this book – primarily archives-oriented rather than records-oriented standards – are identified as appropriate in later chapters. The resources at the end highlight some other standards that the archivist should take into consideration.

The danger with standards is that, on the one hand, they can be over-prescriptive and unrealistic, especially for archival institutions with limited resources. On the other hand, because they are *standards* and not *laws*, no archivist is legally obligated to use them. This lack of enforceability reduces the chance of achieving complete consistency, which is the perceived goal of a standard. Standardization only happens if everyone agrees to use *the same standard*. But as an old saying goes, 'Standards are like toothbrushes; everyone wants to use them but no one wants to use someone else's.'

The importance of respect

It should go without saying that the archivist is in the business of archives because she has an interest in her society: in the lives and loves of individuals; in the work of organizations to act on behalf of their constituents; and in the role of government as a democratically accountable agent within its society. Most archivists want to, and most *do*, have the highest respect for records and people.

Inevitably, archives can have tremendous emotional impact for the families represented in them, and for their descendants, researchers and the public. Even the archivist is not immune. To ignore the emotional impact of archives is to lose sight of their tremendous power as evidence and as a tool for identity and memory. What may today seem to the archivist as an amusing anecdote in a letter from 1825, about how a farmer was kicked by a cow, might at the time been a contributing factor in the farmer's bankruptcy, when he had to wait for his broken legs to heal, so he could not plant the corn, harvest the crops and make an income for his family. A simple petition for divorce might seem commonplace to an archivist in 2017, when divorce is common and accepted, but it might have been earth-shattering a century before to the parties involved. And their descendants might not even know that it took place, so when they find the document in an archival institution all the myths and stories of a happy family might be severely challenged.

The archivist must always remember that she has an obligation, by virtue of her choice of job, to work with all archives to the best of her ability, even when the going gets tough. After all, the emotions she may experience when processing a body of archives are probably nothing compared with those experienced by the people represented in those materials or their descendants. All her interactions with the materials in her care, and with the creators, donors, users and public, should be based on the archivist's belief that, no matter how sensitive or distressing the archives, her job is to help preserve them and make them available as needed, to prove facts and acts, support accountability, enrich memory and foster identity.

Having examined the nature of archival service and the obligations of the archivist, whether a full-time employee or a consultant, and commented on the education of the archivist, the role of archival associations and the importance of respect for the record, one more point of principle needs to be addressed before we can turn to discussions of actual archival practice.

When managing any archival materials, the archivist must balance two competing priorities. The first priority is to support the right of the public to access information about actions, transactions and decisions, particularly but not only for those in society with power and authority. This first right is often enshrined in law, through government archives legislation, access and privacy laws and other legal instruments. The second priority is to support the right of the individuals and organizations represented in archival materials to know that their identity and privacy will be protected as appropriate, ensuring that personal information will not be released inappropriately or that third parties cannot profit from someone's intellectual property, without their express approval, for as long as copyright or related laws allow. While these rights might be guided by law, they are also a matter of morals and ethics. Questions of access and privacy are addressed in the next chapter.

7

Balancing access and privacy

Historically, privacy was almost implicit, because it was hard to find and gather information. But in the digital world, whether it's digital cameras or satellites or just what you click on, we need to have more explicit rules – not just for governments but for private companies.

Bill Gates (1955–) *Wired.com*, 12 November 2013

When an archivist receives archival materials into her care her first interest is, almost inevitably, to make the documentary treasures available for use. What a thrill it is to hold in your hands an original letter written by your favourite artist, or to see the name of a former mayor among the rolls of students in your local high school. As someone once said, archivists get paid to read other people's mail. We love the opportunity to see into the lives of other people and, through them, to understand the way our communities functioned in years past.

But the artist and the mayor have rights too. And these rights do not vanish when documents created or owned by them move into archival custody. The need to balance access and privacy and the need to respect intellectual property rights are perhaps the greatest source of tension for the archivist, especially given the ubiquity of digital technologies today.

The requirements of access, privacy and copyright laws can throw obstacles in the way of achieving the goal of archival service, which, as stated many times already, is to support the acquisition, preservation and management of archival materials so that they can be made available for use. But the creators of documentary materials – the people who kept personal diaries, wrote letters to their sister, took photographs on their holiday, prepared financial reports for their business – did not create those records for posterity. The fact that those records ended up in an archival repository, perhaps decades after their creation, does not mean that the creators of those records have lost all right to control the ways in which those materials may be used.

A brief look at the challenge of copyright, and the need to balance access with privacy, will help outline some of the primary issues that the archivist needs to consider. It must be remembered that these conditions apply irrespective of the medium or form of the archives in question: they are equally relevant for paper documents, digital photographs, home movies or membership databases.

It is neither possible nor logical, however, to delve deeply in this book into the minutiae of copyright or access and privacy laws in different jurisdictions. The legislation around these matters varies so widely that explaining the provisions of the law in one country while ignoring the law in another would only mislead the archivist, who might be left thinking that Law A in Jurisdiction Q is the same as Law B in Jurisdiction Z. That is so far from true that I will instead stick to core principles, with a few fictitious examples only to illustrate concepts. It is the archivist's responsibility to learn, in depth, the specific legal framework in which she is obligated to protect privacy, provide access and manage intellectual property rights in her own jurisdiction.

Respecting intellectual property rights

Intellectual property rights relate to the rights of a creator to own and use his intellectual products, such as artwork, music, photographs, essays or letters. These rights are comparable to a property right, which is the right of a person to own and manage a physical entity, like a piece of land or a car or a house.

Copyright is one form of intellectual property right: patents and trademarks are other forms (outside the scope of discussion here). A person who holds copyright has the sole right to benefit economically from his literary or artistic creations and to be recognized and receive credit as the creator of that work. He also has the exclusive right to reproduce that work, including the right to prevent others from publishing or disseminating the work without permission. As outlined below, these rights do not last forever, but while they are in effect they must be respected to the utmost.

While intellectual property laws appeared as early as the 16th century, the modern concept of copyright derives from the upheaval of the French Revolution, which led to greater emphasis on individual rights instead of collective ownership and state control. The original purpose of copyright was twofold: to encourage people to produce creative products, and to support the development of research and scholarship. By allowing creators an exclusive right to profit from their works, those creators would see the benefit of devoting themselves to intellectual enterprise, perhaps by receiving financial compensation for their efforts. By limiting how long those rights existed, the rest of society would have greater access to literature, art or music once the creator's rights expired.

The archivist faces three major challenges when managing intellectual property rights in an archival environment: confirming copyright, knowing when intellectual property rights expire and distinguishing between physical and intellectual ownership. Each of these issues is explored below.

Confirming copyright

There is no automatic process for documenting the ownership of intellectual property. Unlike the process of acquiring and owning physical property such as land, cars or houses, there is no formal documentation associated with proving the ownership of intellectual ideas or creative thoughts. The first requirement, though, is that the idea be transferred into some tangible form: a poem, letter, photograph or song. That tangible product can be 'registered' as belonging to a particular creator, though only a handful of countries actually provide legal processes for formally registering copyright, and even then this registration process may be voluntary. For the most part, copyright to one's intellectual creations – art, music, manuscripts, personal letters, photographs, sketches and so on – is simply assumed.

The archivist has to remember that every documentary product in her collection was created by someone, whether a government or an individual or an organization. She also has to remember that copyright exists separately for all versions of a documentary product, whether it is the tenth or the 14th draft of a book, the scribbled and the typed notes of a meeting or the negative and the print of a holiday photograph.

The duration of intellectual property rights

The next challenge involves identifying when intellectual property rights expire. Every country administers its own copyright legislation, and the time under which materials are protected by copyright varies from country to country. One of the most important distinctions in copyright law, for archival management, is that published and unpublished works are often governed by different terms, conditions and time frames.

The act of publication, loosely defined as making copies available to the public, means that some creative content, including personal records, has been printed in multiple copies and given to people beyond the limits of, say, a family or a business, or that this content has been made available online through a website, blog or digital exhibition. The terms of copyright in published works is usually relatively easy to determine. The copyright laws in different jurisdictions usually outline precisely when a published item moves into the 'public domain', usually a set number of years after the date of publication. Once an item enters the public domain, it can be republished without permission from the original copyright owner. The law in one country may say that a published work, such as Anne Frank's diary, moves into the public domain 70 years after publication. The law in another country may set the time at 25 years or 50, 60 or 80 years.

Unpublished works, which form the largest portion of archival holdings, are all those materials that were never disseminated widely and intentionally in the first place: they were created and used internally, within families or businesses, and then kept for their enduring value. They were never published in the traditional sense. The terms and time frames for copyright protection in unpublished works can be byzantine in their complexity, especially since those terms change every time a country revises its copyright legislation. A single change in copyright law can leave the archivist scrambling to determine which types of material are still governed by which clauses and which other materials have to be managed according to a new set of criteria.

Untangling copyright in photographs

To illustrate this complexity, let us consider an example of copyright in my own country. In Canada, copyright in photographs was extremely complex before federal copyright legislation was changed in 2012. Before 2012, copyright conditions were based on questions such as whether the photograph was commissioned (such as wedding photographs taken by a professional photographer); whether the image was taken by a photographer on behalf of a corporation or other agency (such as promotional pictures taken by a photographer working for a tourism company); or whether the image was taken by an individual without any obligation to anyone else (such as a mother taking pictures of her children on holiday).

With the passage of revised copyright legislation in 2012, those terms and conditions were streamlined, as follows:

- If a photographer, whether a commercial photographer or a family member taking holiday snaps, is still living, he retains copyright to the images he took.

- If the photographer died within the last 50 years, he (and therefore his estate) still retains copyright to his images until 50 years after his death.
- If the photographer died more than 50 years before the current calendar year, copyright has expired and his photographs are now in the public domain.

However, and here is where things become truly labyrinthine, these conditions only apply to photographs taken after the law passed on 7 November 2012. If the photographs were taken between 1949 and 6 November 2012, the conditions in effect in the previous legislation still apply. But if the photographs were taken before 1949, they are now considered to be in the public domain. Unless they are defined as Crown works, in which case they are deemed to be the property of the government in question, and permission may have to be sought from different government agencies before the images can be reproduced. (One gets exhausted by all the mathematics involved in such calculations!)

Physical versus intellectual property

If determining copyright conditions were not complicated enough, the archivist has to consider another challenge. The owner of an archival document may own the physical item, but he may not hold the intellectual property rights to that item. Therefore, while the donor of a body of archives may be completely at liberty to give the documents to an archival institution, he may not have any authority to transfer copyright.

Imagine the correspondence between two friends: Charles Hampton and Vanessa Singh. When Charles writes to Vanessa, Charles' letter, now in Vanessa's archives, is her physical property. She or her descendants can transfer ownership of that material to an archival institution whenever they choose. But Charles still owns the copyright to that letter until the terms of copyright expire. Anyone wanting to publish the letter must first obtain permission from Charles or his descendants, not Vanessa or her descendants.

Similarly, family photographs taken by Mother of her children at the seaside may be shared with Granddad and Cousin Andrew and her daughter's best friend: as prints in a Christmas card, as attachments to an e-mail message or as posts on a Facebook page. The people who receive those images in their Christmas card or e-mail message may decide to keep the copies they have received as part of their own records. But those recipients do not own the copyright to those images. Granddad cannot copy the image in the Christmas card and use it to promote his surfboard business without obtaining permission from Mother. Cousin Andrew cannot publish the image in a family history he intends to sell without violating Mother's intellectual property rights. The best friend's mother cannot, in theory, even post the image to her own Facebook page without obtaining clearance from Mother.

When the archives of Granddad or Cousin Andrew come into archival custody, they may be valuable contributions to the documentary story, but anyone wishing to publish this photograph, found in their digital or physical archives, would need to seek permission from Mother, her children or her estate, for as long as the copyright period persists. (Which, as noted, can require a graduate degree in mathematics to calculate.)

The archivist's responsibility

The hornet's nest of copyright is enough to drive any archivist to take up a career as a surfer. But the rules must be respected, not just for the sake of the copyright owner but for the sake of the wider society. Laws exist to balance the rights of individuals with the rights of the community. Copyright laws are in place to strike that balance between personal and collective priorities in the care of people's creative and intellectual property, which is the heart and soul of archives.

Ultimately, the most important action the archivist can take is to advise, *clearly and definitively*, that it is up to the person wishing to publish archival material to identify copyright restrictions and obtain permission from copyright holders. The archivist is not and should not be responsible for clarifying copyright or locating copyright holders, except when the institution itself wishes to publish items from its holdings. The archivist's primary duty is simply to warn all researchers that it is their responsibility to locate copyright owners and obtain permission for anything other than personal or research use. To provide that advice, the archivist needs to understand the current requirements of any copyright legislation applicable in her jurisdiction. Only then can she state explicitly and accurately the terms under which certain materials may or may not be published. Becoming knowledgeable about the laws in place in the archivist's own country is the essential first step.

The concept of fair use

The archivist must also remember that *publication* and *use* are not the same. Respecting copyright does not mean that researchers cannot use archival materials. Researchers should be able to use any holdings in the institution, even if publication of the materials is bound by copyright, unless other restrictions apply. Researchers should also be able to obtain copies of the materials for personal or reference use, as long as they do not publish archival materials in their entirety without having first received permission from the copyright holder.

To support research and study, most copyright acts include a 'fair use' or 'fair dealing' provision, which allows a person to reproduce some portion of a work for the purposes of research, private study, criticism or reporting. The interpretation of fair use varies from jurisdiction to jurisdiction, but it almost always limits use to a portion of a work, not the entire work. This means that publishing one paragraph from a 20-page report might not be considered a violation of copyright; rather, that would be defined as 'fair use'. But publishing a single photograph without permission would be a violation of copyright. The entirety of the photograph is the photograph, so publishing the entire image without permission is the same as publishing the entire report without permission.

If a researcher is challenged (usually in court) and found to have reproduced more than a 'reasonable' amount of a work, or if he has otherwise interfered with the rights of the copyright holder, that researcher may be charged with violating intellectual property rights. He may have to pay a form of compensation for the breach.

The archivist reproducing large bodies of material for researchers is well advised to issue clear and firm warnings to them about their obligation to respect copyright. The archivist should also ensure that researchers acknowledge that they have been so warned; this acknowledgement often comes in the form of a formal waiver, which both the researcher and archivist sign, outlining the researcher's responsibilities for adhering to legal requirements. Such a form should be completed before any large reproduction work is carried out or if there is any concern that the researcher may intend to publish the contents and so may be in danger of violating the law.

Copyright and preservation
The archivist must also balance the requirements of copyright with the need to preserve archives. Sometimes preservation demands duplication, such as by microfilming or digitizing. As copyright restrictions have become more complex in recent years, archival institutions and libraries have found themselves caught in the web of confusing and conflicting interpretations of intellectual property laws. For instance, changes to copyright legislation intended to prevent people from pirating music have had serious implications

for archival preservation. The archivist attempting to digitize an analogue sound recording in order to extract and save the content from a deteriorating cassette tape may, in some jurisdictions, be breaking the letter of the law. But is she violating the spirit of preservation?

The archivist must abide by the law, but one can only hope that common sense also prevails. Copying fragile and irreplaceable archival materials so that the content is not lost forever should, in theory, be defined as 'preservation'. If the archivist fears she is stepping over the line, she should get a legal opinion and document all her actions. Then she has a solid base of evidence and opinion on which to defend her decisions.

Copyright and donations

The archivist must do all she can to identify intellectual property rights when receiving archival donations. Even if the archivist cannot secure those rights for the institution, she needs to document as much information as possible about who created the materials, not just about who collected and owned them. Only then can she advise researchers about copyright conditions as fully as possible, even if the information provided is 'no one knows'.

If, at the point of acquisition, the archivist can negotiate the transfer of intellectual property rights from the donor to the institution specifically for those archives he created, then the archivist's job is somewhat easier. She is then able to manage intellectual property rights for at least some of the materials in the collection. But she needs to know what she can control and what is out of her control, so that she can steer the researcher in the right direction when advising on how the materials can be used.

Due diligence

When the archivist wishes to publish materials herself, for the benefit of her own institution, she must do as much as she can to identify and locate copyright holders. For instance, if she wants to republish a 20-year-old report to celebrate an anniversary, publish a personal diary on the institution's website or add historical photographs to a virtual exhibit, she needs to clarify copyright conditions before confirming whether her institution has the right to publish those materials.

Sometimes, even after concerted effort, the archivist is unsuccessful. In those cases, the archivist may end up classifying the materials in question as 'orphaned works'. In intellectual property terms, orphaned works are those archival items in copyright limbo, where the identity of the person or agency holding intellectual property rights cannot be determined, or where the identity of the likely rights holder is known but that person or agency cannot be located.

Having used common sense, researched vigorously and documented all her actions, the archivist may believe the risks of publishing the items are sufficiently low, and the benefits sufficiently high, to decide that she will proceed with publishing orphaned works. However, that due diligence process does not entitle the archivist to authorize researchers to publish materials. They have to do their own research, though the archivist can provide them with her findings to help them on their way.

Knowing whether or not an item is governed by copyright legislation can require that an archivist be both detective and mathematician. Fortunately for the archivist and, some would argue, the common good, intellectual property rights do not last forever. After a certain time, all published and unpublished materials move into the public domain, becoming public property that can be used by anyone. Even the esteemed Mickey Mouse will become part of the public domain in 2024, nearly 100 years after he was first created, at which time anyone will be able to reproduce his image – unless the Walt Disney Company finds a way to extend its ownership of those intellectual property rights.

Addressing privacy concerns

In addition to understanding copyright law, the archivist also has to become familiar with the requirements of access and privacy laws. In many countries, laws with names such as 'access and privacy', 'freedom of information', 'access to information' or 'sunshine', control the ability of governments or organizations to collect and use personal information.

As well as controlling what government may document in the first place, access and privacy laws usually also give the public a right to see public records, whether those documents were created decades before or a week ago. Some exceptions exist: most public-sector agencies have an obligation not to release records that might violate commercial confidentiality, state security or the privacy of other individuals or groups.

In some jurisdictions, access laws also control the way in which non-government agencies such as private corporations or associations manage and disseminate information. The archivist in a hybrid institution, responsible for the archives of both governments and private agencies, has a particular duty to determine restrictions on access for public and private holdings in her care before making them available for use. The basic principle behind most freedom of information laws is that the person asking for information should not have to explain why he wants it, and the office holding that information should not bar access to it except under specific and defined conditions.

Most access legislation includes time frames under which access is managed, with the belief that as time passes the importance of protecting privacy diminishes and the value of providing access increases. The archivist responsible for archival collections covered by access and privacy legislation must become intimately familiar with all terms and conditions, in order not to violate individual privacy rights or withhold access inappropriately.

Privacy as an ethical issue

Even when laws do not apply, the archivist is wise to accept and respect *reasonable* rights to individual privacy when negotiating a donation or considering when and how to make archives publicly available. This becomes a matter of morals and ethics, not law. How does the archivist balance the rights of researchers to access and use personal information with the rights of the people who created or are identified in archives? When, and for how long, do people have a right to keep their lives private? Do individuals truly have a 'right to be forgotten', an increasingly popular principle now that so much personal information is available through the internet? The archivist has to consider whether she has a moral obligation to withhold access to archives if she believes that the information contained in them is too personal or if she thinks that the people identified might be adversely affected, even if no one else sees a concern. Still the bottom line remains the same: *archives are kept in order to be used.* They are society's evidence of itself. Restricting access indiscriminately and unreasonably is not consistent with the archivist's responsibility to make documentary resources available.

There are always circumstances in which it is reasonable to limit access to documents, irrespective of any legislative controls, particularly if the parties involved could be harmed, either by the content of the archives or by the very fact that their personal information has been made public. To consider how this situation may play out in an archival institution, let us return to the two correspondents identified earlier: Charles Hampton and Vanessa Singh.

Perhaps Charles and Vanessa were both prominent artists, whose lives have attracted much attention from the press. Charles, who may still be hale and hearty with many years of life remaining, decides to deposit his archives with a university special collections department. Included in those archives are dozens of letters written by Vanessa, who is equally healthy and still very much alive. When Charles donates his archives, he includes Vanessa's letters in the donation.

Copyright is not at issue here. Vanessa owns the intellectual property rights, so she can control the publication of those letters. But can she control the right of people to read them? She transferred ownership of the pieces of paper to Charles when she wrote him the letters. In most jurisdictions, Charles would have a full legal right to donate those letters to the archives. And unless *he* issues a restriction on access, the public will be allowed to read them. The fact that Vanessa may believe her right to privacy will be violated if her letters are exposed to the public is not a matter for the law, unless she decides to take Charles to court, by which time it may be too late: the letters may already be 'out there'.

The archivist has to walk a fine line here. If she decides to contact Vanessa and ask permission to allow the letters to be used, Vanessa may demand that the letters be destroyed or returned to her. The archivist is under no obligation to carry out Vanessa's wishes. In fact, such an action would violate the archivist's responsibility to Charles. But the pot has been stirred. The archivist may ask Charles to confirm whether Vanessa is happy to have her correspondence open to the public. But he would then need to contact Vanessa, wouldn't he, or make the decision himself and let the archivist – who is the one providing access – face the consequences. Pot stirred again.

In the end, if the letters are particularly sensitive, Charles and the archivist may work together on a compromise. They may agree to impose a reasonable restriction, perhaps by closing the correspondence to public view for a certain number of years. They do not need to contact Vanessa. But Vanessa and Charles and everyone who creates records that might make their way into archival custody someday need to appreciate the difference between owning an object and being able to control how it is used.

The passage of time offers the best resolution to issues of privacy. There is a general belief that personal sensitivities diminish a generation or two after the death of the authors of archival materials. The creators of the archives and their immediate descendants are no longer alive to suffer the consequences of seemingly negative or controversial information. And society benefits from having insight into the lives and relationships of people now long gone.

Restricting access to the archives of living donors or closing archives for, say, 25 years after deposit limits immediate access to the materials but ensures they are available for use in the future. Often the alternative is the destruction of archives, which is within the power of the creator of the archives but not in keeping with the quest to document society, warts and all.

What if there is no one to consult when the archivist is faced with a question of access? The principals involved may no longer be alive, but the archivist may still have to deal with sensitivities in the archives themselves. Consider this example.

On the death of a local psychiatrist, his widow decides to donate his archives to the university where he was a professor emeritus. Among the psychiatrist's papers are professional papers, research notes, personal documents and appointment books documenting all his meetings with psychiatric patients. These day timers show the names of every patient the psychiatrist treated for 30 years, along with detailed scheduling information.

A researcher studying psychiatric practice could extrapolate a tremendous amount of information from those appointment books. How often did patients come to the doctor each week or month? How many years did each patient remain in treatment? Did attendance in the psychiatrist's office change over the course of weeks, months or years? The records present a rich source of information not found in other medical records.

The archivist needs to tread carefully. Do national or state access and privacy laws restrict access to these records? Is there legislation governing the management and use of medical records? The appointment books could be used to identify individual patients, years after they attended the doctor's office. What are the privacy requirements for accepting and managing those materials?

If the archivist keeps the appointment books, she might need to impose restrictions on access for upwards of 100 years. Alternately, she may require researchers to sign confidentiality agreements, agreeing to use the appointment books for statistical analysis only without disclosing identifying information. Researching the issues associated with providing access to these particular archives might take hours of staff time, and the institution may need to obtain a formal legal opinion.

The archivist might also have to confirm that she has the right to keep the books in the first place. In many jurisdictions, doctors are expected to destroy records a certain number of years after they cease to practise, in accordance with the regulations of medical or psychiatric associations. But now that the books are in the archivist's possession, what research potential would be lost if she destroyed them? Does she really have the right to toss them out? Or the right to keep them? And who can she ask for advice, without stirring another privacy pot? Is it better to keep the books and beg forgiveness from posterity than to ask permission and see them shredded now?

Privacy as a cultural issue

The archivist also has to wrestle with another growing concern in society, which relates to the rights of subjects to control information *about* themselves that might be found in the archives of others. Access and privacy laws establish fairly clear parameters around access to such information as individual names or addresses; personal opinions or statements; medical history; financial welfare; or marital status. But how does the archivist address questions of privacy or access as defined by different cultures?

For instance, an archival institution may have in its holdings an extensive collection of photographs documenting a particular ethnic group. These images may be of tremendous value to historians, anthropologists or ethnologists. But some cultures may believe that allowing 'outsiders' to view those materials violates their cultural rights. In some aboriginal communities, for example, it is not uncommon for people to avoid referring to a person, or viewing an image of them, for some period after their death. This avoidance is seen as a mark of respect. The period may stretch from one to several years. When a display including images of aboriginal people is mounted, therefore, the archivist may need to highlight the potential that the individuals depicted may be deceased. That way the members of their family or clan are made aware in advance and can continue to respect their traditions when viewing, or choosing not to view, the images.

In other cultures, family histories can only be passed down to assigned people within the family, clan or tribe. Some ceremonies cannot be viewed by anyone not directly involved. But many such events may have been documented in written or audiovisual records, by anthropologists, sociologists, historians or the people themselves. Those archives may end up in the custody of publicly funded institutions, accessible for anyone to use.

There may very well be no legal restrictions on the use of these materials, but there may be legitimate ethical and moral concerns. Respecting legal obligations to make materials available while acknowledging the privacy concerns of the groups in question can become a delicate balancing act. The wise archivist does not adopt a rigid position one way or the other. She seeks to address the interests of all constituents within her community, while remembering that it is not her place to make or break the law. If the law does not suit the interests of a particular party, the people who are most dissatisfied have the first responsibility to lobby for change. As mentioned earlier, in such cases the archivist must sometimes step away from the fray, letting professional associations, interest groups and lawyers raise public awareness of the issue, which may prompt necessary and valuable changes to the law.

As demonstrated in this chapter, as in the rest of Part I, the archivist must take into account a wide variety of archival principles before she can begin to think about how to put the art of archival management into practice. These principles relate to: the concept of documentary evidence and the nature of archival materials; the realities of archival history and the nuances of archival theory; the different uses of archives and the various configurations of archival institution; and the duties and obligations of the archivist, particularly with regard to access and the right to privacy. The goal always should be to ensure that the archivist helps her society capture and preserve archives so that they may be made available for use as widely as possible. Only then can archives serve as a rich and cherished evidential foundation for a civilized and respectful society. How the archivist upholds and balances these principles in actual practice is the subject of Part II.

PART II
Archival practices

Part II of this book puts into action the principles, theories and concepts introduced in Part I. The following topics are addressed: how does the archivist manage the institution, or understand how it is managed if she is not the decision maker? How should archival materials be preserved so that they remain stable, authentic and reliable over decades and centuries? What issues need to be considered when acquiring archives, and how should those archives be arranged and described? Finally, how should the archivist make those materials available for use: what is involved in providing equitable reference services and in engaging actively with the research community and the wider public? These questions are considered in the following chapters:

Chapter 8: Managing the institution
Chapter 9: Preserving archives
Chapter 10: Acquiring archives
Chapter 11: Arranging and describing archives
Chapter 12: Making archives available.

8

Managing the institution

Let no act be done at haphazard, nor otherwise than according to the finished
rules that govern its kind.

Marcus Aurelius (121–180) *Meditations*, 161–180 AD

Even if she cannot directly shape operations herself, the archivist should
understand the organizational environment in which archival service is
performed. The policy framework includes the legislation, regulations,
policies and strategic plans governing the care of records and archives. The
administrative framework includes financial, logistical, physical and
personnel conditions surrounding archival service in that institution.

As with everything else related to archival service, legislative, regulatory
and administrative frameworks vary significantly from jurisdiction to
jurisdiction and institution to institution. Government archives may be bound
not only by a core piece of legislation, such as an Archives Act, but also by
legislation related to data protection, access or privacy. A museum archives
may need to be aware of the requirements of heritage management
legislation, while a bank archives has to adhere to regulations for the
disclosure of financial data. Even a community or local history society needs
to respect copyright and intellectual property rights, which affect all archival
institutions and – as examined in Chapter 7 – are governed by different laws
around the world.

Imagining the 'ideal' organizational structure

Given that every archival institution is different, there is no 'best' way to
configure operations, but – as emphasized throughout this book – digital
technologies are transforming how information and evidence are created,

directly influencing the ability of archivists to protect authentic documentary evidence for both immediate and future use. An ideal scenario in the 21st century (one that is, in reality, as rare as a feathered alligator) is one that gives the archivist broad powers to oversee the creation, management, use and disposal of documentary evidence, from before information is created to the point at which archives are secured for preservation.

In such a dream scenario, the archival institution is ultimately responsible for major policy decisions about records management and archival preservation for its sponsor agency. The archival institution is directly accountable for the care, custody or control of archives but also guides the development and implementation of records policies. The institution may also provide guidance and training on effective records and archives care.

This broad responsibility allows the archival institution to play a central role in ensuring that the official documentary evidence of the sponsor agency is well managed from the moment of creation, no matter whether it is in digital, analogue or paper form. This archival role supports accountability, increases efficiency and, ultimately, results in the creation of a comprehensive body of authentic archives, available for use now and centuries from now.

In reality, making the case for such overarching authority can be extremely difficult. (How many feathered alligators are there?) But that does not mean it is not a scenario worth aspiring to achieve.

Identifying a strategic direction

While working to achieve this ideal, or whatever dream scenario is best for her particular circumstances, the archivist can continue to provide the best quality service possible by understanding her existing administrative framework and working to strengthen institutional capacity whenever possible. Good management is not a matter of luck; it is a matter of planning. Even institutions such as museums or local history archives, which may not have direct responsibility for the archives of their sponsor agency, need to plan their operations strategically, so everyone involved with the institution is striving to achieve the same goals and objectives.

Developing an institutional vision

The first task in defining a strategic direction is to clarify the duties of the archival institution, both actual and desirable. Will the archival institution be responsible for managing all forms of records and archives, including digital data, from its sponsor agency? Or is the institution responsible for acquiring and preserving documentary evidence from external sources, such as private individuals or community groups? The archivist needs to clarify the institution's reason for being and, from that, determine the ideal outcome of any work performed.

Defining this strategic direction often involves articulating a vision, mission and mandate. A *vision statement* outlines a model future that would come to pass if the institution is able to operate to the best of its abilities. The vision of a national government archives might be 'to guarantee the rights and responsibilities of government and support community identity through the effective management of the government's records and archives'. The vision of an activist archives with a social justice orientation, such as one involved with documenting the experience of Japanese Canadian immigrants to Canada, might be to 'document the struggle against injustice, in order to support the creation of a democratic and egalitarian society'.

A *mission statement* explains how that vision will be achieved. It turns the vision into a reality and establishes the basis for specific actions. For instance, the government archives' vision might be achieved through a mission 'to manage government evidence effectively, irrespective of form or medium, and to acquire and preserve non-government archives in all forms that illuminate and reflect the history, development and state of the nation'. The activist archives may achieve its vision through a mission to 'acquire, preserve and make publicly available the archives, oral histories and other recorded memories of Japanese Canadians, in order to preserve evidence of the immigrant experience'.

The last of the three elements, the *mandate statement* articulates the legal authority and specific responsibilities of the institution, allowing it to achieve its vision and mission. A mandate statement for the government institution might read as follows:

Under the Records and Archives Act 2014, the National Archives of Boratavia exists to acquire, preserve and make available the documentary heritage of the nation through the effective management of government records and archives in all media and all forms, as well as through the acquisition and preservation of non-government archives, regardless of form or medium, that illuminate and reflect the history, development and state of the nation.

A mandate statement for the activist archives might read as follows:

Registered as a non-profit organization under the Societies Act, 2010, the Japanese Canadian Historical and Community Archives of British Columbia is an independent archival agency dedicated to collecting, documenting and providing access to archival holdings, oral histories and related documentary resources that illuminate the experience of Japanese immigrants to Canada, and Japanese Canadian citizens, from the arrival of the first immigrants in the 19th century to the present day.

Vision, mission and mandate statements are sometimes combined, and elements of each may be included in a formal strategic plan or other policy documents. The statements can also be posted on institutional websites, added to staff business cards or displayed in the lobby of the repository.

The process of developing a vision, mission and mandate is not simply a branding exercise, however. A well-considered and clear declaration of purpose helps the institution focus its energies, resources and time on duties that must be performed in order to achieve success. If, for example, the archivist of a government archives decides that its goals include managing government archives effectively, she will need to think twice about whether to sponsor a travelling exhibit of art completely unrelated to the institution's holdings. Similarly, if an activist archives is dedicated to preserving archives related to a particular ethnic group, the board of directors should not divert resources to acquire a collection of Pre-Raphaelite literature, no matter how academically interesting the materials may be.

Conducting a SWOT analysis

The process of defining a vision, mission and mandate helps the institution identify clear goals. But not every goal is achievable, at least not in the short term. Strategic planning allows the archivist to identify opportunities for achieving desired goals and to pinpoint risks that might hinder efforts. To plan strategically, it is useful to conduct a SWOT analysis: a review of strengths, weaknesses, opportunities and threats. A SWOT analysis demands deep thought and wide consultation about all the internal or external issues that might help or hinder efforts to achieve the institution's vision, mission and mandate.

When conducting a SWOT analysis, the archivist should consider the following sort of issues:

- Will the archival institution play an active role in supporting information and records management, not just archives management, for the sponsor organization? If so, how will that role be funded? A formal records management programme may be an invaluable support, but if the archival institution is expected to oversee a records management programme without adequate resources, the chances of success are limited at best.

- What technical, financial, physical or other constraints may affect the work of the institution? Does the institution have the space to acquire extensive collections of archives or the equipment needed to preserve and make available different media materials? For instance, the institution responsible for digital archives will need to be able to establish and sustain a trusted digital repository, or else it will not be able to preserve electronic records and data as authentic evidence. Acquiring archives without being able to preserve them serves no one well.

- Are there any anniversaries, funding opportunities, or other events on the horizon that might provide an opportunity for the institution to move its vision forward? A centennial celebration in two years is a great reason to develop an exhibit. Waiting to design the exhibit until three weeks before the anniversary is poor planning. A grant programme may provide funds to hire summer students, but applying for funds without preparing a clear work plan is unproductive for both student and institution. The municipal government may be offering a heritage house to the community archives for free, but if the house is structurally unsound and far from the centre of town, it might be more expensive than it is worth. How 'free' is 'free'?

The essence of strategic planning involves meshing short-term gains with long-term sustainability. A good example of the danger of poor planning can be found in the increasing number of half-finished or abandoned archival digitization projects that have come to pass now that digitization is seen as archival nirvana. Today, members of the public, and funders of archival services, seem to think that all archival materials ought to be (or already are) available online. Many archival institutions are leaping onto the digitization train, either to meet public demand or to secure otherwise scarce project funds. But what happens when that funding dries up? Who will be responsible for maintaining the technology? Who will add new content to the database? If short-term initiatives are not followed by strategic planning for stability and sustainability, the long-term results may be worse, not better.

Figure 8.1 is a sample of a SWOT analysis for a community archives. In this case, the institution is a small, rural archival facility, run exclusively by volunteers, which collects only private archives related to that local community.

Strengths	Weaknesses
• Dedicated volunteer team • Commitment by local community leaders to the future of the archives • Good quality storage facilities with considerable room for growth • Relatively new computer equipment and a high-speed internet connection • Growing online presence for the community archives through Facebook and the website • Extensive collection of archival materials dating back over a century	• Absence of a trained archivist to assist with developing and executing archival tasks, leaving volunteers without clear leadership • Limited volunteer time, so archival progress is slow and inconsistent • Lack of formal policies or procedures for archival work • Lack of information in accession records about provenance, copyright or privacy, limiting the ability to disseminate archival content on the website or through Facebook
Opportunities	Threats
• Funding programmes, including national and regional funding initiatives, with application deadlines once a year • Promotional and outreach opportunities, including History Week, Archives Day, Community Day and upcoming 100th anniversary of the community's Fire Service in two years • Volunteer engagement, evidenced by high community turnout for special projects such as helping to identify photographs or to conduct oral histories of community members • A local community member wishes to donate archives and money to the institution but wants assurance the materials will be safe and the money well spent	• The current ad hoc approach to digitization risks violating copyright and privacy rights, damaging the reputation and credibility of the institution • There is a limited number of qualified archivists in the region so it is difficult to obtain ongoing professional support • Moving to digital archival management risks shutting out current volunteers, who are not comfortable with computers and prefer paper-based archival tasks such as completing photograph catalogue information on paper forms • Undertaking any significant archival project with grant funds but not building in ongoing support will reduce sustainability

Figure 8.1 *A SWOT analysis*

Once the archivist has identified the institution's strengths, weaknesses, opportunities and threats, she is in a better position to plan for the future. She can then clarify and refine the institution's vision, mission and mandate and define priority actions. Whenever possible, the archivist should translate this information into a formal strategic plan, mapping out priority activities for, say, three, five or ten years into the future.

In the case of the community institution shown in the SWOT analysis, it may be that the strategic plan identifies a series of steps over two or three years. In Year 1 the volunteer team may apply for a grant to bring in a contract archivist. That contract archivist will establish new archival operations, develop policies and procedures and train volunteers. At the same time, the volunteers can lobby the local community for funding to support an ongoing part-time archival position, with the hope that those funds are in place at the end of Year 1, while the contract archivist is still in place.

In Year 2, the donor offering materials and funds could also be approached, now that the institution can demonstrate that the archives and the money will both be well managed. The contract archivist and volunteers can also hire and train the part-time archivist, who can then take over duties by the end of Year 2, when funding for the contract archivist is finished.

By the start of Year 3, the community archives has a strong operational structure, a trained part-time archivist and a group of dedicated and happy volunteers, relieved that they do not have to carry the burden of archival care on their shoulders alone. Further actions taken that year might include holding more outreach events, applying for funding for special projects, bringing in more volunteers and soliciting more archival and financial donations. By the time this strategic plan has been put into action, the community archives has built the basis for a sustainable archival service. It can then prepare another strategic plan (which, in reality, should be developed before the first one expires) to steer activities for the next three years.

Establishing a policy framework

Strategic planning gives everyone in the institution a clear foundation for their work, making them feel they are all striving for the same goal. But whether an archival institution defines a new direction for the future or continues to pursue existing priorities, the institution should be governed by a strong policy framework. Establishing policies and procedures is essential to consistent archival practice, whether the institution is corporate or community based, staffed by 800 employees or one volunteer.

A first requirement is that the institution must be conceived as a permanent facility. Archival institutions are ongoing operations, not special projects or time-limited initiatives. A closet stuffed with boxes of records is not an archival facility, any more than a shelf full of books is a library or a garage full of car parts is a museum. Even a digital repository for electronic records care needs a stable physical and administrative environment.

All archival institutions should have the authority to take physical and legal custody or control of archives and associated materials; dispose of unwanted materials; store archives safely; arrange, describe and preserve them according to archival standards and guidelines; and provide equitable access. If the institution also has wider information and records management duties, those responsibilities also need to be clearly articulated and adequately resourced.

Identifying areas requiring policies

All major archival tasks should be guided by formal policies, which need to take into account not only the institution's needs and priorities but also those of its sponsor agency and the wider society in which that agency operates. Policies must also respect the legal and regulatory requirements in the jurisdiction. Laws affecting the management of archives may relate to:

- copyright and intellectual property
- access to information
- protection of personal privacy
- admissibility of evidence
- data protection and information security
- heritage or cultural property management
- criminal acts
- employment and labour relations
- taxation and financial management.

The archivist in even the smallest and most informal facilities must understand the extent of the regulatory regime in which she works. Even the simplest of archival decisions, such as publishing a photograph on a website, can have legal repercussions if copyright is not respected. In keeping with the principle *ignorantia juris non excusat* – 'ignorance of the law is not an excuse' – the archivist will not be forgiven easily if she acts unlawfully, even if she claims that she did not fully understand the law.

Developing a core archival policy

A core archival policy serves as the foundational statement of the institution's vision, mission and mandate, explained earlier. Policies should also be developed to address specific tasks such as acquisition, preservation, reference and access, as well as records and data management, if the archivist is also responsible for those duties. (Key policies for acquisition, preservation and other archival tasks are discussed in later chapters.) Depending on the placement of the archival institution within its wider organizational framework, an archives policy may be one of several information governance policies that outline responsibilities for the creation and management of records and data as evidence, the administration of access and privacy requirements or the security of records and information systems.

Figure 8.2 shows a sample policy statement for the Cascadia University Archives and Special Collections, a fictitious archival repository based on the west coast of Canada responsible for both institutional records and archives management and the acquisition and preservation of non-sponsor archives.

As seen in the example, the focus of Cascadia University Archives and Special Collections is clear. It provides oversight for the effective creation and management of University records and evidence; acquires, preserves and makes available official University archives; and collects private archives related to the history and development of the University. It also collects archives in specific subject areas, to support academic research and scholarship.

Note that the specific areas of acquisition focus are not identified in this foundational policy. It is almost always better to articulate such details in a separate acquisitions policy, as discussed in Chapter 10. That way the institution does not have to keep changing its enabling policy every time it adjusts its collecting focus, which archival institutions should do as circumstances require.

The core archival policy establishes boundaries around the work of the archival institution, identifies different roles and responsibilities and articulates terms and concepts precisely. As a result, institutional priorities and responsibilities are not left to individual interpretation.

Vision
Cascadia University Archives and Special Collections fosters a spirit of accountability, integrity and identity at Cascadia University by developing and delivering effective and innovative information, records and archives management services, actively preserving documentary evidence of the history, development and activities of the University, and acquiring, preserving and making available documentary materials that support academic research and scholarship.

Mission
Cascadia University Archives and Special Collections serves all members of the Cascadia University community as well as the general public by effectively managing, acquiring, preserving and making available documentary evidence of the University, in all forms and media, including both official University records and information and those non-institutional archives that document the lives and work of people and groups associated with the university or that support research and scholarship.

Mandate
Cascadia University Archives and Special Collections is responsible for supporting the effective, efficient and accountable management of the University's documentary evidence, regardless of form or medium, for appraising, acquiring, preserving and making available for public use both University records and data with permanent value and private documentary materials created or collected by individuals and groups associated with the University, and for appraising, acquiring, preserving and making available archival collections that support and enhance research and scholarship across the University.

Figure 8.2 *Cascadia University Archives and Special Collections policy*

Scope of holdings

The holdings of Cascadia University Archives and Special Collections will include:

1 Official records and other documentary evidence created, received and accumulated by the University's offices and officers and by the various governing bodies of the University, including electronic records and data, produced or received by the University in pursuance of its functions, regardless of the physical form or characteristics or the records.
2 Non-official archives in all media and forms, including the archives of University-sponsored or related activities (such as student or faculty associations or groups), as well as archives that reflect the life of the University community (such as private papers of faculty, staff and alumni); and records created by other individuals, organizations or agencies whose lives and work relate to some aspect of University life.
3 Non-official archives and related historical materials in all media and forms, including rare books, that by their contents and nature provide special insight into topics relevant to the research interests of the University.

Unless deemed to have evidential and archival value and related to the stated acquisition focus of Cascadia University Archives and Special Collections, non-institutional archival materials, artefacts, memorabilia and other objects, whether related to the University or not, will not be retained as part of the holdings of Cascadia University Archives and Special Collections. Instead, Cascadia University Archives and Special Collections works co-operatively with the Cascadia University Library and the Angela Chan-Davies Memorial Museum to facilitate the care and preservation of those materials that merit preservation but that fall outside of the scope of responsibilities for Cascadia University Archives and Special Collections.

Ownership of records

Official records and other documentary evidence created, received, and used by representatives of Cascadia University in the course of University business are the property of the University. Officers, employees and other officers shall follow the instructions of the University Archivist for the management of their official records, data, information and archives. On leaving or relinquishing their positions with the University these officers shall leave all official records, data and information resources for their successors.

Materials donated, bequeathed, purchased and otherwise deposited into the custody of Cascadia University Archives and Special Collections are the property of the University, unless otherwise agreed in writing.

The University Archivist may develop and implement regulations concerning the use and daily operations of the institution.

Roles and responsibilities

The Vice-President, Legal and Administration, has a duty to ensure that the University complies with the requirements of all information, records, data and archives policies and procedures.

The University Archivist oversees the operations of Cascadia University Archives and Special Collections, including developing and approving all policies and procedures; establishing priorities; and managing infrastructure, facilities, staff and other resources in support of the archives' operations. The University Archivist will work closely with University faculty and staff to ensure consistency in the management of information, records, data and archives and to ensure that appropriate advice and guidance is provided to all appropriate staff.

Figure 8.2 *Continued*

Managerial and professional staff members across the University are responsible for ensuring that information, records, data and archives under their jurisdiction are managed in conformity with this policy and other University requirements. All members of University staff are responsible for maintaining these resources in accordance with best practice guidelines in order to support the preservation of authentic and reliable evidence.

Non-official archives and related materials acquired by the Cascadia University Archives and Special Collections will be managed in accordance with archival principles and legal requirements, with the goal of making them available for research and scholarship as widely as possible.

The Archives Management Committee comprises the University Archivist, the University Records Manager, the Vice-President, Legal and Administration and the Manager of Information Technology and Resources or their delegates. The Committee is responsible for considering any management issues, including strategic planning, acquisitions management and decisions related to the deaccessioning or disposal of archives. Separate committees may be established to review retention and disposal criteria, identify information suitable for proactive disclosure or oversee related activities.

Monitoring compliance

The University will follow this policy, along with all relevant procedures and guidance, in the process of creating and managing its information, records, data and archives resources. Interpretation of the policy will be monitored by senior management, with input and advice from the Archives Management Committee. Regular inspections will be conducted by quality services staff and internal auditors to assess how the policy is being put into practice across the University. These inspections will seek to:

- identify areas of strength and weakness in information, records, data and archives management
- highlight non-compliance with established procedures
- recommend performance improvements to ensure compliance is achieved.

Associated policies

This archives policy is a component of Cascadia University's corporate information management programme and is intended to work in concert with other University policies and strategies, including those related to records and data management, copyright, information security, access to information and protection of privacy. This policy also relates to the following specific policies and procedures:

- Cascadia University Information Governance Policy, 2014
- Cascadia University Protection of Evidence Policy, 2014
- Cascadia University and Special Collections Acquisitions Policy, 2015
- Cascadia University and Special Collections Preservation Policy, 2014
- Cascadia University and Special Collections Access Procedures, 2014
- Cascadia University and Special Collections Accessioning Procedures, 2015.

Definitions

Archives   Records, data or other documentary evidence, regardless of form or medium, with enduring value and selected for permanent preservation because of their administrative, financial, informational, historical, legal, operational, cultural, social or scientific value. Archives will normally be preserved in or managed under the care and control of an archival institution.

Figure 8.2 *Continued*

Archives management   The area of general management concerned with ensuring the preservation and management of and access to the official and non-official records and other documentary evidence of the organization that have been deemed worthy of permanent preservation because of their enduring value.

Documentary evidence   Documentary sources, including records, digital data or other sources, regardless of form or medium created, that provide proof of actions, transactions or decisions and that are received, maintained and used by an organization (public or private) or an individual in pursuance of legal obligations or in the transaction of business. See also *Records*.

Non-official records   Documentary evidence or information that relate to the operation or history of the University but that are not created by University officers, employees or designated representatives on behalf of the University.

Official records   Documentary evidence or information created, received and accumulated by University officers, employees or designated representatives on behalf of the University.

Records   Documents or data, regardless of form or medium, created, received, maintained and used by an organization (public or private) or an individual in pursuance of legal obligations or in the transaction of business, of which it forms a part or provides evidence. See also *Documentary evidence*.

Records management   The area of general administrative management concerned with achieving economy and efficiency in the creation, maintenance, use and disposal of the records, data and documentary evidence of an organization and in making the information contained in those sources available in support of the business of that organization.

Approved by
Leah Sigmundson, Vice-President, Legal and Administration, 24 September 2015.

Review date
This document will be reviewed and revised as required on or before 31 December 2020.

Figure 8.2 *Continued*

Administering the archival institution

Archival operations depend not just on a strong policy framework but also on adequate and sustained resources, good quality facilities, reliable, up-to-date equipment and well-trained, dedicated and enthusiastic workers. In many parts of the world though, from Namibia to New Zealand and Canada to Cambodia, archival institutions depend (sometimes heavily) on public or donor funds for their continued existence. The archivist cannot just cross her fingers and hope for the best, which is why strategic planning is so critical.

As a manager, the archivist needs to make daily decisions from the perspective of risk. What is the likelihood of something negative happening, and what are the possible consequences? An earthquake may be disastrous but highly unlikely. The archivist should reduce the risk and plan for recovery in the event of an earthquake, but expending huge sums on bracing shelves and reinforcing storage vaults may not be a priority. On the other hand, a change in staff may seem less threatening but in fact pose a great risk. What if the institution is facing three retirements in the next year, out of a staff of five, and has no succession plan in place? Ensuring continuity of service in the face of such large staff changes needs advance planning.

Below is an overview of administrative issues that any archivist should bear in mind, whether or not she has decision-making power. These issues include: financial requirements and the potential for revenue generation; facilities and equipment needs; information technology requirements; security concerns; and matters related to managing staff and volunteers.

Financial requirements

Archival operations are continuing services that need to be well maintained and adequately supplied. As stated many times, archival administration is not a short-term project. Ideally the sponsor agency – the archival institution's corporate 'boss' – will provide sufficient funding through a formal and sustained budget. The archivist will be expected to identify both short-term and long-term needs so that the sponsor can plan and allocate that budget accordingly, but the archivist should then have the authority to expend the funds in her budget as needed to achieve the institution's mandate.

Ideally, a core budget will cover all essential capital and operating costs, including:

- building rent, lease or purchase costs
- heat, light, electricity, water, taxes, telephone and other operational expenses
- staff, including salaries, benefits and costs associated with training, professional development and business travel
- archival and office supplies, stationery and other goods
- acquisition and processing costs, including, if appropriate, a budget for purchasing archival materials, along with associated travel and shipping costs
- reproduction services, including the cost of purchasing and maintaining photocopiers, scanners, printers, microfilm readers and printers, paper and other supplies
- computer equipment and supplies, including the cost of servers, technical service contracts, software and hardware acquisition and the installation and maintenance of back-up systems
- preservation services, including environmental controls, emergency generators, janitorial services and supplies and the costs of restoration work on high-risk materials

- reference and outreach services, including technology, supplies and equipment for on-site and remote reference services and for developing and maintaining websites or preparing exhibits and displays.

An institution's budget may not cover every desirable archival service, but at the very least the funding available should ensure the continuity of core functions. For example, if the institution is expected to acquire and preserve private archives in all media, resources will be needed to ensure those acquisitions can be preserved and stored adequately, whether they are paper documents, oversized maps or electronic records. If the institution has an obligation to act as a trusted digital repository for the sponsor agency's official electronic archives, then sustained funds will be needed to provide adequate staff, software, hardware and technological or administrative support.

Grants and subsidies may help supplement the budget, allowing the institution to undertake special projects. And the archivist can sometimes include volunteer time and in-kind donations as 'soft' versus 'hard' financial contributions, which can be useful when preparing a grant application. But in the end, an archival institution has a responsibility to its sponsor agency, user community and archival materials to provide effective and sustainable care. If the institution cannot provide basic services with the budget available, those responsible for overseeing the institution need to step back and consider if it is truly a viable enterprise. And if not, what will happen to the archival materials if the agency ceases to exist?

Cost recovery and profit making

Archival institutions exist to provide a service to their society. Their prime function is not to make money. But acquiring and preserving archives is a costly enterprise. The best archival repositories get bigger, not smaller. Aside from the small income generated from photocopy or other reproduction fees, the institution might want to find other ways to recover costs, if not make a profit. Many institutions are funded through tax dollars, however, and tax payers can react negatively when a publicly funded agency adds fees for services they feel they have already paid for in their tax bill. The archivist needs to walk a fine line. The following sort of questions might be considered:

- How much time will a reference archivist spend with a researcher in the reference room, or answering an e-mail or telephone enquiry, before requiring that the researcher continue the work himself or charging the researcher for services rendered?

- Will the institution charge for any additional reference services, and under what conditions?
- Will the institution charge for photocopying or for scanning original documents? Are the fees intended to support cost recovery or make a profit?
- Will the institution charge for the reproduction of photographs? Will those charges vary depending on whether the user wants the image for personal or research use or intends to include it in a commercial product?
- Will the institution develop its own commercial goods, selling archival photographs, postcards, coffee table books, academic histories or audiovisual productions? Why? What is the cost-benefit analysis that supports a sound financial decision? If the motivation is not profit but community engagement, the institution needs to know how the project will be funded and make not just emotional decisions about its value to the community but also financial decisions about its viability and potential for success.
- What is the administrative burden of setting fees, creating invoices, preparing receipts and adding the income to the institution's bank account? If it takes more time to process an invoice for a 25 cent photocopy than to make the photocopy in the first place, charging for occasional copies may not be worth the effort. But if a researcher wants copies of hundreds of pages of fragile documents, which will take archival staff days to prepare, the archivist needs to decide how the institution can be compensated for the time and effort.

The decision about whether to pursue cost-recovery or profit-oriented activities is not a personal one: all decisions need to support the institution's vision, mission and mandate. If it is reasonable to offer services, the archivist needs to figure out how to deliver them without incurring excessive cost. But if the services reach beyond the institution's mandate, the archivist may need to think twice about their viability.

Managing facilities and equipment

An archival institution is, by definition, a physical place. Regardless of their form or medium, archives need to be stored in appropriate containers, from acid-free file folders to digital back-up tapes, and kept in a secure, stable environment, on solid shelves, off the floor or in stable and secure computer storage systems. Even a 'virtual' digital archives that does not cater to users in person requires a physical place to house and maintain computers and servers, as discussed in Chapter 9. Any institution should strive for a facility that has the following qualities:

- high-quality fire suppression equipment and fire-resistant facilities, particularly for storage
- effective and reliable temperature and relative humidity monitors and controls
- protection from insects, rodents and mould
- reliable physical security systems, locks and alarms
- good quality archival shelving and storage units, ideally that maximize the use of floor space and are strong enough to hold the weight of heavy boxes
- protection against flooding or water damage (basements or attics should be avoided if at all possible)
- controlled lighting (ideally there should be no fluorescent lighting, particularly in storage areas, as it emits harmful ultraviolet radiation)
- a separate receiving area to isolate incoming materials until they are inspected (which helps contain insects, mould or dirt, keeping them out of storage areas)
- a secure archival processing area with sufficient space to work on large bodies of archives
- conservation equipment and supplies – ideally in a dedicated conservation laboratory – including, if possible, sinks, work tables, fumigation hoods, vacuums and air filters
- a separate archival storage area for physical archival holdings, large enough to hold existing holdings and, ideally, to grow at a rate of at least 10% capacity a year for at least ten years
- a secure area for digital archival storage, with enough room for computer servers and other technologies needed to receive, process and preserve electronic archives
- a research space, separate from storage and processing areas, that allows for archival supervision
- separate areas for viewing digital archives, microfilm or audiovisual materials
- areas for administrative work, meetings, exhibits and refreshments, including rooms for lunch and coffee breaks for both staff and visitors.

Aside from standard office equipment and supplies – tables, chairs, desks, telephones, fax machines, computers, stationery and so on – the institution will also need to purchase specialized archival supplies such as acid-free folders, boxes and envelopes.

Information technology requirements

The archivist also has to consider information technology requirements. Buying a desk and chair can be an investment; good quality furniture will last for decades or centuries. But computer technology is not a one-time cost. As long as computer manufacturers and software designers keep making new systems and tools (and planned obsolescence seems to be the mantra of many technology companies), computer users have to keep pace, so equipment, software and related tools need to be replaced with painful and expensive regularity.

Budgeting for technology, therefore, involves planning not just for the cost of purchasing hardware, software, licences and supplies in the first place but also for upgrades, training, maintenance, repairs and replacement. The need for continuous improvement in information technologies is particularly acute if the institution has taken on responsibility for managing digital records and archives. But even if the institution is not responsible for its sponsor agency's digital records, it will still need high-quality, well maintained information technologies, to support tasks such as accessioning, arrangement and description, location management, digitization, reference and access. An archival institution needs:

- adequate and up-to-date hardware and software, including servers, peripherals (such as printers and scanners) and software licences and contracts
- reliable technical support services, including training, software installation, repairs and upgrades, troubleshooting and maintenance of facilities and equipment
- the highest quality security systems and services, including remote storage and back-up systems for digital archives and institutional records, firewalls to prevent unauthorized access to the institution's computers and strict protocols for the management of passwords and access to systems and data
- technical and design support for developing and maintaining web pages, virtual exhibits, internet-based resource information and online reference services.

Security requirements

The protection of archives from environmental and human threats is considered in Chapter 9, but it is important to emphasize here the need to protect everyone in the institution from threats to their safety and security. Staff and the public can be victims of theft, physical attacks or vandalism, as well as identity theft, online fraud, computer viruses and privacy violations. The archivist should establish policies and procedures that safeguard the institution against these dangers and protect staff and volunteers from personal harm.

Enhanced security can impact access, though, if protocols interfere with daily operations. What happens if the individual who established the password controls for the computer in the reference room is not available to provide access to the system, and the researcher is told he has to come back another day? How can different staff members work seamlessly if they are given different levels of access to information systems? How does the archivist find out if electronic records are worth preserving if she cannot make her way past encryption barriers set up by the records creator? The archivist needs to take steps to mitigate digital security risks while ensuring that the institution can still work efficiently and archives can be managed effectively.

Managing people

Many people imagine archival institutions as storage depots filled with shelf upon shelf of hundreds of plain brown boxes, guarded by a lone caretaker decked out in lab coat and white gloves. In reality, archival institutions are people places. They are managed by people and for people, and everything they hold is, ultimately, about people. The quality and nature of the people who work in the institution can set the tone for all its services.

Choosing quality staff, finding dedicated volunteers and supporting them so that they stay for the long term is critical to institutional success. The archivist needs to think about who will work in the institution, how much they will be paid, what qualifications they will need and what training they will receive. Whether the archival institution is a local archival facility relying on unpaid helpers or a federal government agency with a staff of hundreds, all workers need to be supported adequately so that they may perform their duties to the best of their abilities.

An effective archival manager will determine the most appropriate human resources, from archival staff to advocates and spokespeople, and will foster sustainable relationships. The importance of engaging the right person for any job is undeniable. And the right person for archival service will often be a professionally trained archivist who brings university or college qualifications to the job. But there is also a legitimate place for para-professionals, support staff, students and people with few formal qualifications but great enthusiasm, such as volunteers. Community supporters and political champions are also essential. Positive connections with people across the jurisdiction should be nurtured.

Of course, not every person who wants to work in the institution has the temperament for archival work. There is usually a formal vetting process for hiring paid staff, but it can be harder to turn away volunteers. The archivist must not feel pressured to find a job for every person who wants to join up. Some people may contribute more helping with fundraising or hosting social events rather than processing archives.

The archivist must remember, though, that volunteers sign up because they want to provide a useful service; they do not just want to warm a chair. They need and deserve adequate training, consistent supervision and ongoing encouragement. Formal agreements should be drawn up between the institution and individual volunteers, confirming their mutual responsibilities and duties.

Students, particularly those pursuing formal archival qualifications, can also be a great asset to archival institutions. They bring enthusiasm above all else. What fresh recruit to a discipline does not plan to change the world before she has finished her course work? Students also bring the energy and commitment of those keenly aware that they need both practical experience and a good reference.

In some countries, university or government funding programmes may help the institution provide a stipend for summer students or interns, which can be an incentive for involving newcomers in the profession. Some universities offer course credits for practicum or work placement experiences. But the archivist should not forget that working with students can be extremely time consuming. They may be uncertain about their duties, unsure of their knowledge or so keen on applying newfound theories that they exhaust staff with their fervour. Involving a student is a commitment to training, not just a way to solicit cheap labour. All members of the institution, staff and volunteers, need to offer students their support and guidance in order for everyone to benefit from the experience.

Measuring success

All archival services need to be measured. Comparing actual results against intentions provides valuable insight into how well the institution is doing against its strategic objectives. If no one is looking at a virtual exhibit, how can the institution justify keeping it on the website? If the benchmark for digitizing photographs was 2000 images in a year and only 1000 were processed, what went wrong? Was it a case of poor planning, faulty execution or unreasonable expectations? The archivist cannot know if descriptive tools are useful, if reference services are adequate or if digital content is engaging if she does not periodically survey users and gauge their level of satisfaction. Just as the archivist needs to plan any initiative before beginning work, she also needs to measure success after the fact. The following need to be measured:

- *Inputs*. What staff time, resources, money or facilities were used to create and deliver a particular initiative? How much time was required to develop a tour for school children or design a new database? What were the actual costs of arranging and describing a particular collection?
- *Outputs*. What actual products or services were generated? Can they be quantified or measured? How many images were scanned? How many children visited on how many different tours? How many storage boxes were used? How many maps were flattened?
- *Outcomes*. Never mind the statistics, what has been the impact of the programme or service? It is extremely difficult to measure short- and long-term effects, but the archivist cannot just cite the number of boxes carried to the reference room as evidence of success. Perhaps the researcher asked for so many boxes because the finding aid did not clarify which materials were located where in the collection. While it is impossible to draw a direct link between a school tour in 2016 and the decision of a 10-year-old girl to become an archivist years later, some outcomes can be measured more precisely. If, for instance, the intention of an exhibit was to engage with an immigrant community by displaying archives related to their history, the archivist should be able to learn from that community if the *output* generated – the exhibit – provided good *outcomes* – a greater sense of belonging and a belief that their community archival institution saw them as legitimate members of their society.

As a rule, the archival community has tended not to pay as much attention to programme or service evaluations as our colleagues in museums and galleries have done. This may be a consequence of the lower public profile of archives, harkening back to the days of service to king and crown. But if archives are for the public, then measuring the public's response to archival services is an essential management task.

Before turning to the specifics of how to arrange and describe archives and make them available for use, one more overarching matter of archival practice needs to be addressed. Establishing a robust preservation programme for archives is essential to ensuring that the holdings are as safe as possible. The requirements for preserving archives are discussed in the next chapter.

9

Preserving archives

What boots it at one gate to make defence,
And at another to let in the foe?

John Milton (1608–74) *Samson Agonistes*, 1671

In theory, archival materials should be safer in archival custody than they were in the basement or attic of the person who created the records. Otherwise, one could argue, the archival institution should not acquire the materials in the first place. Many archivists would refute that statement, saying that if they did not bring a particular archival collection into their institution, the documents would be lost forever: shredded by a business that did not want to pay for storage or burnt by a family that had to clear out grandfather's home immediately after his death. Both positions have merit. But even if the archivist cannot achieve quality preservation controls today, she should not be ignorant of the best scenario for archival care. This chapter addresses the ideals of preservation and the realities of achieving them.

It is critical to emphasize at the start that the profession of conservation is a recognized specialty, quite distinct from archival management. Ideally, the first course of action for any archivist needing to address matters of preservation and conservation would be to work with a professional conservator or a digital preservation specialist to identify risks and establish priorities for action. In reality, though, the vast majority of archival institutions do not have the resources to employ conservators or digital preservation specialists. Compromises must be made.

Fortunately, the greatest success with preservation comes not from active repairs but from basic housekeeping efforts. Keeping the facility clean, monitoring the environment, establishing temperature and relative humidity controls and reducing the risk of disasters can be much more beneficial in the long run than spending scarce resources to get cellotape off a fading map.

It is also important to remember that, whatever the ideal might be, every archival institution needs to determine its own preservation needs, in keeping with its particular social and geopolitical realities. An archival institution in northern Europe faces different preservation challenges from one in sub-Saharan Africa, and the developers of a digital repository will prioritize different preservation concerns from a special collections department with a large number of medieval manuscripts. Blanket statements about what is best in theory do not necessarily translate to achievable results in practice. The resources included at the end of this book provide a small sample of the information available about aspects of archival and digital preservation.

Unlike in other chapters in this book, the scope for story-telling here is limited at best; there are few case studies to liven up the details about quality environmental controls and the importance of good housekeeping. But managing the conditions in which archives are kept is one of the most important jobs an archivist can do, so understanding these principles is essential. This chapter considers the major hazards that might compromise the security and stability of archival materials, the ideal conditions in which archives should be kept, the different requirements for handling and storing materials in different media, and the steps the archivist can take to identify risks and establish priorities for action. The first thing to understand is what archivists actually mean when we talk about preservation.

What is preservation?

Many people incorrectly equate archival preservation with conservation and restoration, and too often they mistakenly believe that the repair of individual documents should be an archival priority. Most archival conservators would respectfully but vigorously disagree, arguing instead that the establishment of a stable environment is much more important. It is necessary, therefore, to clarify the differences between preservation (including digital preservation), conservation and restoration.

The term 'preservation' is used to describe the passive protection of archival material, in which no physical, technological or chemical treatment is performed. Preservation is the total sum of processes and tasks performed in order to protect records and archives (in any form) against damage or deterioration. Actions include developing sound preservation policies; maintaining adequate environmental and storage conditions; housing records and archives in stable storage environments; and handling and managing archives in order to ensure they are safe from harm.

Digital preservation is the formal action of ensuring that digital information and evidence remains accessible and usable over time. Paper or analogue preservation usually seeks to preserve both the *content* and the *original form* of an archival item, often because the form helps clarify context and structure. On the other hand, digital preservation seeks to preserve the *content* but is less concerned with the form, because the context and structure of digital archives are not defined by the medium on which they were stored.

For example, the preservation of an original black and white or colour photograph would involve storing the item in an appropriate container so that the original image remains stable, even if copies are made for reference use. The preservation of a digital object such as a PDF document or TIFF file might involve receiving the items on a USB stick, transferring the items (the content, with metadata attached) into a digital repository, ensuring that the transferred items are complete and authentic copies of the original, then deleting the contents on the USB stick so there is no confusion about which is the original. In the digital environment, then, the *form* in which the incoming digital object was stored (such as a USB stick or CD or a folder in a cloud computing system) is not as important as the fact that the content is now safely stored in such a way that it will remain authentic and reliable evidence over time. The safe storage of authentic digital archives is essential, especially as those materials are likely to be transferred to another storage device at a later date.

Conservation can be defined as the active protection of archival material (and here we are talking primarily about paper and analogue materials), often by using physical and chemical treatments to repair damaged or deteriorating items or to minimize further deterioration. Repairing maps, cleaning works of art or removing the dust from bound ledgers are all conservation actions.

Restoration involves the repair of an item, either to return it to its original appearance or to improve its aesthetic qualities. Restoration is often undertaken when the look of an item is important or when the item is in grave danger of complete deterioration. If stabilizing an item is all that is required, the focus should be on conservation instead: removing staples and tape, storing items in archival-quality containers or removing dust and debris from files.

Restoration is not usually a high priority activity for the care of paper-based materials. The cost and time required to treat one item such as a map or photograph can take resources away from other preservation priorities, particularly the priority to create a safe storage environment. The restoration of audiovisual materials is a much greater concern, especially as the equipment needed to access and use old cassette or reel-to-reel tapes, VHS recordings or other magnetic media is becoming so hard to find. The restoration of digital objects is another matter entirely. Digital restoration is a highly complex and expensive technological exercise, but because it is often the only way to find out even what is stored on a corrupted or damaged storage device such as a floppy disk or hard drive, digital restoration can be an essential action even though, unfortunately, the archivist cannot know if the investment is worthwhile until she finds out what is actually on the corrupted device.

Understanding and responding to hazards

Several environmental hazards can affect archival materials, including fluctuations in temperature and humidity; mishandling and abuse of materials; high levels of acidity in archival materials or storage containers; excessive exposure to light or pollution; fire and water damage; and deterioration caused by biological agents such as mould, insects and rodents. Loss of power and damage to digital storage equipment are among the most severe risks to digital archives because power cuts can result in malfunctioning equipment and lost data. The intentional or accidental destruction of paper and analogue materials and the corruption of digital archives are also serious risks, and the archivist needs to protect both traditional and digital holdings – including digital storage devices – against unauthorized access.

Below is a brief overview of major archival hazards, followed by a summary of actions that can be taken to mitigate their effects.

Power and electricity

What is the risk?

Without stable electricity or other consistent power sources, lights, heaters, air conditioners, dehumidifiers and other critical equipment simply will not work. Computers cannot be turned on, so digital data cannot be accessed. Telephones may not operate; automated door locks protecting storage vaults may not function; and power-generated moveable shelving units may only work with considerable manual effort. Simply put, without electricity, all normal operations in a modern archival institution come to a halt.

What can be done?

If the institution is in a location where sources of power are unreliable, back-up generators may be an essential investment. Funds should also be set aside for regular maintenance of such equipment. The archivist does not want to discover in an emergency that the generator is out of fuel or so badly rusted that it will not start. If acquiring a generator is not feasible, the archivist needs to plan strategically how to maintain operations in the event of a power failure. Should digital databases be backed up daily instead of weekly? Should the institution invest in static shelving instead of moveable? Should all staff be supplied with cellular telephones, so they can reach each other if landline telephone service is interrupted?

Temperature and relative humidity

What is the risk?

Temperature (level of heat or cold in a substance or in the surrounding environment) and relative humidity (the amount of water vapour in the air) can significantly affect the life span of archival materials. Conservators suggest that every increase in temperature of 5°C doubles the reaction rate of media, so archival materials such as photographs or maps stored at 20°C only survive half as long as materials stored at 15°C.

Similarly, the higher the humidity, the greater the risk to archives. High relative humidity promotes the growth of mould and causes archives to absorb moisture, swelling them and deforming their shape permanently. Cutting relative humidity in half may double the life of archives. But if the humidity is too low, it can dry archival materials, leaving them brittle.

The greatest danger comes not from temperature and humidity levels that are consistently too high or too low but from excessive fluctuations in those levels. As the levels rise and fall, materials heat up and cool off, or become more or less laden with moisture, so they expand, shrink and expand again, weakening the bonds holding together the fibres of paper or layers of film or plastic. Over time, items become increasingly fragile and their life span decreases. Changes in temperature and humidity can also negatively affect computer equipment, which can compromise the integrity of digital storage systems.

What can be done?

Stabilizing temperature and relative humidity can markedly increase the life span of archives, even if the levels themselves are not optimal. Temperature and relative humidity should be monitored regularly, daily if possible. The results should be logged, including the day, month, year and time of day; the temperature; the relative humidity; and if possible also the outside weather conditions (including outside temperature and any precipitation). This log will help the archivist track changes in the environment, so she can make decisions about storage based on facts, not speculation. A variety of equipment is available to monitor temperature and relative humidity, some devices more complex and expensive than others; the resources on preservation management at the end of this book offer specific guidance.

If possible, temperatures in the storage repository should not drop below 18°C or rise above 20°C. Relative humidity should range from 35% to 40% and should not exceed 50%. Providing a cool, dry environment benefits the entire archival collection, but certain materials benefit from more precise controls, as discussed later.

A number of simple steps can be taken to control temperature and relative humidity. Ensure there is good ventilation throughout the building, including good air circulation around all computers and digital storage devices. Store materials away from outside walls to encourage air circulation, and keep records out of basements or attics. Pack documents in archival-quality containers if possible, and store extremely fragile materials together in a safe location so their condition can be monitored easily.

Portable humidifiers and dehumidifiers can help adjust the relative humidity, but plugging in a portable dehumidifier and turning it on is not enough. Without enforcing a strict monitoring regime there is no way to know if the equipment is actually helping. And relying on such equipment when power supplies are dubious is not a wise strategy. Investing in a generator might be a higher priority, before investing in humidifiers or dehumidifiers. When considering an investment in such expensive equipment, seeking the advice of a professional conservator might be the best first step.

Abuse and mishandling

What is the risk?

Whether intentional or accidental, poor handling of archives causes irreparable harm. Mishandling includes cracking or pressing on bindings, writing on documents, touching photographs with bare fingers, eating or drinking near archives, tearing or folding pages or handling documents with wet or dirty hands. (Or, in reality, insisting that everyone wear white gloves and watching as they drop books and papers on the floor because the gloves do not provide a solid grip on the object.)

Digital archives can be damaged if original digital documents are deleted or overwritten, or if files are not backed up and the master copy is lost when a storage device is corrupted. The lack of anti-virus software and security systems to prevent hacking into computer systems can lead to permanent damage or loss to archival materials, never mind personal information or the corporate records of the archival institution. And inadequate housekeeping and poor storage are serious threats to the safety of all holdings, irrespective of medium.

What can be done?

Reference and storage areas should be supervised, and extra oversight should be given when particularly valuable materials are being used. Security screening of staff should be regular and rigorous. Visitors should register and provide identification before using archives, so the archivist knows who has been in the reference room and when. To balance access with protection, the archivist has every right to impose conditions on the behaviour of visitors.

No one should be allowed to eat, smoke or drink in the reference room or near archival collections. If possible, the institution should provide a location in the building where visitors can take refreshments, especially if the institution is far removed from restaurants, cafés or other commercial operations. While the idea of wearing white cotton gloves when handling any archives has fallen out of favour, as noted, gloves are still useful when handling anything made of film, like photographs, negatives or moving image materials.

Storage areas should be off limits to the public, and visitors should not be allowed to retrieve archival materials themselves. Researchers accessing digital archives should always be working with copies, not originals. All archival storage areas (including digital storage systems) should be inspected at least once a month (weekly if possible) to look for any threats and to ensure physical materials have been returned safely to the right storage locations. Researchers should not be allowed to access unprocessed archives, regardless of medium: the risk of loss is much greater if the contents are not known.

Still, the archivist has to balance restricted access against the reality that it may take years to process archives fully. This is one reason archivists should strive for general arrangement and description of all holdings as a first priority. This approach – referred to as processing 'from the general to the specific' by some and given the name 'more product, less process' by others – is premised on the belief that it is always better to have *some* knowledge of and control over everything in the repository than achieving item-level processing of 5% of the collection and gaining no control over the rest.

While unglamorous, basic housekeeping, including dusting, vacuuming, wiping down floors and walls and so on, can be extremely effective in protecting archives from risks. A clean facility and firm access protocols also send the message that the institution is serious about its stewardship responsibilities.

Acidity

What is the risk?

Acidity is the quality of being acid or 'sour', as opposed to alkalinity or the quality of being alkaline or 'sweet'. Many archival materials, particularly paper-based records, are often composed of substances that are acidic, so the items are inherently fragile. The level of acidity (or alkalinity) in an object is measured on a numerical pH scale that ranges from 0 to 14. An item is acid neutral if it measures 7.0 on the pH scale. Anything above 7.0 represents increasing alkalinity, and anything below 7.0 represents increasing acidity.

The pH scale is logarithmic, so each change in numbers reflects a tenfold change in acidity or alkalinity. For instance, a pH of 5 is ten times more acidic than a pH of 6, and a pH of 4 is 100 times more acidic than a pH of 6. While acidity and alkalinity can both be destructive to archives, acidity is considered the more damaging of the two.

Acids can be introduced into paper during manufacturing. For example, in the early decades of the 19th century paper was made primarily from cotton and linen fibres. This rag paper, as it is called, tends to be chemically stable, having a neutral pH, and can have a life expectancy of several hundred years. On the other hand, paper made after the middle of the 19th century was often composed of wood pulp fibre, so it contains high levels of the acidic chemicals lignin and hemicellulose and is inherently unstable. Newsprint is almost always composed of extremely poor quality wood pulp and is therefore highly acidic.

Acid can also be present in the inks used on paper. Iron gall ink, actively used in the 12th to 19th centuries, is particularly damaging. Made of a combination of iron salts and tannin (an astringent chemical found in plants), iron gall ink was popular because it was durable; it bonded mechanically with the writing surface and did not come off easily. Iron gall ink was ideal for writing on vellum (animal skin) since it would adhere so well to the skin, but the ink is so strong it penetrates paper fibres, causing records to deteriorate.

Acid can also migrate from one substance to another. Even high-quality materials deteriorate faster if stored in acidic file folders, and especially if they are kept next to newspaper clippings or in close proximity to items such as staples, metal fasteners or glue. Cardboard boxes or food containers, which are often used by businesses or families to pack archives destined for an archival repository, can contain high levels of acid. The containers can also be home to biological threats such as insects or mould.

What can be done?

Testing the pH of paper archives, file folders or other fibre-based storage containers is one way to determine acid levels. Some pH testing processes require access to specialized equipment such as a pH meter, while others (like a pH pen) leave permanent marks. Testing acidity is best done only if the archivist suspects that a large volume of materials might be acidic or if there is a chance the archives may be able to deacidify materials through chemical treatments. In those instances, accurate measurements are needed before any treatment begins. The testing process is time consuming and expensive, however, and because it reveals but does not resolve a problem, a better first step is to store archival materials securely, ideally in good quality archival storage containers. Mass deacidification – the chemical reduction of acid in large volumes of archives – used to be a common conservation practice, but increasingly archivists are turning to digitization as a preservation tool.

Archival-quality envelopes, folders and boxes provide a stable microenvironment, reducing the spread of acid and mitigating the effects of fluctuating temperature and relative humidity. Plastic enclosures such as envelopes or folders must be inert: no chemical activity should be present in the materials. Mylar, which is a clear, uncoated polyester film, is considered the most stable plastic container for archival materials. Polyvinylchloride or PVC containers contain harmful gases and should never be used.

The cost of archival-quality storage containers is very high, though, and there is ongoing debate about how much stability they provide, in comparison with good quality records storage boxes. The archivist should consider the risks and the costs when deciding when to use top-quality materials and when, perhaps, to wait a few years before moving holdings from one container to another. Not all materials have to be in acid-free containers from the moment they arrive in the repository. Ideally, the archivist should be able to plan ahead with a potential donor to use good quality storage containers, even plain records boxes instead of orange crates, so that when the archives arrive in her custody, they do not have to be repacked right away.

Items should never be attached to other items or to envelopes, plastic containers or folders in any permanent way. Encapsulation – the action of enclosing a document within sheets of polyester and sealing the edges to keep the item in place – is an acceptable storage method if appropriate procedures are followed. Lamination, on the other hand, which is the process of permanently attaching an item to plastic using heat or adhesives, is irreversible. The archivist should never undertake actions that she cannot reverse, and lamination is one of the most dangerous and damaging actions that have been taken in the past to 'protect' archives.

The archivist responsible for current records management as well as archival preservation can lobby her sponsor agency to use archival-quality paper when creating permanently valuable records, based on one of the standards defining the qualities of permanent paper. (Standards for archival-quality paper are noted in the resources at the end of the book.)

Ultimately, the archivist has to balance risk with reward when dealing with acidic materials. The cost of housing large volumes of archives in acid-free containers can be high, and the containers should ideally be replaced every few years, as the acid in the archives themselves will leach out onto the folders and boxes, reducing their 'acid-free' quality. Archivists today tend to use acid-free containers for highly vulnerable materials first, while regularly assessing the state of other holdings before deciding whether and when to transfer them to other storage containers.

Light

What is the risk?

Light speeds up oxidation (a process that occurs when oxygen is combined with other elements), which can hasten the deterioration of materials such as paper. (Oxidation is also responsible for the rust on metals.) Light also breaks down chemical bonds, causing ink to fade, and generates heat, which damages archives. Ultraviolet light is most harmful, because the wavelength of ultraviolet light generates more radiation, increasing chemical deterioration. Ultraviolet light is found in sunlight and in fluorescent light, so both those types of light need to be controlled in order to protect archives.

What can be done?

Light can be measured to determine the overall level of light (measured in lux units) and the level of ultraviolet radiation emitted from a source. Measuring ultraviolet radiation involves specialized and expensive equipment. Most conservators recommend that institutions focus instead on reducing overall light levels, removing ultraviolet lighting or placing filters over ultraviolet lights, rather than spending scarce resources measuring a situation that ought to be remedied anyway.

To understand the impact of excessive light, it is worth pointing out that an archival document left on a table about one metre away from a 150 watt incandescent bulb is exposed to a light intensity of 50 lux, which is within reasonable limits. But the longer that item is exposed or the closer it is to the light source, the more damage the light can cause. Thus the ideal light levels for the storage or display of most archival materials is 50–100 lux. Photographs, oil paintings and wood objects can be exposed to up to 150 lux.

The best light level is none at all, if archives are stored in an environment with controlled temperature and relative humidity, but as working in pure darkness is impossible, the best action is to reduce the exposure to light as much as possible. If the environment is excessively humid, though, it is best to keep some lights on all the time, in order to increase the temperature, lower relative humidity and discourage mould, insects and rodents.

Archival materials should be stored in boxes or containers whenever they are not in use, in order to reduce light exposure. During processing, materials should not be left uncovered or near sources of strong light for any length of time. Curtains, blinds or filters reduce ultraviolet radiation from outside, but if light levels remain high, the archives themselves may need to be stored in a cooler, darker location.

To control artificial light, a first step is to identify all fluorescent lights in the building and determine whether they are close to archives storage or reading areas. Conservators have long recommended replacing fluorescent lights with incandescent lights, which do not generate the same level of ultraviolet radiation. Both types of light, incandescent and ultraviolet, do generate heat though, so lights should be kept off whenever possible (bearing in mind the concerns for excessive humidity noted above). Unfortunately there is growing social pressure on archival institutions to use compact fluorescent lighting, which is considered more environmentally friendly, but these lights still generate ultraviolet radiation and so are less appropriate than incandescent lights for archival use.

Photocopying and scanning can generate tremendous exposure to light and heat, damaging materials. Ideally, materials to be photocopied or digitized will only be exposed to high light levels once, the first time they are copied or scanned. Once a master physical or digital copy is produced, that copy should be used to make further copies and the original should be safely stored.

Pollution

What is the risk?

Pollution is a serious archival hazard. External pollutants such as gases, chemicals and toxins come from factories, automobiles or trucks. Internal pollutants come from photocopiers, cleaning supplies, paints, untreated wood, plastics, adhesives and even tap water. The particles that make up pollution are abrasive and acidic, and if these particles settle on archives and then become moist, they can leave stains. Dust can also seriously damage the interior of a computer; it can slow down fans and act as a form of insulation, causing the computer to heat up. High heat levels can then cause computer components to fail unexpectedly, and repairs can be complicated and expensive.

What can be done?

The best way to reduce pollution is to install air filtration systems that screen out polluted air particles. This process is expensive and requires regular maintenance, so it is not an easy option for many archival institutions. Storing materials in archival-quality boxes, containers or cabinets also limits their exposure to pollutants. Untreated wood shelving can be sealed with an interior latex paint (not an oil-based paint) to keep acidic wood particles from damaging records or storage boxes.

No one should be allowed to eat, smoke, drink or cook near records or archives. Poor quality holdings such as newspapers are best stored separately from original archival materials, at least in different containers. Dusting and cleaning storage and public areas regularly keeps dirt and dust to a minimum. Areas around computers and storage devices should be kept as free of dust as possible. Ideally computer equipment will be kept in a separate location with high-quality environmental controls, at least for master storage devices holding irreplaceable digital data. Computer equipment in the reference area should also be kept free of dust but the secure, dust-free environment so important in a trusted digital repository is not necessarily required for equipment in public or office spaces.

Fire and water

What is the risk?

Fire is a devastating threat to archives, not just because of the all-consuming losses brought by the fire itself but also because of the damage caused by the water or chemicals used to extinguish the flames. Water damage from leaks, floods or rain is equally hazardous. Because paper absorbs water so quickly, damage to textual and photographic materials can be immediate, widespread and irreversible. Inks may run or dissolve, mould can grow, pages can become stuck together and glues soften. Water can also damage the inner workings of a computer, and extracting data from drives damaged by fire or water could be impossible.

What can be done?

To reduce the threat of fire and water damage, hazardous materials such as chemicals, paints, solvents and other flammable substances should never be stored near records. Archival materials should be kept at least 15–25 centimetres (6–8 inches) off the floor, to minimize damage in the event of flooding or water leaks. Materials should not be stored in basements or attics, since those areas are often the first places in a building to be damaged in fires or floods.

No open flames or sources of heat, such as lighters or cigarettes, should be allowed anywhere in the facility. If portable heaters must be used to keep staff warm when working with archival materials, the archivist needs to assess not only the risk of fire but also the changes in temperature and humidity that occur when the heat source is turned on and off regularly. If using portable heaters is necessary, they should be turned off when no one is in the room. The risk of fluctuating temperature levels is less worrisome than the risk of fire, should the heater short-circuit for any reason.

Exposed water pipes should be wrapped to slow down leakage, should the pipes crack or burst. Computers should be stored well away from any sources of water and away from high-risk areas, like windows or on the floor. Fire alarms and portable fire extinguishers should be installed throughout the facility, even if centralized fire suppression systems are installed. The array of fire suppression systems available today is bewildering, including as 'wet pipe', 'dry pipe', deluge', 'foam water' and 'pre-action' systems. The archivist should consult the local fire department and conservation specialists before selecting any new system for the repository. Everyone in the institution should be taught how to use emergency response devices, from handheld extinguishers to alarms to complete suppression systems, and all equipment should be checked or tested regularly to make sure it is operational.

Biological agents

What is the risk?

Mould, insects and rodents can damage archives. Mould is prolific in environments with high temperatures and humidity, such as dark, unventilated storage rooms or buildings with no environmental controls. Insects such as silverfish, cockroaches, booklice and beetles are attracted to paper-based products and they also gravitate toward damp, dark corners. While an occasional insect in a repository is not uncommon, a large number can be a sign of an infestation. Rodents such as rats and mice seek out warm, dark environments, using paper products to build nests. They also chew paper, bindings, boxes and even electrical wiring, resulting in short circuits, power outages and fire.

What can be done?

Storing archives in climate-controlled environments, keeping relative humidity low, and cleaning storage and reference areas can reduce the risk of mould outbreaks or pest infestations. Detailed and regular inspections of computer and electricity cables can identify if pests have damaged the wires. To reduce the chance that rodents will enter buildings, screens should be placed over exterior windows and doors. If rodents do make their way into the facility, they are best caught in traps. Poisons kill rodents, but if the dead rodent cannot be found quickly, rotting carcasses can attract insects or other rodents, exacerbating the pest problem.

Archivists can clean mould, for example by drying damaged records and then vacuuming off the mould using a low-suction vacuum, which prevents spores from being dispersed. Alternately, dried mould can be removed with a soft paintbrush. Both techniques should only be practised in an area isolated from other records to prevent mould spores from landing on clean material. The techniques required to clean mould, while not complicated or expensive, require specialist knowledge. The archivist should seek advice from a trained conservator before attempting the process.

If mouldy archives simply cannot be salvaged, they can be duplicated either manually or digitally and the originals destroyed. Any equipment used to copy mouldy items, like photocopiers or scanners, should be cleaned thoroughly afterwards to ensure mould spores are not transferred to other holdings. Archival materials can also be fumigated or treated with insecticides, but this process exposes materials and people to toxic gases. Conservation professionals should be consulted before any such work is considered.

Caring for materials in different media

A brief overview is given below of the major issues associated with the storage of archives in different media, including paper documents and cartographic records; photographic prints; photographic negatives, slides and transparencies; photograph albums; bound volumes; parchment, vellum and seals; newspapers; works of art and framed materials; motion picture films, including cellulose nitrate films; analogue audio and video recordings; microforms; and artefacts. While the storage requirements for some materials fall within the general norms identified earlier, other items, from cellulose nitrate negatives to colour prints to parchment scrolls, may be better protected in highly specific microenvironments, as discussed below. It is important for the archivist to be aware of different requirements, even if they cannot be achieved in the foreseeable future. The preservation of digital holdings is discussed in a later section, as the actions required for digital preservation relate more to the need for strong policies and clear procedures than particular environmental conditions.

Paper documents and cartographic records

Acidity is a frequent condition in paper records, including correspondence, reports, minutes, cartographic and architectural records and other textual materials. As paper ages, the acid weakens the fibres. Ideally, paper archives should be kept in darkness whenever they are not used and should be exposed to as little light as possible, especially ultraviolet light. Blueprints are particularly susceptible to fading and so should always be kept covered when not in use. The best temperature and relative humidity levels for storing paper materials are 18–20°C maximum and 35–45%. If paper records are to be exhibited, light levels should be no more than 50 lux. Original blueprints are rarely displayed in exhibits as they are too susceptible to fading.

Paper archives should be flattened and stored in good quality (ideally acid-free) file folders, at a thickness of no more than 1–2 centimetres of documents per folder. Metal clips and staples can be replaced with plastic fasteners if time and resources allow, as long as the original order of documents can be maintained and only a small number of pages are fastened together, to avoid bending the paper. The folders should be stored in sturdy boxes, again acid free if possible, to keep out light and dust, and the containers should be placed on shelves or cabinets so that they not overhang the sides. If particular paper archives are in high demand, the archivist may wish to reproduce them to facilitate access while reducing wear and tear on the originals.

Photographic prints

Photographic prints consist of two layers: one provides the support and one holds the image. The support layer is usually made of paper but may also be made of glass, metal or other materials. The image layer is made up of a variety of chemicals. Black and white photographic images consist of silver, embedded in a binder, called the emulsion layer, which may be made of substances such as gelatin, albumen or collodion. Colour images are composed of a number of organic dyes embedded in layers of gelatin.

All photographic prints can be damaged by ultraviolet light, pollutants and dust. Black and white photographs are often more stable than colour photographs, which are much more sensitive to changes in light, temperature or humidity. Photographic prints are best stored in total darkness, with any exposure to light as minimal as possible; as with paper archives, a light level of 50 lux is acceptable for exhibitions.

The most important factor in the preservation of photographic prints is to house them in an environment with stable temperature and relative humidity. If possible, the temperature should be below 20°C and the relative humidity at 30–35% for black and white photographs and 25–30% for colour photographs. A relative humidity lower than 20% is hazardous; the dry air causes the photographs to become brittle.

The oils in fingers damage photographic prints, so these particular items are best handled with gloves and only by their edges. Items should not be bent or folded or attached with paper clips or staples. If possible, individual prints should be stored in acid-free, non-buffered envelopes or folders, non-buffered photographic mats, Mylar sleeves or inert plastic holders. Enclosures should not contain coated plastic (such as plastics with anti-static coatings), nitrate or chlorinated plastic (such as polyvinylchloride or PVC) or any material containing sulphur or adhesives. (It is critically important not to assume that because a stationery store has labelled photographic storage materials as 'archival quality' that the materials are okay to use; check with conservation specialists or go to websites for conservation associations to confirm which supplies are suitable.) Popular images should be digitized or otherwise reproduced so that the copies can be used for reference.

Colour photographs and photographs and negatives produced on cellulose acetate or cellulose nitrate paper can be protected by placing them in vapour-proof packages and storing them in frost-free freezers, with a relative humidity of 20–30%. This cold storage principle only works if the items placed in freezers or lockers are left there for extended periods, however. Removing and replacing materials every few days or weeks defeats the purpose. Further, because cold storage facilities are expensive, cold storage is a strategy best developed in conjunction with digitization or other reproduction, so that users can access copies and originals remain undisturbed. Professional conservators should be consulted before any cold storage system is considered.

Photographic negatives, slides and transparencies

Like photographic prints, negatives are made up of a support layer and an image layer. The support is generally polyester, cellulose acetate or cellulose nitrate film. The image layer of a black and white negative is usually made of silver particles in gelatin. The image layer of a colour negative also contains silver, but the particles may have been bleached during development, adding acid to the negative and making it less stable. Slides also consist of a support layer and an image layer. The chemical dyes used to produce slides can destabilize the slide over time.

Negatives and slides are damaged by light and heat; chemicals and pollutants; and high temperatures and humidity. Negatives are best stored with as little exposure to light as possible, at temperatures below 20°C if possible. As is the case with photographic prints, the maintenance of a stable relative humidity is the most important action to support preservation: at 30–35% for films and slides and at 25–30% for glass plate negatives and glass slides.

As with photographic prints, negatives should be handled by the edges only and never with bare fingers. They should be stored in acid-free, non-buffered envelopes or folders. The enclosures used for prints are usually also suitable for negatives. Slides are best contained in inert plastic holders, never in glassine envelopes and never in enclosures containing coated plastics, nitrate or chlorinated plastics (such as PVC) or sulphur or adhesives. If negatives or slides are used often, they should be copied and the originals stored. Negatives should only be copied photographically as the light from photocopiers is too damaging.

Photograph albums

The established order of images in a photograph album is an integral part of the album's evidential value. But the albums themselves can be physically unstable, particularly if the pages include adhesives or poor-quality plastics. If an album is in poor condition, the archivist needs to decide whether to keep it intact or take it apart. If it is made of self-adhesive pages, which were particularly popular from the 1960s to 1990s, the pictures should be removed and the album discarded. It can be difficult or impossible to remove the images without damaging them, though; if a first, gentle attempt to detach the images from the page is unsuccessful, the better option is to photocopy or digitize the pages and then store the album securely, with a plan to disassemble it safely in the future.

Albums are best stored individually in boxes to keep out light and dust. Individual pages can be separated with acid-free paper. Albums should be stored in the same environmental conditions as photographs, ideally in total darkness and at temperatures below 20°C and with relative humidity below 45%. The archivist should always describe an album's contents and structure in as much detail as possible so that its original physical form is well documented, even if the original is taken apart.

Bound volumes

The pages and bindings of bound volumes, including ledgers, diaries, publications and scrapbooks, might be made of paper, leather, vellum, cloth, boards and adhesives. Bound items are best stored at temperatures of 18–20°C maximum, with a relative humidity of no more than 45–50%. The storage environment should be as dark as possible and the volumes should be protected from strong light during use. Items used in exhibits should be kept in light of 50 lux or less.

Extremely fragile items can be stored in boxes or tied with cotton tape; the pages might be interleaved with acid-free tissue to reduce the transfer of acid from one page to another, particularly in scrapbooks. Damaged books should never be repaired using elastic bands, adhesive tapes or glues. In situations where the archival institution is housed in or associated with a library, it is expected that a trained librarian will be available to provide advice.

Parchment, vellum and seals

In some parts of the world, many archival documents are made from parchment (made from the skin of a sheep or goat) and vellum (made from the skin of a calf). Both parchment and vellum are quite durable and not easily affected by acid, but both are susceptible to changes in temperature and relative humidity. In a dry environment, they become brittle, while in a humid environment they are susceptible to mould growth. Parchment and vellum should be exposed to as little light as possible; they are best stored at a temperature of 18–20°C or cooler and a relative humidity between 50% and 55%. The temperature and relative humidity need to be as stable as possible, to reduce the chance of stretching and shrinkage.

Parchment and vellum documents should be stored flat in boxes or drawers or in file folders on shelves. Before parchment or vellum is flattened, the skin must be softened by exposure to humidity. Any seals attached to documents should be wrapped in acid-free paper and stored with the document itself. If the seals are no longer attached, they can be stored separately in boxes. A separation sheet should be included with each item – document or seal – indicating where the other is located. (The process of creating a separation sheet is outlined in Chapter 11.)

Newspapers

Newsprint is a highly unstable medium, wholly unsuitable for the long-term preservation of information. If the institution wishes to provide access to historical copies of newspapers, the best course of action is to microfilm or digitize issues and use those copies for reference. If the originals must be kept, they should be stored separately from other archival materials, in boxes or folders to keep out any light, with temperatures below 20°C and relative humidity of 40–45%. Binding newspapers is a poor use of time and money, as it speeds up deterioration of already acidic pages and complicates other efforts to conserve the items.

If the institution wishes to keep newspaper clippings, they should be digitized or copied onto acid-free bond paper. The originals may then be destroyed. Rarely do original clippings contain critical evidential value, and the acid in the paper is often so destructive that keeping the original clipping only damages other materials in the same folder.

Works of art and framed materials

As discussed in Chapter 2, archival institutions might acquire art work as part of an archival acquisition. An artist's sketches, drafts and artworks may very well be kept with the artist's body of archives as evidence of his or her work. Deciding whether to acquire art as part of an archival collection depends on the mandate of the institution and the merits of the acquisition.

The preservation problem is how to store and preserve works of art if they are kept in the institution. The archivist needs to use her discretion. Framed works are usually left within their frames, unless the frames are highly acidic or are clearly damaging the art itself. Framed pieces with less 'artistic' value could be removed from their frames, if doing so increases the stability and security of the items. Unframed items are best stored in boxes or containers to protect them from dust and light.

If works of art are to be displayed, light levels should be kept lower than

150 lux. For storage and display, temperatures are best kept at 18–20°C and relative humidity between 45% and 55%; both temperature and humidity should be as stable as possible. Art should not be cleaned without guidance from an art conservator. A digital or print photograph can be created to provide a substitute for the original for description or reference purposes.

Other framed items, such as certificates, diplomas, photographs or posters, often find their way into archival collections. The frames and mats surrounding the documents can be highly acidic. The archivist has to ask if the frame itself is an important part of the evidence, or if there is any reason the item should remain in the frame. If not, the item should be removed from the frame and stored separately. It should just be discarded if it does not add any specific evidence or information.

Motion picture film

Moving image films and film strips are composed of an image layer of gelatin emulsion on top of a support layer of polyester, cellulose acetate or cellulose nitrate. Storage temperatures should be as cool as possible, no more than 20°C, with relative humidity at 35–45%. Films should be stored in film canisters or other containers that keep light out.

The film itself should be touched as little as possible and handled only with gloves to keep oils off the film. Copies should be made for reference use and the originals stored for long-term preservation. If films need to be repaired, professional conservators should be contacted, as the process is highly technical and damage can be irreversible.

Cellulose nitrate film

Cellulose nitrate-based film, produced from the late 1800s to the 1950s, is extremely fragile. The film can is highly flammable, can deteriorate rapidly and can produce acidic fumes that will damage other materials stored in the same area. To identify nitrate-based film, look for the word 'nitrate' embossed on the film's edge. If the word appears, the film is nitrate based. If the film is marked 'safety film' then it is not nitrate based. If no words appear, the archivist should check if the film is curling on the edges or if it appears thicker on the sides. Manufacturers of nitrate film added more gelatin to reduce the curling process, which was common with nitrate films; the added thickness can be a sign the film is nitrate based. Also see if the film feels sticky, has brown stains or smells unpleasant. These are all signs the film is nitrate based.

In the past, nitrate film was removed from storage areas immediately and destroyed as soon as a suitable copy was made. Now archivists prefer to adopt a wait and see approach: identifying nitrate-based materials, storing them separately from other holdings and monitoring them regularly. As soon as significant deterioration appears, the archivist can take action, but until then monitoring their condition is a reasonable option. A professional conservator should be contacted for advice before any attempt is made to duplicate or dispose of nitrate-based materials.

Analogue audio and video recordings

Many archival institutions house sound recordings such as phonographic records, cassette or reel-to-reel tapes and videotapes. Less common are wire, cylinder or wax recordings. (Archivists are also acquiring more and more digital audiovisual recordings such as WAV files (waveform audio file format), MP3 files, CDs or DVDs, which need to be managed as digital archives according to the guidance suggested later in this chapter.)

While light is not particularly damaging to most analogue sound or video recordings, the heat generated by light can cause the recording media to swell or shrink, damaging the item. The temperature is best kept below 18°C, with relative humidity at 40–45%. The archivist should preserve any associated materials; commercial recordings, for instance, may come with album covers or liner notes that may contain valuable descriptive information. The recording itself is best stored separately from any additional items.

One of the challenges with arranging, describing and storing analogue audio or video recordings is being able to access the equipment needed to play them. If they cannot be played, they cannot be appraised or used. The archivist should make reference copies of recordings as quickly as possible to support access to the content and store the originals so they can be reproduced again in the future. Today, that reproduction will most likely be digital, not analogue. It does not make sense, for instance, to transfer the contents of a cassette recording onto reel-to-reel tape only to have to acquire the reel-to-reel equipment to play the tape, and then to have to transfer that recording to another format a few years from now.

Unfortunately, the equipment needed for audiovisual duplication is becoming harder to access; archivists have been warned that the window for completing such work is only years. As a result, many specialists suggest that if analogue audiovisual materials have not been transferred to better formats by the early to mid-2020s, it may be impossible to find the equipment needed to support that work, so duplicating audiovisual recordings is perhaps the greatest archival preservation challenge today.

Microforms

Microforms – whether microfilm or microfiche – resemble film in their physical properties and storage needs. Temperatures are best kept at 18–20°C and relative humidity at 35%. Fluctuations in temperature and relative humidity are particularly hazardous and should be avoided. Storage in total darkness is best, and microforms should only be handled with gloves. Rolls of film should be stored in boxes or containers that keep out light and dust. Duplicate copies of microforms are useful to facilitate reference and reduce wear and tear on originals. Master originals of the microforms can then be stored offsite and duplicates used for reference, so that (theoretically) the master version is safe in the event of an emergency.

Artefacts

As outlined in Chapter 2, archival institutions sometimes acquire artefacts, such as globes, coins, medals and trophies, even tools, clothing or animal specimens, as part of archival acquisitions. The storage and preservation requirements for artefacts vary dramatically, depending on the qualities of the object in question.

Theoretically, the best course of action in most instances is to transfer artefacts to an appropriate museum environment, just as one might send publications to a library or works of art to an art gallery. But, as already argued, it can be difficult to draw a firm line between the different domains. The archivist needs to consider how important the attachment – the artefact or object – is in contextualizing the evidence provided in the documentary material. If objects are transferred elsewhere, the archivist needs to document their content, context and structure in detail before they are removed, so that the different elements – archives and artefacts – can always be reunited intellectually, if not physically. Separation sheets are useful here too, as discussed in Chapter 11.

Digitization for preservation

Digitization – the transfer of analogue or manually created items such as documents, photographs or sound recordings into digital form for electronic access and use – has become extremely popular in the first decades of the 21st century. Digitization is considered a tool for both preservation and access. In many countries, a great deal of public money is being devoted – or, some might argue, diverted – to the task. In this section, the practicalities of digitization are introduced, with a focus on the value of digitization as a preservation strategy. The topic of digitization is raised again in Chapter 12 in relation to its benefit as a tool for reference and outreach.

If a document or image is digitized and made available electronically the original does not have to be handled repeatedly, which reduces wear and extends the life of the original. As a preservation tool, digitization is today what hand copying, microfilming and photocopying were in decades past: a means of extending the life of documents by reformatting them for easier and less invasive use, and then storing the originals safely.[1]

Planning a digitization programme

Digitization is time consuming, costly and potentially damaging to archival materials, so any digitization initiative must be well planned so that it is efficient, cost-effective and sustainable. As always, the first step is to clarify the nature and scope of the digitization programme and balance that initiative against the institution's core mandate. A municipal or local authority archives may choose to provide electronic copies of council minutes because the records are in high demand and the originals are at risk from excessive handling. A historical society archives, on the other hand, may wish to digitize photographs related to an upcoming community anniversary, and a university special collections department may prioritize the digitization of a collection of politician's papers to support academic research. Whatever the reason, a digitization programme should be based on a long-term vision, not a reaction to immediate pressures.

The longevity of digital information

As emphasized many times already, digital information is highly susceptible to damage or loss, given the speed with which technologies become obsolete. An archival image may only have to be scanned once, but the digital copy needs to be reformatted periodically, to ensure it can be accessed when computer technologies change. The archivist should assume that she will need to reformat or convert digital products from one digital format to another every three to five years to ensure their continued preservation. Still, digitized copies of archives should not be considered replacements for analogue or paper originals. Archivists today have adopted the philosophy that original records should be retained in their native format, so documents, photographs, sound recordings or other physical items should be preserved. Born-digital archives would be considered the 'original' and preserved in digital form, and any paper copies would be for convenience only. This approach of keeping originals even if digital duplicates have been made may not continue forever, but it is considered the best strategy now.

Beyond planning for the long-term preservation and management of the physical original and the digitized copy, the archivist also needs to consider the sustainability of the overall digitization programme. Digitization is not just a matter of placing a photograph on a flatbed scanner and pushing the start button; the process must not harm original items and should result in an authentic replica. A poorly reproduced sound recording is of little benefit to a researcher. A badly scanned photograph may not contain sufficient detail to be useful. A scanned copy of an official document with the top and bottom of the page cut off may not be accepted as evidence for legal or administrative purposes. The institution needs to do the job right the first time and every subsequent time.

A range of standards and guidelines exist to support digitization, including many identified in the resources section of this book. These standards address issues such as choosing appropriate file formats for storage; selecting software and systems for reproduction and storage; determining whether and how to compress digital files to save space; and confirming digital reproductions are of high quality and will remain stable and usable over the long term.

These digitization protocols and standards can be highly technical and inevitably change with every new technological development. The archivist has to be prepared to commit the energy and resources required to ensure a digitization programme follows best practice standards in the present and the future.

Issues of authenticity and copyright

Enhancing digital images may make them easier to view, but such alterations diminish the fidelity of the images. A digital copy is not exactly the same as the original but it should be as faithful a reproduction as possible. When old black and white movies and television programmes were colourized, the process of adding colour made the productions look more familiar to modern audiences, but the enhancements meant that the 'new' films were not authentic reproductions of the originals. The distinction may not matter to a viewer watching an old detective movie on television, but the differences change the accuracy of the copy: the archivist should avoid editing digital copies whenever possible and always document any changes made so that the digitization process is completely transparent.

According to most interpretations of copyright laws around the world, creating a digital copy of a document or an image and then making it available on an internet-accessible environment is, in effect, publishing it. Therefore the archivist must consider copyright, privacy and publicity rights, as well as other donor restrictions, when deciding which materials to digitize. The easiest way to avoid such complications is to limit digitization only to items or collections already in the public domain. (The challenge of understanding copyright, given the diversity of legislation in jurisdictions around the world, was discussed in Chapter 7.) However, if digitization is essential to preventing the loss of archival content, copyright may be a lesser concern than urgent preservation.

If the archivist decides to digitize copyrighted materials and provide public access, she may want to add a watermark, such as a word or logo overlaying the image, which shows up whenever the digital item is displayed or printed. The watermark does not prevent others from reproducing copyrighted materials without permission but it does limit opportunities for further use by interfering with the aesthetics of the image.

Alternately, the archivist may choose to digitize materials using less than production-quality techniques. The resulting images will be suitable for reference but if digitization is for the purpose of preservation, the reduced quality may defeat the purpose. Anyone interested in publishing an item would need to obtain permission from the copyright holder, after which they could order a better quality copy from the archival institution. Note that editing for digital publication can violate copyright, as the archivist is 'reworking' an image without the permission of the copyright holder.

Digitization, priorities and resources

The archivist also needs to fit digitization into larger institutional objectives, paying particular attention to resource implications. Too often, digitization is considered in isolation and not as part of a wider, more strategic approach to records and archives management. The archivist has to know that her institution can provide the technological infrastructure to ensure digitized materials are secure and stable and can afford to install and maintain specialized software to facilitate online access. Staff will no doubt be diverted from other projects to work on digitization activities, and the archivist has to consider the impact on overall operations.

Digital technologies present the archivist with a tremendous opportunity to disseminate information from and about archival holdings while protecting original materials from further deterioration. But digitization can also become a bandwagon, which people get on without asking where it might be going. The institution needs to be sure that any digitization initiatives accommodate strategic priorities for preservation as well as for reference and outreach.

Preserving digital archives

Electronic records, from e-mails to word-processed documents to digital photographs and databases, are a growing component of archival holdings. Whether a digital object arrives in the archival institution as part of a donation, or is the result of a digitization programme, the archivist needs to ensure that a digital object with archival value is preserved with its authenticity intact. Managing these materials is not simply a matter of storing them safely and checking on them periodically. As introduced in Chapter 5, the creation of a sustainable programme for digital preservation depends on the co-ordination of policies, procedures, technologies and people, all working in concert to achieve a technologically, financially and administratively sustainable storage process for the long term.

Digital preservation is far too complex a task to be covered adequately in only a part of a chapter; whole books are devoted to outlining policies, procedures, technologies and system requirements for the secure care of digital archives, whether they come in as donations or are the creations of the archival institution itself. I have, yet again, to direct readers to the valuable resources at the end of the book. Still, it is possible to highlight some of the primary conditions that must be met to ensure the success of digital preservation. If the archivist familiarizes herself with these requirements, she has enough introductory knowledge to know what questions to ask and issues to consider when pursuing options for digital preservation. As a starting point, any digital preservation programme must meet the following fundamental requirements:

- Clear, sensible and enforceable policies and procedures need to be established and maintained for all aspects of digital preservation, including technological specifications, operational requirements, and financial commitments.
- All the archives or other digital objects stored in the digital repository need to be managed in accordance with legal requirements such as evidence, intellectual property and privacy laws.
- Strict controls have to be established to ensure that any new content is quarantined and scanned for viruses or malware and then disinfected before any data or archives are added to the digital repository. (This is the digital equivalent of holding new paper archives in a separate room to check for insects, mould or pests.)
- Robust security systems need to be developed to protect both the archives and the technology. The archivist also needs to define clear roles and responsibilities for anyone accessing and using the digital

repository, from staff to volunteers to contractors, and she has to ensure that everyone complies with all necessary requirements.

- The digital repository must meet best practice standards for the storage of digital media and technology, including the implementation of stable environmental controls and monitoring systems. (Some relevant standards are noted at the end of the book.)
- The archivist has to establish strategies for maintaining, upgrading and replacing hardware and software, to ensure systems remain operational and up to date.
- The archivist also has to establish effective preservation strategies, including procedures for dealing with power losses, environmental emergencies or other external hazards.
- A regular and consistent process needs to be implemented for creating back-ups of electronic archives, including offsite storage and duplication of holdings as needed.
- Everyone adding archives to the digital repository or preparing descriptions of holdings has to adhere to standards for metadata management and archival description, so every item in the digital repository is clearly identified and contextualized.
- Decisions have to be made and enforced about the minimum metadata to be captured when archival material is brought into the repository (what metadata *must* exist) and about the range of allowable metadata that might be acquired if space, time and resources allow (what metadata *can* exist).
- The digital repository needs to be able to support information sharing and export as much as needed, so that digital content and associated metadata can be reused easily.

Other requirements for digital archives preservation are the same as those for analogue and paper, including ensuring that digital storage systems are housed in safe surroundings; that measures are in place to prevent, reduce or eliminate dust, pollution or mould; that power supplies are consistent; and that emergency back-up systems are operational. Beyond those, the archivist has to develop specific standards for digital preservation such as how to define a digital object as authentic, how to ensure the actual process of digital transfer is robust and how to maintain the stability of the digital objects throughout their life in the digital repository (which one assumes is a life without end).[2]

Developing preservation and emergency response plans

In order for the archivist to achieve all of the conditions outlined in this chapter for the safe storage and physical protection of archives, whatever their form or medium, she needs to develop a preservation plan and an emergency response plan. This section outlines the specific tasks involved with developing both of those plans.

For both plans, the first step is to conduct a preservation survey. The survey provides a snapshot of the current condition of all archival holdings and of the different storage facilities. A preservation policy should then be drafted. This policy lays the groundwork for ongoing preservation management by articulating the institution's responsibilities and priorities for preservation, establishing guidelines for the handling and storage of materials and outlining conditions that may be imposed in order to protect archives. Based on the policy decisions made, a strategic plan for preservation can be developed, identifying priorities for action over a certain period. This strategic planning process is comparable to that outlined in Chapter 8, with a particular focus on physical and environmental conditions and storage and handling requirements.

Conducting a preservation survey

The best way to determine preservation priorities is to conduct a survey of the institution, in order to assess the severity of any and all hazards. Without identifying environmental conditions, the archivist does not know which threats exist and which are most severe.

An initial preservation survey, sometimes called an environmental assessment, creates a baseline measurement of the status of the archival facility and holdings. Following the first survey, the archivist can update information annually (or after any emergency) to identify any changes or new concerns. Like other management tasks, an environmental review is not a one-time action but should become part of the regular oversight of archival operations. (The resources at the end of the book include guidance on devising preservation surveys and environmental reviews.)

The preservation survey assesses conditions such as:

- the general condition of the interior and exterior of all buildings
- the condition of all storage facilities
- the nature and condition of archives in all media (including digital holdings)
- the existence and location of vital records

- the extent and effectiveness of security systems and procedures
- the type of potential environmental or other threats and the risks of damage
- the existence and nature of emergency response procedures
- the existence and scope of locally available preservation services and support systems.

The importance of identifying vital records

The process of review should include the particularly important task of identifying vital records. Vital records (also referred to as essential records) are those records needed by the institution to support its own recovery after a disaster or emergency. Other vital records may also be needed to help the organization protect its assets and protect employees, volunteers or the public. (This use of the term 'vital' is different from the sense of a vital record as a document of a significant life event, such as birth, marriage or death.)

The vital records of an archival institution might include its accession records, which identify everything in the institution's custody or under its control. Other vital records might be staff and volunteer contact information, needed to locate everyone in an emergency and ensure they are safe; and reference room or building entry registers, which can identify anyone in the facility at a particular time, so everyone can be located and protected in an emergency. Other vital records might include building leases, essential service contracts or other documents that prove the institution's rights and responsibilities. Once these vital records are identified, the archivist needs to develop mechanisms for protecting them and build that guidance into her institution's emergency plan, discussed later, so action can be taken to protect and access the records in an emergency.

Drafting a preservation policy

A preservation policy articulates the institution's goals and priorities specifically for preservation. It is important to develop the preservation policy in keeping with the goals and strategies established in the institution's core archival policy. All decisions about archival management, from preservation to acquisition to reference, need to work coherently to achieve the institution's larger vision, mission and mandate.

Figure 9.1 on the next page shows a sample preservation policy, which outlines the priorities of the fictitious Wickham County Archives, an institution that maintains its collection in a relatively stable physical environment and is responsible for preserving not only traditional paper-based archival materials but also a small but growing collection of digital archives and a collection of medieval and early modern documents in vellum and parchment. The institution also acquires modern government archives and private papers in all media.

Introduction

The Wickham County Archives holds more than 10 million discrete items, documenting all aspects of life in Wickham County from the 12th century to the present day. This preservation policy establishes the management framework for preserving these archives in the best possible physical condition so that they may survive for as long as possible and remain usable for both their evidential and informational value.

Preservation principles

The core principles of preservation management for the Wickham County Archives are outlined below:

- Archives will be preserved in their original format, with their historical, textual, visual and physical nature protected, for as long as possible, with a view to preservation in perpetuity.
- Preventative measures will be employed as a priority to protect and preserve all collections and individual items as effectively as possible.
- Active and remedial conservation treatments will be used when there is a clearly identified need but in most cases will be restricted to the minimum treatment required to stabilize an item or a collection and allow for use or reproduction.
- Original material will be made available for use whenever possible, but surrogate copies may be substituted if original materials are badly damaged or fragile, in order to protect those originals from further deterioration.
- All archival items will be managed with the highest standards of professional care by archivists and conservators.

Treatment principles

Actual conservation or restoration treatments are only carried out if they are deemed essential to the preservation of the original item and if other alternatives such as reproduction or digitization are not appropriate. When performed, treatments will be carried out in accordance with the following general principles of archive preservation and conservation:

- All treatments will preserve the integrity of the original document.
- Only the minimum treatment necessary to stabilize an item will be undertaken in the first instance.
- All treatments will be fully documented.
- Any new materials added during any treatment will be removable, so that changes are not permanent.
- No action will be taken that prevents further examination or other treatments in future.

Figure 9.1 *Wickham County Archives preservation policy*

Preservation functions
To support the goals of this preservation policy, the Wickham County Archives commits to the following specific duties:

- The Archives will regularly and systematically assess the condition of the institution's facilities, holdings, policies and procedures and will upgrade or amend conditions as required to ensure the appropriate care of archival holdings in all media.
- The Archives will provide a safe and secure environment for the storage and use of all holdings by monitoring, recording and maintaining standards for temperature, relative humidity, lighting and air quality control.
- The Archives will protect archival holdings from damage caused by pests, fire, flood, vandalism, theft and poor handling.
- The Archives will ensure staff members are trained in appropriate preservation techniques and methods in order to support their responsibility for the care and management of archives.
- The Archives will dedicate resources to projects that help extend the life span of archives and enhance access to the collections, including reformatting, reproduction and individual treatments as appropriate.
- The Archives will commit ongoing resources to the safe management and protection of all its digital archival holdings, whether received from private donors or from government agencies in Wickham County.
- The Archives will review this policy regularly and will update it as required.

Associated materials
- Wickham County Archives Acquisitions Policy, 2012
- Wickham County Archives Processing Procedures, 2012
- Wickham County Digital Archives Accessioning and Processing Procedures, 2014
- Wickham County Archives Reference Policy, 2014

Approved by
Chester Edmonds, Wickham County Clerk, 9 June 2015.

Review date
This document will be reviewed and revised as required on or before 31 December 2020.

Figure 9.1 *Continued*

Developing a preservation management plan

Once a preservation assessment is completed and a policy developed, specific priorities for action can be identified and formalized in a preservation management plan. A preservation plan helps focus the institution's energies and resources and can be a useful tool to demonstrate to the institution's sponsors – the resource allocators – that the archival operation is moving ahead in a deliberate and well thought-out manner. Without such a plan, senior management may ask why the institution should provide funds for, say, archival storage containers or why the repository needs new fire suppression systems. Being able to justify such expenditures, and ensure they are in fact the best use of funds, helps the archival institution carry out its mandated responsibilities effectively and strategically.

Immediate priorities will depend on the results of the preservation survey, but it is normal to carry out seven different subsequent actions in the order shown below:

1 Establish a regular environmental monitoring programme.
2 Implement and maintain stable environmental controls.
3 Develop and maintain an emergency response plan.
4 Identify and protect vital records (those records the institution must have easy access to in an emergency).
5 Store archival materials according to the requirements of their particular medium.
6 Maintain a regular and thorough housekeeping programme.
7 Identify and treat high-risk materials.

Developing an emergency response plan

The emergency response plan, identified as the third priority in the list above, is sometimes also referred to as a disaster recovery plan or a business continuity plan. An emergency response plan identifies potential emergencies and categorizes their potential danger to the institution and its holdings. The plan also outlines the procedures to follow during and after an emergency to protect people and holdings, restore order and salvage damaged materials.

An emergency is defined as any unexpected occurrence requiring immediate action. Losing electrical power in an archival building is an emergency, especially when staff members are in the middle of updating databases or a large collection of irreplaceable photographs are stored in cold storage freezers. But an emergency does not have to be a disaster. A disaster is an unexpected occurrence with seriously destructive consequences. A power loss turns an emergency into a disaster when the institution does not have a process for backing up databases or keeping freezers running until the main power supply is restored.

A comprehensive emergency response plan addresses mechanisms for protecting both physical and digital archives. It normally includes the following information:

- detailed evacuation procedures, including information about emergency meeting points as well as maps and diagrams
- floor plans for the building, identifying the locations of power and water

supplies, drains, emergency exits and other critical areas

- full contact information for all staff, with a separate section for those staff members who may need to be involved in emergency response, with a description of their roles and responsibilities
- contact information for any organizations or suppliers who have agreed to provide emergency support, such as companies that provide salvage services
- the identification and location of vital records, or particularly valuable or fragile items or materials, which need to be prioritized in an emergency
- a list of emergency equipment and materials held in the institution, with their locations clearly marked
- instructions about how to restore the contents of digital collections from back-up copies
- the names and contact details of experts who can help restore or protect electronic data sources in an emergency
- up-to-date details about the hardware and software used to create, store and manage electronic records and data, so the institution can act immediately to replace or repair damaged equipment or software
- copies of or access to all critical documentation related to electronic information systems or other primary management tools, such as operating manuals or procedures documents.

The archival institution might also decide to maintain insurance to cover losses in the event of an emergency. While insurance will not cover the replacement of archival materials – they are irreplaceable, after all – insurance can reimburse for the loss of equipment or supplies. The policy should cover the institution against theft, fire, water damage and other hazards, and it should provide adequate coverage for the costs associated with obtaining emergency storage or restoration services, including digital restoration. The institution should have liability insurance, in the event that anyone, staff, visitor or researcher, is injured on the premises.

———————————

Preservation is essential to ensuring that archives are protected as safely as possible for as long as possible. But, ultimately, what those archives *are* is a decision made by the archivist, in keeping with the goals and aspirations of the archival institution. The next chapter considers issues associated with acquiring and appraising archival materials. Where do they come from? How do they go from the creator's office to the archives' storage bay? How does the archivist decide what is or is not worth keeping?

Notes

1 There is not enough room in this book to address microfilm and other reprography practices in detail; given the decreasing prominence of film or paper-based reproduction, in favour of digital, readers are directed to the general preservation resources identified at the end of the book, which provide general insights and identify further reading.

2 Critical to digital preservation is ensuring the authenticity of the digital bits and bytes being brought into the digital repository. Data need to be validated using checksums, which is a type of algorithm used to confirm that every bit of data arrives intact once the digital object is moved from one storage device to another. Archivists are also exploring the use of different technologies to ensure accuracy and improve efficiency when receiving digital content. Blockchain technologies are the latest development in this regard. These highly technical topics are well outside the scope of this book; useful introductory resources are cited at the end of the book.

10

Acquiring archives

One cannot collect all the beautiful shells on the beach; one can collect only a few, and they are more beautiful if they are few.

Anne Morrow Lindbergh (1906–2001) *Gift from the Sea*, 1955

How does an archivist decide which archives to acquire? How does she decide which specific items within a particular acquisition should be kept? Whatever an archivist decides to keep becomes valuable in large part because it has been kept. And whatever is not kept is, in the normal course of events, gone forever. Appraisal decisions can be daunting, to say the very least.

This is one reason appraisal is considered the most important and the most difficult aspect of archival work. If every record were valuable, and if every archivist had all the money and space in the world, there would, in theory, be no need for appraisal. The archivist could pack up all the documents in her care, put them in acid-free boxes or store them on a stack of computer hard drives and tell researchers to come and get them. Many archivists and digital experts are arguing this very idea, suggesting that with the unlimited capacity of cloud computing systems and the tremendous potential for research into 'big data', keeping more – in theory, keeping all – is easier and potentially more fruitful than ever before.[1]

Others, and I count myself among them, prefer to think about Anne Lindbergh's seashells. What is the point in keeping everything? What is the point in trying? If archivists and society decide just to keep everything, how can we actually know which bit of information is core evidence and which is just dross that clutters our hard drives and our minds?

In order to cope with the challenge of deciding what to keep and what to reject, archivists have invented (and rejected and redefined and reinvented) a range of theories and principles surrounding the appraisal and acquisition of archival materials. Some of these approaches are highly objective, others exceedingly subjective.

As suggested in Part I of this book, archivists centuries ago did not even consider the idea that they might keep only some of the archives offered to them. Everything from 13th- and 14th-century scrolls, 16th-century government records, handwritten pioneer diaries to parchment treaties were deemed worthy of preservation. The archivist of the 18th or 17th centuries rarely identified one codex or treaty as having more or less value than another. Both would be kept. As a result of the increase in literacy, burgeoning paper boom, growth in documentation and parallel expansion in the number and nature of archival institutions, the archivist of today has to make a choice about what to acquire, and how much of that acquisition to keep.

This chapter looks at issues associated with two stages of appraisal: deciding broadly which groups of archives should be acquired to fulfil the institution's mandate, and deciding which materials within a specific acquisition are actually worth keeping. The archivist needs to think about the variety of appraisal criteria that might be applied at both stages. The processes by which archives may be acquired are also discussed here, along with the legal and administrative actions involved with documenting the transfer of custody or control from the creator to the archivist. The chapter ends with a brief look at the difficult question of monetary appraisal.

Appraisal for acquisition

Appraisal for acquisition involves identifying appropriate collections of archival material to add to the holdings of the archival institution. No matter how 'valuable' a body of archives may seem, if the materials do not fit in with the mandate and scope of the institution, then the archivist who acquires them is doing a disservice not only to the creator of the records but also to potential users and the archives themselves. Researchers will not look for the archives of a sports star in an institution devoted to the history of architecture. Citizens of a city should not find their local government's records in a museum in another country. Taxpayers may object to public expenditures to purchase a manuscript of a Mozart symphony if their local, publicly funded library has insufficient budget to maintain regular reference services. The collections of an archival institution should make sense. 'Making sense' requires – what else in a heavily policy-driven discipline? – developing a firm policy and defining a strategic plan for action.

Defining an acquisitions policy

The logic behind an institution's acquisition focus should be articulated in an acquisitions policy. Building on the core archives policy examined in Chapter 8, an acquisitions policy defines the scope of collecting. What will the archival agency acquire and what will it exclude from its holdings? Why?

Often an archival institution's primary responsibility is to manage its own sponsor records and archives. The fictitious Cascadia University introduced earlier might be responsible for University records, but it might also acquire non-institutional archives directly related to the University, such as the records of alumni, faculty, staff, associations, clubs or groups. The institution might also collect archives related to the research priorities of the university: fishing or forestry, for example. The University needs to be sure it can support any acquisition path chosen, with resources, space, staff time and tech-nologies. Any acquisition is a commitment that will, ideally, be honoured *ad infinitum*.

When developing an acquisitions policy, the archivist needs to consider the following:

1   What related activities are under way in the same jurisdiction or wider region? Are other archival institutions interested in similar records, such as sports archives, women's studies archives or literary papers? The local historical society archives may want to preserve archives related to Polish immigrants in the area, but the Polish Community Centre may already be acquiring similar materials. To prevent competition, one or the other agency may need to step aside, or they may choose to work co-operatively. The archivist needs the Wisdom of Solomon to prevent the archives from being lost or damaged through a battle of wills.

2   How will the institution receive archival materials? Will it accept loans? Will it purchase materials? Will it receive transfers of digital archives directly from departments within the sponsor agency? A clear understanding of the scope and boundaries of acquisition will ensure the archivist does not end up making ad hoc decisions.

3   How will the institution fund not only acquisition but also preservation and storage? What is the cost of keeping those archives as permanent holdings? The archivist needs to be accountable not just for acquiring archives but for supporting ongoing care.

4   Will the archivist have sole authority to negotiate and accept acquisitions or transfers, or will an advisory board or other stakeholders play a role? If more than one person is making acquisition decisions, it can be very difficult to ensure efforts are co-ordinated. One party may feel compelled

to 'do a favour' by accepting one acquisition, and then the next thing the archivist knows, a dozen people are hoping for the same favour.

5 How will the institution administer restricted or confidential material? Breaching privacy and access laws or policies is a serious infraction. For instance, in some government institutions, volunteers are welcome supporters, but they are not allowed to work with restricted archives. Such conditions may be required by law, but they may limit the scope of volunteer service, which changes the archivist's calculations around how long it will take to process acquisitions and make them available.

The imaginary Cascadia University has brought all its archival services together under one agency, Cascadia University Archives and Special Collections, which manages official University archives and also collects archival materials and other resources related to areas of scholarly focus within the University, including fisheries, forestry, mining and the development of railways in western Canada. The sample acquisitions policy shown in Figure 10.1 sets out the collecting focus of this hybrid institution.

Introduction
Cascadia University Archives and Special Collections, established in 1955 and administered as a department of Cascadia University Library, houses a significant collection of rare books and archival materials that support research by scholars, students and the general public within the University, from the region and around the world.

Role of Cascadia University Archives and Special Collections
Cascadia University Archives and Special Collections is responsible for the selection, acquisition, care, preservation, storage, exhibition and use of published and unpublished materials designed as rare or special, and also for the acquisition of archives created by and specifically related to the University and its students, alumni and surrounding community.
   Cascadia University Archives and Special Collections collects official University archives; archives of associations, groups, faculty members, researchers or others with a relationship to Cascadia University; archival and historical materials that by their contents and nature provide special insight into topics relevant to the research interests included in the institution's acquisition mandate; and rare books relevant to the acquisition mandate of the institution.

Acquisition priorities for research collections
When acquiring archival and manuscript materials, or rare books, associated with research areas beyond the life and activities of Cascadia University itself, Cascadia University Archives and Special Collections prioritizes the collection of materials related to fisheries, forestry, mining and the development of railways (primarily but not exclusively related to the west coast of Canada both before and after Confederation).

Figure 10.1 *Cascadia University Archives and Special Collections acquisitions policy*

The archival collection is founded on two significant archival acquisitions: the personal and research papers and personal library of Dr Cedric Arthur Galloway (1869–1953) and the research collection of Robert Allison (1901–93). Dr Galloway, a professor of history at Cascadia University from 1907 to his retirement in 1946, developed a vast collection of published and unpublished resources related to the history of the Pacific fishing industry. Mr Allison actively collected archival and reference materials related to the development of railways across the country. The Special Collections Department has expanded on these original donations and developed additional acquisition areas, as described below.

West coast fisheries

The research collection related to fishing focuses on the development of the Pacific fisheries industry, on the west coast of Canada and the USA. Included in the research focus are publications and archives related to First Nations fisheries; the commercial fishing industry from the 1800s to the present day; the lives of immigrant populations in the fishing industry, including the Japanese, Chinese and Europeans; the development of canneries along the Pacific coast; fishing boats and equipment; and the state of fishing and canning in the 20th and 21st centuries.

Forestry

The research collection related to forestry focuses primarily on the softwood forest industry, as the primary focus of forest business in western Canada, including both coastal and interior logging. The archives and rare books collected relate to logging companies and individual loggers; sawmills; environmental management of forest areas to support sustainability; land management issues related to forestry and other activities; community involvement in the forest industry; logging equipment and the lives of loggers and sawyers; and the marketing, sale and use of timber products within and outside of Canada.

Mining

The research collection related to mining focuses on the history and development of the mining industry across western Canada. Activities documented include the mining of oil, natural gas, copper, coal, gold, zinc, molybdenum, silver, lead and other minerals. Materials, which relate mining from pre-historic times to the present, document such activities as exploration and prospecting; the development and management of mines; the reclamation and reuse of lands; processing and refining of minerals; marketing and sale of mineral products; and equipment and machinery used for mining purposes.

The development of railways

The research collection related to the development of railways focuses on the history of railways across Canada. Included in the collection are archives and rare books related to the history and development of railways in Canada, including the Canadian Pacific Railway, the Canadian National Railway and other national, regional and local rail projects. Archives relate to the history and development of rail services; the impact of rail services on the economic, cultural and social life of the country; rail equipment and supplies including rolling stock and engines; ancillary services such as the development of hotels; the relationship between rail services and tourism; and the restructuring of rail services across the country in the 20th and 21st centuries.

Figure 10.1 *Continued*

Reference collection
Cascadia University Archives and Special Collections also maintains a more general reference collection in support of academic research, including bibliographies and other reference materials in support of the University's research interests intended to facilitate academic and student studies throughout the University.

Limitation of scope
When considering possible acquisitions, Cascadia University Archives and Special Collections will take into consideration the following issues:

- the authorized mandates of other archival institutions, in order to avoid conflict of interest or overlap in acquisitions
- the availability of appropriate storage facilities and the resources required to make the material available for research purposes within a reasonable time after acquisition
- the physical condition of the materials and any costs associated with ensuring their physical stability and security over time
- the nature and extent of any conditions on access to or use of the archives, including access, privacy and copyright restrictions
- the relationship of potential acquisitions to existing holdings and the benefits of or drawbacks to investing the resources and time required to acquire, preserve and make available the materials in question.

Cascadia University Archives and Special Collections will review its acquisition strategies annually and revise its services as required to make most effective use of all resources available.

Approved by
Clifford Leach, Chief University Librarian, 18 October 2015.

Review date
This acquisitions policy will be reviewed and revised as required on or before 31 December 2020.

Figure 10.1 *Continued*

Acquisition planning

As an acquisitions policy is developed, the archivist must keep thinking about how the goals and priorities outlined in the policy will be achieved. A clear acquisition plan helps ensure that the institution stays on track and that its efforts do not overlap with the work of other relevant institutions. An acquisition plan should set out a clear, well focused and constructive approach to building collections.

Sometimes an area of potential interest is not yet represented in archival holdings. For instance, a local archives based in a community with a growing ethnic population may find that its existing collections do not represent the story of that ethnic minority. By actively seeking out and acquiring relevant archives from that community, the archivist may help the society move away from one vision (a society with a marginalized sub-group) to another (a society with several groups in greater balance). Such a shift may be seen as political, but it may also be seen as a forward-thinking effort to reflect the reality of the community within the archival collection, by filling gaps or weaknesses in the existing holdings.

Any effort to identify collecting areas should be done co-operatively. Acquisition strategies can be developed by bringing together representatives of institutions in a region or country, or institutions with academic or research mandates, to devise a collaborative approach. The members of the group can identify spheres of acquisition activity and 'divide the pie', so that different institutions acquire particular sets of archives without (too much) competition.

Some archivists have extended this concept of strategic planning even further, arguing not only that the archivist should *collect* materials related to a particular topic or issue but also that if records on that topic do not exist, the archivist should actively *create*, or support the creation of, documents to fill the gaps. Activist archival institutions are particularly engaged with this type of interventionist archival service. Many see their role not just as protecting the existing archives of one group but as supporting the creation and care of records to represent the interests of marginalized groups or under-documented activities.

While the principle of co-operation is laudable, the move toward interventionist archival services, whether out of a concern for social justice or any other reason, is fraught with risk. Some detractors present philosophical objections, suggesting that the archivist should be a record *keeper* not a record *maker*. Other critics are more pragmatic, arguing that most archivists simply do not have the time or resources to manage the archives in hand, let alone manufacture new records.

Ultimately, the wise archivist turns back to the core principles of service, as outlined in Chapter 6, taking into account the legal, social and political framework in which her agency is placed. What are the legal requirements of the archivist as a member of her institution? What are her duties as a citizen? If they diverge, how can she find a balance between doing her job and sleeping comfortably at night?

Representative or comprehensive?

Another question to consider is whether the institution's acquisitions will be representative or comprehensive. The institution interested in the archives of forestry may acquire archives representing different aspects of that work:

from forestry companies, environmental groups, individual loggers, forestry consultants and so on. But how many collections from different logging companies in the region need to be acquired before enough is enough? How many are enough to represent a strong and balanced documentary record, and how many are too many for time and space and resources to support? The archivist has to decide if the objective is to provide evidence of every logging company in the region or if the goal is to preserve a strong, but not exhaustive, collection of forestry archives to document this particular part of the community's story.

The archivist also has to consider the politics of saying no. Will a logging company find another home for its archives? Should it preserve the materials as part of its own business? Destroy the archives? When an institution starts to acquire archives in a particular geographic, thematic or other area, a message is sent out to the community that *this subject* is *that institution's* responsibility. The institution needs to decide if it can and should accept that expectation of service years or decades into the future, before it agrees to head down that path.

In the end, if a potential acquisition does not fit with the institution's acquisitions criteria as outlined in its acquisitions policy, the archivist needs to present a very strong argument for accepting the material. Inevitably, there are times when the archivist may agree to take in archives that are seemingly out of scope. Perhaps a potential donor is offering a large donation with great research value, and he also agrees to provide the funds to arrange, describe and preserve the materials. The archives may be about events on the margins of the institution's acquisition mandate, but there may be no other suitable repository for the archives. Maybe the donation presents an opportunity for an overdue course correction in the institution's acquisition focus. In the end, the benefits of acquisition may outweigh the fact that the archivist will have to revise her institution's policy. Still, any time the archivist reaches beyond stated directions, she needs to have a clear and justifiable rationale, or else the archival programme loses coherence.

Acquiring digital archives

In general, the criteria for appraising digital archives are the same as for analogue or paper archives. Do the materials fit within the institution's acquisitions policy? What terms and conditions govern their access and use? Do the materials provide best evidence? Acquisition issues specific to digital archives also need to be considered: does the institution have the capacity to accept and preserve digital objects, which come with such enormous technological requirements for care?

There are four ways in which digital materials may come into archival custody or control:

- as a formal, planned process of transfer from a creating agency, with all metadata intact
- through transfer from a creating agency but with custody elsewhere
- as a deposit into storage systems directly managed by record creators
- as part of a donation or after-the-fact rescue attempt.

Each presents its own challenges, which are discussed below.

Formal, planned transfers from a creating agency

Digital archives may come as a formal, planned process of transfer from a creating agency to the archival institution, with all the metadata intact. If the archivist can plan for the receipt of digital archives from her sponsor agency, she can establish processes for ensuring they are managed effectively as evidence, with no loss of context, content or structure. She still needs to invest in all the technologies required to develop a trusted digital repository to preserve those materials safely and provide reference access to the information in them.

Transfer from creating agency to archival control, but with custody elsewhere

Control of digital archives may be transferred from a creating agency to the archival institution, but actual custody may be somewhere else: with the originating office, in a cloud computing environment or in a shared digital repository. In this case, the archival institution is responsible for preserving materials and supporting access, but the digital objects and the technology needed to manage them are kept in another location. This is the approach taken with digital collaboration projects, and it is also a feature of commercial online storage systems. The savings in equipment and technology costs need to be weighed against the risks associated with not actually having the materials themselves in hand. There is also a greater risk, especially when relying on commercial services, that the 'trusted' requirement in the 'trusted digital repository' does not meet best practice standards.

Deposits into storage systems

Digital archives may be deposited into storage systems (whether in archival custody or control) directly managed by records creators. This approach is common when organizations establish electronic document or records management systems for staff, allowing employees to 'declare' something as an official record and add it to a digital storage system. The archivist responsible for ensuring archival materials in this system are protected may decide to set up mechanisms for identifying records with archival value and 'transferring' them to safe storage sooner or later. The transfer could involve actually moving files from one storage location to another, or 'locking down' a record to prevent further changes, so that it retains its value as evidence. Both scenarios require that the archivist play a central record-keeping role, building policies, procedures and technologies associated with accountable records care into the system.

Donations or after-the-fact rescue attempts
Digital archives may arrive as part of a donation or through an after-the-fact rescue attempt. For instance, the archivist may be handed a USB stick from a local resident, who says, 'This is everything copied off Uncle Frank's computer, and by the way he was an avid photographer who took thousands of digital pictures of trips to Iceland and Costa Rica and other wonderful places. Good luck.' The archivist is faced with opening every file on that USB stick before she can decide which materials are worth keeping. What are the costs of such after-the-fact donations, and will the resulting growth in the archival collection be worth the effort?

Appraisal for selection

Having constructed an archival acquisitions policy, established acquisition priorities (ideally in collaboration with allied institutions) and formalized decisions in an acquisition plan, the archivist is then equipped with objective measures for deciding whether any particular donation fits within her institution's collecting scope. Her next challenge, when archives come through the door, is to decide which materials within the new acquisition are actually worth keeping. This process is known as appraisal for selection.

No matter how relevant the topic or scope of the acquisition, not every piece of paper in the box or every digital document on the CD will be worth keeping. A potential acquisition of archives from a fish packing plant may include digital copies of original audited financial statements and annual reports, along with 20 boxes of paper receipts for the sale of fish products over 20 years. The financial statements and annual reports provide valuable summary information about the operations of the plant. The receipts show individual sales, and the total figures should have been summarized in the financial statements and reports.

Despite the remote possibility that a researcher might someday be interested in the details of individual fish sales, the archivist has to take a risk-based approach. What is the cost of keeping all the receipts as well as the financial statements and reports? Is the effort worth the time and resources? The summary financial records carry greater evidential value and require considerably less space and fewer resources to preserve than the receipts. Usually the decision is clear: keep the reports; destroy the receipts.

On the other hand, if only *one* receipt was left from the fish packing plant, and no reports exist, the archivist would likely keep that lone document. It may be the only evidence, however meagre, of the plant's financial transactions. It may also provide unique evidence of the cost of fish a century ago, or it may be a rare example of a type of financial record never seen before.

The archivist needs to balance potential research interests and evidential value with time, resources and space. But she also needs to remember, as discussed in Chapter 2, that sometimes an item may be worth keeping even if it does not provide the best evidence. A Brazilian land grant from the 1800s or a 16th-century ledger showing household accounts in rural Belgium may be as valuable for their rarity as for their content. The only manuscript copy of the 11th-century saga *Beowulf* is an irreplaceable treasure, in large part because it has survived for several centuries.

Criteria for selecting archives
So what criteria can the archivist use as a basis for selecting archives for permanent preservation? No amount of archival theory can provide a definitive answer: there is no scientific formula or master checklist. But some common appraisal guidelines can help the archivist consider the questions to ask.

Focus on evidence
As emphasized throughout this book, the first value of archives is as evidence, particularly in these days when the absence or mismanagement of documentary evidence is bringing governments and organizations into disarray and disrepute. If materials contain core evidence of actions, transactions or decisions, their archival value is greater than if they offer nothing more than discrete bits of information. The archivist has to sort the

evidential wheat from the informational chaff. She can start by asking herself if the archives under consideration were originally created and used for the following purposes. If the answer is yes to these questions, then these records usually provide 'best evidence':

- Were the records used to help the creator make, confirm or remember decisions, particularly about policies, operations or significant actions?
- Were the records used to help the individual or agency remain accountable to himself or itself and to others?
- Were the records used to identify or confirm the individual's or organization's legal, financial or other obligations?
- Were the records used to identify or support the rights and obligations of others who may be involved with or affected by the work of the individual or organization, such as business partners, clients or the public?

Functional appraisal

When the archivist works closely with the creators of records, perhaps in the post-custodial records continuum favoured by many, determining evidential value is not about assessing actual archives in hand but identifying important functions and activities and then targeting relevant records for preservation. Functional appraisal or macro-appraisal (a concept first articulated by the Canadian archivist Terry Cook, as introduced in Chapter 3) focuses on an analysis of the functions and activities performed within an organization, not on the content of extant archives, with the goal of deciding which records should be kept on the basis of which functions are more or less significant.

Following the macro-appraisal approach, the archivist would not sift through all the archives of a particular agency to find those materials that best reflect past actions. Instead, she would work with the agency to identify core functions and activities, particularly those that support the agency's central responsibilities, and together they would identify the documentary materials that ought to be kept to provide best evidence of those functions and activities.

As already discussed, functional or macro-appraisal encourages (if not actually demands) that the archivist play an active role in record keeping, not just in archives management. Functional appraisal would ideally take place as part of the process of classifying and scheduling records in the office, so that the need for valuable evidence is identified even before actual records are created. Then, the records can be created and managed securely, regardless of whether they are in paper or digital form, and brought into archival custody or control at an appropriate time with their evidential value protected. (However, as argued in Chapter 3, this approach is built on the premise that creating agencies will document their activities accurately and fully, a presumption not always borne out by reality.)

Other appraisal criteria

While evidential value is a primary concern, archives can be used for many other reasons, as discussed in Chapter 4. Thus the archivist also needs to consider if archives provide informational, aesthetic or symbolic value. Does their preservation help foster community or individual identity or support collective or personal memory? Archives may not provide best evidence, but they might shed light on aspects of life and work that give the community a richer image of itself. A certificate of achievement may provide evidence that Ashley Fonseka received top marks in speech and debate in university. The framed document may also be beautifully illustrated, a testament to the work of an unknown artist. An author's first royalty cheque might have no value as financial evidence, but it is a powerful symbol of a literary milestone. If the archivist considers not only pure evidential value but also the wider worth of archives in her society, she will likely succeed in keeping wheat, not chaff.

Selecting digital archives

The biggest challenge with appraising digital archives for selection is that, in the absence of a formal record-keeping process, the archivist must review every item, sometimes painstakingly, to assess value. Software tools and technologies can help: computer algorithms can be employed to search for duplicate documents or to locate keywords that identify high-value records. But after-the-fact digital appraisal still demands infinitely more time and effort than defining minimum expectations for records preservation and receiving specific materials as a result.

The archivist who wants to expand her institution into the digital age – and there is no going back on that road; every institution operating today needs to deal with the consequences of computers – needs to equip her institution, and herself, with the technology, skills and knowledge required to do the job well. The most important question the archivist has to ask, and be able to answer to her and her institution's satisfaction, is whether the institution can afford to acquire, preserve and make available digital materials, knowing they will receive the best possible care.

Going down the digital road requires starting with a solid and sustainable digital records management strategy; the journey must be carefully planned. A box of paper archives will likely survive a century, even sitting in a broom closet. A USB stick of unidentified digital documents should not be accepted today in the hope that the archivist will find time to figure out what to do with it a month or a year from now. The chances of success are too slim.

Sampling, weeding and culling

The archivist might consider sampling, weeding and culling when faced with large volumes of archives, such as individual case files. Case files are digital or paper files related to particular interactions between individuals and agencies. Examples include military service records, student files, employee files or client records.

Weeding and culling can be a relatively straightforward, if time consuming, process. With paper files, the process involves sorting through physical files and taking out duplicate records or obsolete documents. In the digital environment, the process can involve searching for documents with a particular title or keyword, such as 'draft', or using algorithms to search for duplicates, and then deleting them. With paper, the process is intensive but the results fairly reliable: if two identical copies are found, the archivist can destroy one knowing the other remains. In the digital process, the archivist has to know that every draft was a draft and not a final version that was never properly renamed; the risk of losing a valuable document is quite high.

Sampling, which aims to identify and retain a representative portion of a group of case files rather than keep every file, is more complicated. Sampling requires that the archivist formulate a structured approach to deciding which portion of the archives to keep, based on scientific or random criteria. Sometimes an entire series of case files might be digitized but only some files might be kept in paper form. Or the archivist may judge that not all the case files need to be kept as evidence, whatever medium, so she establishes a process for keeping only a representative sample.

Before deciding to sample archives (keeping some and destroying others) the archivist has to ensure the records as a whole contain no enduring evidential value. A complete set of pension case files might not need to be kept permanently if no one represented in the pension files has been alive for several decades. But a complete set of land registry case files would likely have permanent value: the history of ownership of a piece of land can serve as essential legal evidence, even decades or centuries after the first land title record was put in the file.

Sampling for paper and analogue archives

There are two approaches to sampling for paper and analogue archives: statistical sampling (which can be either random or systematic) and targeted sampling. Both approaches have benefits and drawbacks.

Statistical sampling

Random statistical sampling involves selecting files based on a random numbering table: files numbered 1, 3, 35, 57, 99 and so on would be kept. In systematic sampling, the archivist might keep every tenth file, such as every file created in 1932, 1942, 1952 and so on, or every file for people whose last names end in R or T. In order to select files, they need to be numbered or named in the first place, which can be an onerous job.

Systematic statistical sampling is easier than random sampling to carry out, but it can result in a less arbitrary sample. If the archivist decides to keep only files for people whose names start with a particular letter, has she taken into account the naming conventions in her society? Choosing 'Mc' and 'Mac' to sample case files in Scotland may not reduce the volume of archives noticeably. Choosing 'Q' or 'Z' may leave the archivist with very few files. Therefore, the criteria for systematic sampling must be carefully considered against the purpose of the records and the nature of the community in which they were created and used.

The archivist also has to take into account historical events over time. Say she wants to sample a sample of 150 years' worth of individual student records at an American community college. She needs to take into account the effect the Depression and Second World War might have had on enrolment. Sampling specific years, even though the dates were arbitrarily chosen, might leave a misleading impression of the number and nature of students over time.

Targeted sampling

Targeted sampling is not designed to capture a representative sample of archives. Some people argue it is not really sampling at all. Targeted sampling preserves archives that contain evidence or information the archivist believes merit retention, irrespective of other appraisal decisions. For instance, the archivist might retain all files related to police incidents involving firearms while destroying other incident files. Or she might keep all the personnel records for management staff but none for support staff. Archivists sometimes also look for what are called 'fat files': large or voluminous files that, it is assumed by their size, are likely to be more complex and thus more informative.

Targeted sampling leaves a highly selective body of materials. Therefore the archivist has an even greater responsibility to explain in detail the criteria used. Otherwise, researchers may end up thinking that all police incidents involved firearms or that an organization did not have any support staff at all.

Digital data and 'big data'

Sampling digital archives is such a new concept that little has yet been written on the topic. Indeed, as already suggested, the question is reversed. Rather than focusing on whether to sample a selection of electronic files to reduce the bulk of holdings, the archivist has to decide whether it is better to keep everything, in the quest for sources of 'big data' analysis.

The research benefits of large data sets are important, but the challenge of storing, preserving and protecting huge aggregations of digital evidence can be significant. And the responsibility to protect the privacy of individuals is only harder when preserving large data sets of personal information, such as found in medical or financial records. Big data can be a boon to research, but such large volumes of digital archives still need to be preserved and managed effectively.

Appraisal and the cost of ownership

An archival institution is not a business, and decisions should not be driven by an economic bottom line. But even the archivist has to put on an accountant's hat periodically and step back to consider the very real costs associated with collecting and preserving archives. A repository's holdings inevitably continue to grow, and a strategically minded archivist has to develop a tough shell, acknowledging both the benefits and the costs of archival acquisition, preservation and access.

The archivist needs to assess the 'total cost of ownership', a term first used in the financial sector and later by software developers to assess the costs and benefits of technology upgrades. What are the real hard and soft costs of owning archives in perpetuity? The archivist assessing the total cost of ownership of a potential acquisition should ask the following sort of questions:

- If materials are going to be purchased, what is the total cost of purchase, including any taxes, legal fees or administrative costs?

- What are the costs of boxing, moving, receiving and storing the materials until they can be processed?
- What are the costs of arranging, describing, processing and conserving, and housing materials in acid-free folders, boxes and other containers?
- Will the archives need to acquire more shelving space or storage cabinets and what will that equipment cost?
- How long can the archives be kept in storage containers, whether acid free or not, before they need to be moved to new folders or boxes? What would be the total costs of changing the storage containers periodically over the next ten, 20 or 50 years?
- What are the costs of acquiring *and maintaining* the digital technologies needed to open, appraise, preserve and provide continued access to digital holdings?
- What are the indirect costs of storing the materials, such as heat or electricity, floor space, technological support, security systems or staff time? Will those costs increase dramatically with a particular new acquisition?

After assessing costs, the archivist can then calculate benefits. The donor might be willing to provide some resources to help process the collection. The materials might be a source of income through permission fees, reproduction rights or other revenue-generating activities. Are those anticipated revenues reliable, and would they be a one-time benefit or an ongoing income stream? Acquiring the collection might increase the institution's profile, perhaps encouraging other donations, monetary and otherwise; that benefit may warrant the expenditures of time and resources.

After doing the maths and considering all the benefits and drawbacks to acquisition, the archivist can make a much more informed decision. In the end, she needs to balance costs with the wider benefits to society. Will adding the collection to the archives' holdings strengthen the community – by enhancing its sense of itself, improving the scope of its documentary heritage or preserving touchstones of identity – such that, in the end, the financial cost of ownership is offset by the value of the archives as tools for accountability, identity and memory?

Other appraisal considerations

The archivist needs to consider other criteria as well, particularly when appraising non-sponsor archives. Many of the issues raised here have already been introduced in earlier chapters. Some involve archival theory and principles; others are highly practical.

Physical condition

The physical condition of the acquisition can affect the cost of ownership. Are materials so poorly damaged that restoration may not return them to a reasonable state? Or are the items so historically significant that no cost is too high? A tattered copy of a municipal newspaper from 1939 may not be worth keeping, let alone treating, even if it does commemorate a visit by the King of Norway. The original treaty between two aboriginal groups may be precious beyond belief, and no expense should be spared to protect it.

Volume

Can the archival institution manage the volume of archives in the acquisition? While the solution to a space crisis is not simply to reject all donations larger than four boxes or 100 GB of data, the archivist needs to assess current and future capacity for preservation, storage and reference before committing to an unexpectedly large and complex acquisition.

Medium

Archivists argue that a record is a record is a record, and that the medium on which the content is held is not relevant to the value of that record as evidence or information. From a preservation perspective, however, the media used to create records can significantly affect the time and resources needed to manage them, especially for digital archives, as discussed already. The archivist must not forget the practical realities of preserving archives in different media when considering new acquisitions.

Uniqueness

All archival materials are unique in their context. A duplicate item may be 'archival' in the sense that it provides evidence because of its particular location within a larger body of archives, such as the different copies of meeting minutes considered in Chapter 1. And a published item may be unique within its context, as shown in the example in Chapter 2 of Ashmole's book with Newton's handwriting. But an entire series of Frank Sinatra's records in the collection of a music lover, while valuable in many other ways, especially to members of Frank Sinatra's fan clubs, may not be unique. It would be a rare archival institution indeed – aside from the Sinatra fan club or the institution housing Frank Sinatra's own papers – that could justify their preservation.

Accessibility

The archivist needs to determine if there are any legal restrictions on access to materials within a potential donation and then decide if those restrictions will place an excessive burden on the institution or hamper access to an unacceptable degree. It may be reasonable for the donor and archivist to agree to close all personal correspondence for 50 years. It is not appropriate for the donor to demand that people of a particular gender, sexual orientation or colour be prevented from using archives.

Potential use

It is impossible to predict how archives will be used. But sometimes, perhaps foolishly, archivists try. While it is dangerous to overemphasize the immediate research value of archives, it is equally risky to choose not to keep archives because no one can see a possible use for them today or next week. Decisions about use should be linked to questions of preservation and cost, not to the perceived research value of a body of archives today. Who would have thought 50 years ago that ships' logs or farmers' crop charts would be used to track weather patterns and climate change today? The lure of big data is a timely example of the value of keeping more, not less.

Acquisition and personal bias

As discussed in Chapter 6, the archivist has to guard against letting personal preferences interfere with her duties, including (especially?) with acquisition. The archives of poets may be more enticing to one archivist, and the archives of scientists more compelling to another. To avoid bias, the archivist must always return to the institution's acquisitions policy as an objective and formal guide. But bias can creep into institutional policies too; appraisal has always been influenced by political and social conditions.

In the 1950s, environmental issues were far removed from the everyday lives of people, governments and corporations. Few governments had separate offices responsible for environmental issues; those agencies that did exist may have been more concerned with managing parks or servicing recreational facilities. Only the smallest quantity of public or private records created in the mid-20th century might overtly relate to environmental management as we define it today. In 2017, the environment is top of mind for many around the world. It is perhaps not surprising to know that archivists today are increasingly focused on preserving evidence of climate change.

But the only constant in life, or in archival service, is change. In her quest to document the story of climate change or political protests or economic inequality in 2017, what topics is the archivist of today *not* considering, some of which might become pivotal issues 50 years from now? Rather than dust off her crystal ball, all the archivist can do is respect her institution's acquisitions policy, work co-operatively with other archival institutions and revisit acquisition strategies regularly, so that the wider archival community moves forward in a strategic and sustained fashion.

Dealing with donors

In theory, the archivist should only acquire material that fits with the criteria in the acquisitions policy, and she should be able to document all acquisitions so that they can be received and managed in an effective, accountable and efficient manner. In reality, the archivist has to deal with the donor who leaves a folder of photographs on the desk when no one is in the reference room, or with the couple who donate one or two items as a test, to see how grateful the archivist is before they bring in more materials. The archivist also has to negotiate with the organization that threatens to destroy records if the archivist does not come and take them away immediately, as well as with the departmental officer who refuses to transfer records at all, even though he is bound to by company policy, because he believes they are 'safer' in his own filing cabinet.

Sometimes, the archivist becomes a combination of psychologist and politician, striving to serve the institution's interests while still keeping on the right side of the community. The biggest political challenge is to avoid making so many 'side deals' with individuals that the institution's policies and procedures no longer apply. At that point, the archivist might have lost so much credibility that she cannot stand firm on any point of policy. The person on the other side of the desk may legitimately ask, 'If it was good enough for Fred, why isn't it good enough for me?'

In the end, any appraisal decision is a judgement call. If the archivist decides that good donor relations outweigh a strict adherence to policy, it is up to her to make the call. And to deal with the consequences.

The process of acquisition

Having considered issues of acquisition and appraisal, the next topic to address is how exactly – administratively and legally – archives move from the creator or donor to the archival institution. The archivist may receive archival materials in four ways: through transfer, donation, loan and purchase. Each method is explained below.

Transfers

Transfers come from within one agency: from a creating office to an archival facility. Transfers can take place as part of a formal records management programme or they can happen periodically or informally, such as when a department needs to make more room in the office. Whenever a transfer takes place, the process should be formalized and the transfer documented, in order to maintain the chain of custody and to identify the specific materials transferred. Because archives are being transferred within one organization, legal ownership does not change; the archival institution is a unit within the larger creating agency. But administrative custody and control will shift from the creating office to the archival institution. This shift in control allows the archivist to carry out appraisal, arrangement, description and access tasks unimpeded. Typically, the transfer process is documented in paper form or in an electronic archival management system, in order to ensure the transfer is formally executed. Even if the actual archives, such as digital records, are stored in another location, the archivist needs to record the transfer of control from creating agency to archival institution. At that point, the creating agency no longer has the authority to decide to destroy or change any of the materials transferred; they now serve as enduring evidence of the organization's activities.

Donations

A donation is typically defined as the permanent deposit of archives from person or group to an archival institution, with legal ownership transferred and no payment provided. If the materials are only to be left in the archives for a certain time, then the transmittal would be considered a loan, discussed below. (Archivists have been known to negotiate 'permanent loans', but these are ungainly and somewhat illogical arrangements, best avoided if possible. The institution should have legal authority for the materials, or else how can it justify the expenditure of time and space on archival care?)

A donation is executed through the completion of a legally binding donor agreement. If any of the conditions in the agreement are violated by either party, the other has every right to seek a legal remedy, so the archivist and the donor must each negotiate the transmittal in good faith, according to core principles, such as the following:

- Both parties must be legally capable of entering into the agreement.
- The agreement must not be contrary to public policy (such as a contract based on fraudulent information or a contract that supports criminal activity).

- The agreement will be considered void if it is based on misinformation or errors that, had they been known, might have prevented one or the other party from agreeing, or if either party has been coerced.
- The major elements of a donor agreement form should include:
  — the names and signatures of the donor (or an authorized agent) and the representative of the archival institution, confirming the transmittal according to the criteria outlined in the agreement
  — the date ownership is transferred and (if different) the date the materials are physically transferred
  — confirmation of copyright ownership and a clear indication of whether or not copyright, when known, will be transferred to the archival institution
  — a clear, if necessarily brief, description of all the materials conveyed
  — information about the physical condition of the materials, including documentation about potential preservation concerns
  — a clear explanation of any restrictions to be imposed (as emphasized earlier, every effort should be made to avoid unreasonable conditions)
  — a description of the procedures the archivist is to follow in order to dispose of unwanted materials (return to the donor, shred, burn and so on).

A sample donor agreement is shown in Figure 10.2.

The Nakouru City and Community Archives (the Archives) gratefully acknowledges the gift of the archival material described below, received from

Martin Kisembi

The donation described below has been received by the Nakouru City and Community Archives as a gift, and the owner or his/her agent confirms full authority to transfer full title, thereby completely transferring to the Archives and its successors the property described below, without any restriction, unless noted on this form. This transfer is permanent and forever and includes (when applicable) the transfer of any copyrights held by the donor in the materials donated.

Description of acquisition
Three items: a 25-page scrapbook containing newspaper clippings related to Alfred Kisembi's family and his career as Mayor of Nakouru from September 1959 to March 1964; a 20-page photograph album containing 100 colour prints of a visit by Alfred Kisembi and his wife Maude and son Martin to Ghana in November 1963; and one reel of 16 mm film, unidentified, that apparently includes footage of Alfred Kisembi at an official function in Nakouru sometime in 1960.

Figure 10.2 *Sample donor agreement*

Donor name and address:
Martin Kisembi
1209–1667 Canterbury Street
Nakouru West 2000

E-mail address: mkisembe447@internet.nk

Telephone: 02 9999 9999

Please indicate below how you would like to be acknowledged in any news releases, exhibit labels, or other publicity regarding this donation.

Credit line: Dr Martin Kisembi

Restrictions or conditions: none

Care of your donation
The following is a list of services the Archives will provide regarding your donation:

1 The donation will be arranged and described according to archival principles, and it will be preserved in non-damaging containers and stored securely in the Archives.
2 The donation will be available for researchers and the public after it has been arranged, described and prepared for storage and use.
3 The Archives will provide reference services for the donation and, if appropriate, will add information about the donation to online databases to support public access.
4 Should the donor agreement contain restrictions on portions of the donation, the restrictions will be strictly enforced.
5 When applicable, the Archives will alert researchers to existing copyrights relating to the donation and will include such copyright statements in archivasl descriptions.
6 The Archives will require that appropriate and complete citations be included in all information relating to the donation, such as exhibitions or publications.
7 The Archives will permanently maintain confidential files documenting the donation.

Donated by
_____
Date   signature of donor

Accepted on behalf of Nakouru City and Community Archives
_____
Date   signature of archivist

Figure 10.2 *Continued*

Loans

Loans can be of three kinds: reproduction or copy loans, exhibit loans or indefinite loans. (As mentioned, a permanent loan is an oddity that should be avoided if at all possible.)

Reproduction loans

A reproduction or copy loan allows an institution to receive archival materials in order to photocopy, photograph, microfilm or digitize them. Once the work is done the originals are returned to the lender. The lender needs to surrender the materials for an agreed time, and the archivist must ensure that the originals are protected while in the archival institution.

At the time the loan is negotiated, the archivist and the lender need to clarify the ownership and transfer of intellectual property rights to the copies. For instance, if the archival institution copies individual images in a photograph album but the lender of the album retains copyright to all those images (assuming the lender holds those rights in the first place), anyone wanting to publish an image from the album would need to contact the lender first.

Exhibit loans

More common in museum environments than in archival institutions, exhibit loans traditionally involve the temporary deposit of a physical archival object (such as a photograph, map or diary) for the purposes of display. Most often, an exhibit loan is agreed between two institutions, though borrowing an item from an individual is not uncommon.

Whenever the archivist wishes to borrow something, she must ensure that the item will be safe and well managed from the moment it leaves its original home to the moment it is returned. The lender of the item, whether an individual or institution, may want to confirm the environmental conditions under which the item will be displayed; the security and emergency systems in place to protect materials; and the borrowing institution's insurance coverage in case anything is lost or damaged. The lender and the institution will both want to know that any objects in an exhibition have not been secured through inappropriate or illegal means; proof of ownership and records showing provenance and custodial history may need to be shared.

Virtual exhibit loans

The archivist might also borrow materials in order to create digital copies to add to virtual exhibits. In this instance, the archivist will negotiate a reproduction loan, not an exhibit loan, collecting additional information such as answers to the following questions: Who owns the intellectual property rights to the original, and will that owner agree that a copy can be added to a virtual exhibit? Will that agreement expire at the end of the exhibit? What will happen to the copy in the archives once the virtual exhibit is over? Will the copy be destroyed or added to the archives' holdings? Will the virtual exhibit itself be maintained as an archival record, and if so how can the archivist respect the intellectual property rights in any of the items used?

Indefinite loans

Similar to agreeing permanent loans, taking on indefinite loans is not considered good archival practice. Why should an archival institution spend money, often public money, arranging, describing and preserving archives it does not legally own? Someday the owner could take all the materials back. What happens to the 'value-added' components, such as the acid-free folders and boxes, never mind the archivist's time, if everything is returned to the owner? In almost all cases, receiving materials through an indefinite loan is an unsound approach to archival management.

There is one particularly worthy exception, though. An archival institution might agree to accept archival materials indefinitely on behalf of an organization or group that simply cannot care for its own archives. A local community group, for instance, might value its archives but might not be able to manage them for another couple of years, as it upgrades its storage facilities. A larger institution in the region could step in for a year or so to provide storage, if not access.

Temporary custody can also be critical to safeguarding archives in an emergency. In 2016, the National Archives of Finland took control of digital copies of archival materials from Syria, materials that have been in grave danger throughout the Syrian Civil War. While it is hoped that the original documents will survive and that a functioning archival service can be re-established in Syria when the war ends, the decision by Finland to step in and provide a safe haven for these copies ensures that the evidence is preserved in some form, whatever happens in Syria in the near future.

No matter how noble the intent, the action needs to be formally structured. A service agreement should be executed, transferring custody of holdings to the stable institution while the other improves capacity or waits for war to end. The original owners of the records should retain legal control, and the two parties would agree how much work the receiving institution will do to address storage, preservation and access requirements. The agreement should be reviewed regularly and renewed or cancelled as circumstances allow.

Purchases

Sometimes, archivists do purchase materials, from individuals, book and manuscript dealers or auction houses such as Sotheby's or Christie's. Many large institutions such as university libraries or national or state archives have a dedicated budget for purchases, but most small institutions have only limited funds, if any. In the event that an archivist is considering purchasing archival items, she needs to decide not only if funds are available but also whether the cost is warranted. When the archivist does purchase archival materials, she needs to maintain complete documentation, including sales receipts, invoices and records confirming the seller's right to own and dispose of the item.

Managing copyright

As discussed in Chapter 7, to own copyright is to own the right to be recognized as the creator of an intellectual product and to be credited for that work. A copyright holder has the exclusive right to reproduce his work and the right to prevent others from publishing or disseminating that work without permission.

When archives are transferred from one part of an organization to another, such as from the Legal Department to the Corporate Archives, copyright is still held by the overarching agency, so administering copyright is relatively straightforward. But when archival materials are donated, loaned or purchased, managing copyright becomes a challenge. When the archivist is negotiating donations or loans, she must strive to identify who owns copyright to the materials in question. If possible, it can benefit the archival institution to obtain the rights to archival items, allowing it to reproduce and publish those materials without having to seek permission from the copyright holder each time. Any transfer of rights must be explicitly included in the donor agreement. The archivist will also want to clarify copyright issues if possible when purchasing materials, though this may not be easy, particularly because purchases are so often made through a third-party dealer.

Accessioning archives

After the negotiations are complete and the materials have been donated, purchased, transferred or loaned, the next step is to document their legal and administrative transfer into the archives.

Accessions, archives and accruals

Accessioning is defined as the process of transferring legal and physical control of archives from the creating agency or donor to the archival institution. The materials received at any one time, as part of one specific accessioning process, are referred to as an accession. An accrual is an accession of archives added to an archival unit, such as a *fonds* or group, already held by the same archival institution.

Sometimes, an accession will represent an entire body of archives. The personal papers of Marie Lévesque or the official records of the defunct Itsabanger Motor Company are one archival collection *and* one accession if they all come in at the same time as part of the same process of transfer from owner to archival institution. But five boxes of archives from the poet José Salazar are one accession if they come in to archival custody on 22 May 2013. Three boxes of Mr Salazar's archives that arrive on 13 October 2014 are another accession, and the boxes also constitute an accrual, since they are an addition to existing holdings.

Consider this example. Lee Yuan Chang, a prominent local author, may negotiate an agreement with the archivist in the university library for the regular deposit of his literary and business papers. Each year, the archivist meets Mr Chang to review new files to be transferred, after which the archivist completes legal agreements as needed. Each donation is a new accession, legally and administratively separate from any donations that come before or after. Each donation is also a new accrual: an addition to the existing holdings of Mr Chang. Every new accession and every new accrual form a new part of the author's personal papers.

The archivist arranges and describes each new accession and adds information about each to the entry for Lee Yuan Chang in the descriptive database. The archivist also updates administrative documentation about how each new accession has been managed. The goal is to ensure that, while the 'whole' body of Lee Yuan Chang's archives is now larger and more complex, each separate accession can still be identified as needed.

When Mr Chang dies, and the last accession of his papers comes after his daughter has cleaned out his office, the archivist processes this new accrual and updates descriptive and administrative records. At this point, it is quite reasonable to assume that no further archives *from* Mr Chang will be added to his archives, as he is not around to create any more. Should the daughter find an errant box in the basement, those materials would be added as a new accession and an accrual. But if someone else comes in with archives *about* Lee Yuan Chang, those materials would be considered a different acquisition and not part of Mr Chang's archives.

The distinction between archives, accessions and accruals applies equally in the digital environment, though applying a series-based approach can help immeasurably. Each distinct series can be managed administratively as its own entity, and the linkages between functions and agents can be made through descriptive tools. Building up a totality of archives from one creating agency ceases to be the focus, replaced by the task of documenting each archival unit as it comes into archival control and linking information about it to the different agencies responsible over time. (More information on how to apply this series-level control in description is given in Chapter 11.)

The purpose of accessioning

Accessioning is not just a tracking process. It is an integral step in gaining legal and administrative process over archives, which is one reason that a clear distinction is made between archives, accessions and accruals. Accessioning supports the following two functions: it documents the transfer of title from the owner(s) to the repository; and it documents any restrictions on access, copying and use. In the case of donations, the accession record can also document the donor's preferences for disposing of unwanted materials, information that should also be captured in the donor agreement, as discussed above.

Accessioning usually involves two steps. The first is to complete and execute formal authorizations confirming the legal transfer of ownership from the creating agency or donor to the archival institution. These authorizations may be transfer forms, purchase receipts or donor agreements. The second step is to document the existence of the new accession in the archival institution, by completing an accession record. This record is an internal document that identifies and briefly describes each new accession so that the materials can be identified, stored and tracked. Information captured in an accession record should include, at a minimum:

- a unique identifying code or number
- the date of the acquisition
- the name of the source or donor
- the type of accession, such as donation, transfer, purchase or copy loan
- a brief description of the materials acquired, ideally including:
  - an estimate of quantity or extent (as precise as possible)
  - the medium or format of the material (photographs, textual records, maps and plans and so on)
  - the years covered by the archives
  - a general statement of the content, subject or scope of the materials

- a brief description of how materials were stored before arriving in the archives, particularly to highlight any changes in custody that could affect what remains and the organization or physical condition
- an indication of any conditions or restrictions on access
- whether or not the accession is an accrual or shares provenance with other archives in the institution
- a note on physical condition, particularly if there are immediate preservation concerns
- the present storage location of the materials.

The accession record will be updated whenever new materials come in, showing each new accession separately. As mentioned in Chapter 9, the accession record should be considered vital and must be protected in an emergency. It is also a permanent record, giving the full picture of all the holdings of the institution from its beginnings to the present moment. The archivist needs to protect accession information, along with the legal records associated with transfers and donations, more securely than almost any other items in her institution.

Accession records are permanently valuable, as shown in this example. Imagine if Lee Yuan Chang's grandchildren came to the institution 50 years after his death, claiming that he never meant to donate his archives and arguing that the institution should give them back. The archivist in charge – who will certainly not be the same one who worked with Mr Chang in the first place – will need to turn to the evidence (the accession record, which is part of the institution's own archives) to demonstrate proof of ownership. Similarly, if ten boxes of archives disappear when the institution moves from one building to another, the accession record will be an essential tool as staff try to find out what is missing.

The accession record also serves a valuable descriptive purpose: if the archivist is not able to arrange and describe archives right away, the summary information in the accession record can serve as a high-level description of what was received, when and from whom. While confidential details in an accession record would not be made available to researchers, the archivist is able to use the data to extract a summary of new or unprocessed holdings, thus helping researchers understand everything in the custody of the institution.

It is unwise, by the way, to use accession records as location registers. The archivist will just have to update accession documents every time she rearranges her storage room. It is better to maintain information about where archives are stored in a separate location file, discussed in Chapter 11, and only identify the first location of a new accession in the accession record, so that materials can be found immediately after they are brought into custody. The archivist can then make a note later, when the items have found a more permanent home, that the initial information on the accession record is now obsolete.

Increasingly, the process of accessioning and overall archival management is carried out using software technologies such as purpose-built or off-the-shelf software tools. A variety of software packages are available to support all types of archival duties. Every archivist will need to decide which tools are best for her own situation. A commercial vendor in England, for instance, may not be able to provide technical support easily for an archival institution in Sri Lanka. A tool that supports one set of archival standards may not be useful if the institution does not follow those standards. And open-source tools, while seemingly inexpensive, may not have all the features needed by an institution with complex requirements, such as an integrated institution that wants to manage its archival, museum and library acquisitions in one database. The best course of action when investigating options for archival management software is to solicit advice from staff in relevant professional associations and national archival institutions, who can help steer the archivist in the direction of tools or resources best suited to her particular environment.[2]

Monetary appraisal

The extreme prices paid on eBay or the jaw-dropping value of treasures on *Antiques Roadshow* can leave the public with a misconception about the value of 'old' books and papers. The reality is that few 'treasures' that come into archival institutions are worth the thousands of dollars a donor may wish. But donors still come into the institution hoping to discover that their archives have monetary value. The archivist needs to know how to react.

As with any financial transaction, an assessment of the monetary worth of archives is based on an understanding of fair market value, which is the highest price that the material would bring in an open and unrestricted market. But fair market value is not always a meaningful benchmark with archives. Just because an archival collection *might* have a high commercial value does not mean it has any meaningful value to an archival institution.

A classic example is a collection of autographs. The original signatures of politicians, actors or musicians may claim a high price at auction, but if the documents containing those signatures are taken out of their original location, the value of the collection as evidence is pretty much erased. The collector may see dollar signs, but the archivist sees an example of lost provenance.

When deciding to purchase archival materials, the archivist cannot just set a price, write a cheque and take hold of the items. She needs to be accountable to her sponsor agency for the sums paid and to have sufficient budget for the acquisition. The sponsor agency may demand that she prepare a monetary appraisal, and the institution may be bound to carry out due diligence to comply with legal or financial regulations for the acquisition of cultural or historical property.

When appraising archives to provide a tax receipt for a donation, the evaluation process can be even more drawn out. Both the donor and the institution will likely be bound by legal or administrative requirements such as the following:

- The donor needs to confirm he holds clear title to the archives and can and will transfer ownership fully to the institution.
- The two parties need to draw up a formal donation agreement before a monetary appraisal can be completed. Conducting an appraisal in the hope that materials will be donated is not logical and may not even be legal.
- Monetary appraisal is based on an assessment of the materials the institution intends to keep, not all the documents in the donor's basement. The donor may have 30 boxes of archives but the institution might only decide to keep five after it has completed its appraisal. Thus the archivist has to finish that archival appraisal before anyone can assign a monetary appraisal.
- In many countries, monetary appraisals have to be undertaken by specialists if the anticipated value is above a certain threshold. For instance, in Canada, the rule of thumb is that an archivist can provide an in-house appraisal if the material has a value of less than $1000 or so, but an independent appraiser may have to be brought in if the value is between $1001 and $5000. If the materials are anticipated to be worth more than $5000, the appraisal may have to be done by two or more appraisers, in order to comply with Canadian tax law.
- A conservation assessment may also have to be carried out, especially if materials are in poor condition, are stored on fragile or high-risk media (such as audiocassettes) or are unidentifiable without technological intervention (like unlabelled floppy disks or CDs). The costs of preservation or restoration may have to be factored into the monetary appraisal.
- In many jurisdictions the institution pays for the monetary appraisal, but

if the donor does not like the results he will be responsible for paying for a second review.

- The tax receipt is invariably issued for the year in which the donation was finalized. If the original donation arrives in the institution in 2014 but the materials are not appraised, arranged, described and valued until 2016, the tax receipt will be issued for the 2016 tax year. The archivist needs to be realistic with herself and the donor about the time frames involved in processing the collection.

Monetary appraisal is a complex area of archival work, and few archivists engage in monetary appraisal often enough to build up a store of knowledge and expertise. The websites of government revenue offices or tax departments often include information specifically related to issues of cultural property management, and so that is the best place to start researching issues of monetary appraisal and archives.

Deaccessioning archives

How should the archivist dispose of unwanted materials? The first and fundamental principle is this: *all* archives that are not going to be kept in the institution must be disposed of legally and with respect for both the materials and the creator or owner. It is not appropriate for an archival institution to sell individual items from an acquisition, put archives in an insecure recycling bin or keep documents as personal property. Such actions tarnish the image of the archivist as guardian, leaving potential donors wondering what might happen to their own materials in the same situation.

Deaccessioning is the act of removing archival or other resource materials permanently from the physical control and legal ownership of the archival institution. The best way to deaccession is not to have to deaccession in the first place. The archivist should appraise archives as soon as possible after they are received, identify those materials not worth keeping and return them to the donor or destroy them right away, depending on the donor's wishes, which should be documented fully in the donor agreement.

If items *are* to be destroyed, that process must be secure. Paper archives should not be recycled until they have been shredded or pulped. Computer disks should not be erased and reused but should be destroyed entirely, unless the archivist can confirm that all electronic data have been removed. The archivist should not sell items, give them to another institution or otherwise dispose of them unless those actions are fully legal and in keeping with original donor agreements.

A difficult scenario is when a donor takes back boxes of materials rejected by one archival institution and then offers them to another, perhaps without even telling anyone at either institution that the records do not represent a 'whole' body of archives. The unwanted materials likely have little or no enduring value; otherwise the archivist would have kept them in the first place. But now the donor has created what is sometimes called a 'split *fonds*', creating confusion among archival institutions and the research public.

Such a situation comes up most often when celebrity figures, such as authors, musicians or politicians, 'shop' their personal archives around from institution to institution looking for the best 'deal'. The archivist on the other side of the desk would be wise to have a conversation with the donor about notions of provenance, original order and archival value. If the archivist decides that having some of the materials on offer would be a good decision archivally, so be it; she needs to decide how firmly she will stand on archival principles of unity and totality. (As already discussed, the idea of an archival 'whole' is not realistic anyway.) But yet again the point must be made, the goal of archives is not empire building; it is documenting aspects of society to leave an authentic and valuable record of the past.

Dealing with the backlog

Sometimes the archivist opens a closet door and finds shelves filled with dozens of boxes of unidentified stuff. The materials may bear no relation to the institution's current acquisitions policy. There may be no administrative or legal paperwork. The story of their arrival in the institution may have been buried with the first community archivist, who died 20 years ago.

In these cases, if the archivist cannot locate a donor, a creator or some likely descendants, she has to consider whether she should even keep the archives. What are the risks of arranging, describing, preserving and making available a body of archives and then discovering you had no legal right to do so in the first place? But equally, what are the risks of destroying materials with wonderful archival value?

There may be some comfort in remembering that the more complete the body of archives, the more likely it is that provenance and source may be identified, somehow. The records themselves may tell at least some of the story. The archivist may be happy to pitch a single newspaper clipping in the recycle bin, but she may find it worth her while to settle into the detective work involved with figuring out the origins of five boxes of personal diaries.

Appraisal is considered by many archivists to be the most important and the most challenging of archival tasks. The decision to keep can be continually reassessed; the decision to destroy is, by definition, final. Digital technologies are forcing archivists to reconsider the foundation of traditional appraisal criteria, and another edition of this book in five years may present an entirely different approach. There is nothing that today's archivist can do but make the best, most thoughtful decision she can given the circumstances she is in now.

Once archives are under the institution's legal or administrative custody or control, the archivist's next task is to bring them under intellectual, physical and/or virtual control. Arrangement and description are addressed in the next chapter.

Notes

1 Without getting sidetracked into a discussion of the value of statistical analysis and data sets, it is useful to define big data, a term that refers to extremely large data sets that may be analysed using computer technologies. The goal of big data analysis is to search for patterns, identify trends or find commonalities across different pieces of information. Such analysis, largely but not only statistical, can provide deep insights into human and social behaviour. But the analysis relies on data, which often takes the form of records or evidence.

2 Two open-source software packages in common use in archival institutions in 2017 are *Access to Memory* (*AtoM*) and *ArchivesSpace*, which are described briefly in Chapter 11, since their most prominent features relate more to description than to administrative control. The information given in that chapter is intended to be illustrative only and not an endorsement of those packages. Every institution must make choices based on its own needs and priorities.

11

Arranging and describing archives

Watch out for the fellow who talks about putting things in order! Putting things in order always means getting other people under your control.

Denis Diderot (1713–84) *Supplement to Bougainville's 'Voyage'*, 1796

Arrangement and description are central to the preservation of archives as documentary evidence. Arrangement and description are also the least stable of archival activities: the 'best' way to arrange a collection of archives a century ago is not considered by archivists to be the best way – at all – today.

A Mesopotamian record keeper placed clay tablets into clay pots and onto clay shelves, relying on his memory to know which tablets related to what topics. No one could access the archives without his permission, and only he knew what was there. One suspects he rarely went on vacation. A librarian in 19th-century Connecticut, on the other hand, described manuscript collections by writing and filing catalogue cards for each new arrival: a complete description of the materials on a 'main entry' card and cross-references to subjects or people in 'added entry' cards. Banks and banks of cards filled the archives, and if the front door was opened as the archivist was adding new entries and a stiff wind blew through, half the day was spent picking up cards off the floor and putting them back in order.

Today, the computer is king, and even the smallest and least secure of archival institutions wants to create a database of archival holdings, not put binders of paper finding aids on a bookshelf or add cards to a catalogue in the reference room. (Few institutions rely on clay tablets, though it has been suggested that they are perhaps the most stable medium around these days.) As archives themselves keep changing, the ways in which they can be arranged and described keeps changing. This is why arrangement and description is the area of archival effort most infused with theory, and why those theories can become such contentious areas of debate.

This chapter provides an overview of central issues in archival arrangement and description. The following questions are examined: what are core principles of arrangement and description? What are the different units or categories – or elements or entities – within a body of archives that need to be arranged and described? What are the qualities, and strengths and weaknesses, of focusing on the description of a whole body of archives in custody versus focusing on the management of archives by function in order to gain control, even if the materials are not in hand? The chapter also looks at the ways in which archivists standardize descriptive practice and the tools used to control the names, terms, geographic locations and other matters of language. The chapter ends by illustrating different ways in which descriptive information might be presented to the user.

Principles of arrangement and description

Arrangement is defined as the process of ordering materials intellectually or physically, in keeping with provenance and original order, to support physical security and control, and to illuminate content, context and structure. Description is the act of establishing intellectual control over archives, by creating tools that identify and describe the content, context and structure of archives, as well as their origins and their relationship to the creating agency or individual. Description also sets out the actions taken by the archival institution as custodian and caretaker to receive, appraise and process the archives.

The outcomes of arrangement and description

Together, arrangement and description achieve three specific outcomes:

1   Arrangement supports the security and control of archives by identifying and, if appropriate, ordering materials so that they may be described and then safely stored and protected, whether physically in boxes on shelves or electronically in digital storage systems.
2   Description reveals the content, context and structure of archives, and the actions the archivist has taken to care for them, which supports their value as evidence and helps make them available for use.
3   The descriptive outputs (database entries, finding aids or lists of boxes or files) demonstrate the work performed by the archivist to receive,

appraise and process materials, holding the archivist and archival institution accountable for their actions and decisions.

The act of arrangement and description serves not only to prepare archives for research use but also to help maintain their authenticity and integrity as evidence. Through the integrated process of arrangement and description, the archivist demonstrates how original records or data were created and used; what actions, transactions, subjects, people or places they represent; and how the archives came into custodial care and were organized for access. In an age when it seems impossible to claim pure objectivity, the archivist can still strive for transparency, which is an important outcome of arrangement and description.

Respecting provenance and original order

The archivist respects provenance and looks for some sort of order that supports the value of the archives as evidence, as discussed in Chapter 3. The order may be reflected through physical arrangement, as files are placed into different boxes to represent the functions and activities identified, or the order may be demonstrated through an intellectual arrangement, which is a representation of different series or files in relation to functions or activities, even if the actual items are not actually moved around.

In the absence of a discernible original order, the archivist must determine and impose some logical structure. While an archivist could argue that an unfathomable mess of papers dumped into an orange crate represents an 'original order', this literal interpretation is, indeed, too literal. It is also rather disrespectful to both the creator and the potential user. Part of the value-added service the archivist provides is to 'make sense' of archives, while remaining transparent about her actions throughout the process.

Capturing core information

Regardless of whether the archives are in physical form in boxes or in digital form in computer servers, the archivist's job is to organize the materials so that they serve as evidence of the different people or groups reflected in the archives; this involves identifying, at a minimum, *who* (the person or agent responsible), *what* (the actions performed) and *how* (the way in which those activities were performed and documented, as shown in the records):

- *Who* as carrying out actions or transactions, decisions or communications?

An organization, a department or agency within that organization, a person or family or a community group? What was their role in society and mission in life; what were their interests, passions and priorities?

- *What* actions or transactions did they carry out, what functions did they perform to achieve their goals and objectives in life and work?
- *How* did they carry out those functions, as demonstrated by the records or data they created and used in the course of carrying out their work? What documents, databases, photographs, maps, reports, correspondence or e-mails did they generate (or leave behind) that provide evidence of their actions, transactions, decisions and opinions?

(Information about *when*, *why* and *where* are also captured, as discussed later.) As emphasized many times already, respect for content, context and structure is a critical underpinning of arrangement and description. The archivist strives to keep archives together according to who created or used them and in the order in which the materials were kept when they were brought into custody.

Therefore if 40 boxes of paper archives and five computer hard drives, comprising the personal archives of the engineer Dr Kikeri Absolom, are acquired by the university archives in 2014, they are managed as one acquisition, under the provenance of Kikeri Absolom, and they are arranged in keeping with the order Dr Absolom applied when he created and used the evidence in the first place. They are then described to reveal the life and work of Dr Absolom and to make available the documentary evidence of that life.

If Dr Absolom returns in 2015 with another box of paper and electronic records, these new materials are recorded as a new accession, but the provenance remains the same: they are part of the archives of Dr Absolom. The archivist may integrate the old and the new physically, by adding new files to existing series, or intellectually, by updating existing descriptions to present information about the new holdings. She keeps clear records of the different accessions (accruals) though, for legal and administrative purposes and to provide transparency about how she has arranged and described the materials.

If the Department of Engineering at the same university transfers its own archives in 2016, and these archives relate to Dr Absolom's research but were created by this separate department, the archivist would not integrate those records physically or intellectually with Dr Absolom's archives. Rather, the archivist would arrange and describe the new materials as part of the archives of the Department of Engineering, respecting provenance, and then she would provide links between the two records creators (the engineer and his department), so that anyone seeking information about either Dr Absolom or the department can find all these materials easily.

As introduced in Chapter 3, archivists have adopted different methodologies over the years for arrangement and description, beginning with organization by form or date, subject or place, and eventually ending up (à la de Wailly) with approaches that respect provenance and original order. But archivists also came up with competing philosophies of where and how the archivist should embark on efforts to arrange and describe the archives.

Should the work wait until the archives were in custody? Should arrangement and description happen before the materials come into archival hands? Is the best strategy to consider arrangement and description part of a fluid post-custodial process, within a continuum of records care? The best way to explain how archivists have approached arrangement and description in line with chosen theories, custodial or post-custodial, is to look at how the processes have been codified in descriptive standards. It is important to clarify here that while these tools are often called *descriptive* standards, they either explicitly or implicitly provide guidance on how to arrange archives as well.[1]

Custodial arrangement and description

As a reminder, the custodial approach assumed that records followed a life cycle and that archival intervention happened at the end of that life cycle, when archives were safely in archival custody. At that point, the archivist carried out appraisal, arrangement, description and preservation. Most archival manuals up to the 20th century focused on how to manage archives in custody. Principles for caring for office records – if principles existed – were described in completely different tools, intended for records creators and records managers, not archivists.

In the 1980s, books such as Michael Cook's *The Management of Information from Archives* was an essential guide in the UK, as was Steven Henson's *Archives, Personal Papers and Manuscripts* in the USA. The influence of librarians on arrangement and description, particularly in North America, was seen in the popularity of the *Anglo-American Cataloguing Rules*, which included a chapter on archives, and in the growing use of MARC, or M*Achine-Readable Cataloguing*, a tool designed by the Library of Congress in the 1960s to control and share bibliographic information electronically, which by the 1980s included a section on how to catalogue archives.[2]

In 1990, the Bureau of Canadian Archivists' Planning Committee on Descriptive Standards published a standard for Canadian use called *Rules for Archival Description* (*RAD*). Revised in 2008, *RAD* codifies the capture of 12 basic descriptive elements, such as title, dates, extent, administrative history or biographical sketch, as well as a number of additional descriptive elements.

Its purpose is to help create consistency in arrangement and description, but the original developers also believed that adhering to the guidance in *RAD* would also help facilitate the development of digital descriptive databases, which were just starting to emerge in the early 1990s.

The first edition of *RAD* focused heavily on the *fonds*, in large part to urge archivists to complete general arrangement and description of whole bodies of archives first before moving on to more detailed item-level work, which had been the hallmark of archival description to that point. But as discussed in the example of the Hudson's Bay Company *fonds* in Chapter 3, the word *fonds* came to mean some body of archives more 'total' than occurred in reality. Taking this weakness in interpretation into account, the authors of the second edition of *RAD* scaled back the discussion of the *fonds*, suggesting that archives could be arranged and described at different levels as long as provenance and original order were respected as much as possible.

Internationally, the primary descriptive standard for many years has been the *General International Standard Archival Description (ISAD(G))*, published by the ICA in 1994 and republished in 2000. *ISAD(G)* defines 26 data elements that should be captured in order to create consistent descriptions, including title, date, creator, biographical history, scope and content, conditions governing access and so on.

In 2004, the Society of American Archivists approved a content standard called *Describing Archives: a content standard (DACS)*, consisting of 25 descriptive elements, including creator, dates, physical extent, administrative history, scope and contents and so on. A second edition of *DACS* was published in 2013.

All of these descriptive tools focus on custodial care: the management of archives in situ. *Fonds*, archive, archives, archives group, record group, manuscript group, papers, collection: the terms vary but the concept is the same. Do not describe until you arrange, and do not arrange until you have custody.

Custodial arrangement and description were defined according to hierarchies, as outlined in Table 11.1. Because the standards were originally developed before digital archives became such a pervasive reality, the levels were originally intended to apply primarily to paper and analogue archives. Their applicability in the digital environment and some additional comments on each level are included in Table 11.1.

To apply the hierarchical approach that uses these different levels of description, the archivist's first job is to identify whether archives actually exist in relation to the anticipated hierarchy: *fonds*, series, sub-series and so on. To provide this assessment, the archivist must examine the materials to discern or decide an order. Then the archivist organizes the materials so that they reflect this chosen order. (Let us not pretend that arrangement happens in

Table 11.1 *Hierarchical levels of arrangement and description*[3]

Level	Definition	Comments
Fonds or group	The whole of a body of documents, regardless of form or medium, created or accumulated by a particular individual, family, corporate body or other agency as part of life and work and retained because those materials have ongoing archival value as evidence of those functions and activities.	As a conceptual framework, the *fonds* can be applied equally in an analogue or digital environment. The challenge with identifying a unified group in digital record keeping is that the work of digital arrangement and description needs to begin well before archives end up in archival storage, so the work begins before there is any custodial 'whole'.
Sub-fonds or sub-group	The archives of an administrative unit directly related to or, usually, subordinate to a larger creating agency, identified as the creator of a *fonds*; the creator of a sub-*fonds* or sub-group will likely have its own distinct record-keeping system and organizational structure. With personal papers, the sub-group could be an individual within a family, whose papers form a significant grouping within the archives.	In the digital environment this level remains conceptual, but records of different subordinate agencies might have been created and managed in completely different electronic records systems, owned and managed by one or another person or group and never actually brought together 'physically', which adds to the burden of creating these relationships between *fonds* and sub-*fonds*.
Series	Aggregations of files or other records within a larger *fonds* or group that relate to the same processes or that are evidence of a common form, purpose or use.	The series is conceptual and so can exist in analogue and digital environments. Whereas the functional approach demands a precise articulation of functions, the series in the custodial context has been interpreted in many ways: form (correspondence or reports), filing system (case files A–L, case files M–Z), date (1932, March 1988), medium (photographs, maps, plans) and so on.
Sub-series	A body of documents within a series that can be readily distinguished from the larger series by filing arrangement, type, form or content.	As a conceptual layer, the sub-series can be applied in analogue and digital environments. It is less valuable in the digital, because technology allows the person seeking records to cut past all the layers that might have existed in a hierarchical paper filing system and get straight to the file or item.
File	An organized assembly of documents within a series, brought together intellectually or physically according to a particular topic, activity or event in one or several folders.	The file is a relevant level of organization in both the analogue and digital environment, though technology can allow the user of digital archives to locate items without having to bother going through a traditional file. The physical file is also an integrated unit but the digital file could be conceptual: several digital objects could be identified as belonging to one 'file' but they may actually be stored in completely different locations in a computer server.
Item	The basic physical unit within a file, such as an individual letter, report, photograph, audio cassette, film reel or scrapbook.	In a digital archival environment, the item would be equivalent to a digital or electronic record.
Piece	The single indivisible unit within an item, such as each sheet of paper comprising a 20-page letter or each photograph in a photograph album.	In the digital environment, the piece is replaced by the concept of a data object, which is one component of a larger electronic record. A word-processed DOC file – an electronic record – might consist of the word-processed file and a TIFF image file embedded within the electronic document. Both would have to be managed appropriately. In paper and digital environments, the actual term 'piece' is increasingly outmoded.

the time it took to read this sentence. The process can take weeks, months or years. The practicalities of arrangement are discussed later, but for the moment let us assume the job has been done, and done well.) Once the arrangement is complete, the archivist captures information about the now-organized archives to prepare a description, which can then be shared with researchers.

Table 11.2 highlights some of the core descriptive elements in each of the three main custody-oriented standards used today: *RAD, ISAD(G)* and *DACS*.

Table 11.2 *Core descriptive elements in custody-oriented standards*

Descriptive element	Definition of element	Information captured in relation to?
Title	The title of the materials, either as shown on the archives themselves or, more often, applied by the archivist after reviewing the materials and researching the history of the creating agency or individual.	*Who* (creator) + *What* (archives)
Dates	The inclusive dates in which the archives were created, from the date of the earliest record to the most recent. While inclusive dates are preferred for large bodies of archives, the assignment of dates can be complex, from single dates to inclusive dates. Different descriptive standards provide their own suggestions for how to express dates.	*When* (archives)
Extent and physical description	The physical extent of the archives, usually following a standard metric measurement, with a description of the materials, which includes information about the different media in the archives being described.	*What* (quantity of archives) + *What* (type of material)
Administrative history or biography	When describing the archives of a corporate entity such as a business or government, core historical information is captured, including the dates of founding and dissolution, mandate and sphere of responsibility, predecessors and successors, administrative relationships and structure, names of the corporate bodies, name(s) of chief officers, and other significant information. When describing the archives of a person or family, the following historical information is captured as a minimum: names and vital events; place of residence; education; occupation, life and activities; and other significant information. The importance of the individual or family in relation to the mandate of the archival institution would also be identified, if appropriate.	*Who* (creator) + *What* (functions) + *Where* (creator and functions) + *When* (creator and functions) + *Why* (creator and functions) + *How* (creator and functions)
Scope and content	A description of the contents of the archives themselves, including types of materials and the topics or issues they cover.	*What* (archives) + *Where* (archives) + *How* (archives)
Archival or custodial history	A description of the physical location and movements of the archives from the time the records were created and used to the time the archives arrived in the archival repository, to identify changes in provenance or management and explain any gaps or overlaps in the archives.	*Who* (creator or other agents) + *What* (archives) + *Where* (archives) + *When* (archives) + *How* (archives)

For each descriptive element, the reason the information is captured – whether it answers 'who, what, where, when, why and how' – is explained.

As noted, *RAD*, *ISAD(G)* and *DACS* include other descriptive elements, such as information about arrangement, restrictions on access, finding aids, the existence and location of copies or related materials, the language of the archives and so on.

This custody-oriented approach works relatively well if the archivist is working with a discrete body of materials that have come into archival care after they are no longer being actively used. The personal papers of deceased individuals come to mind, as these are a 'closed' *fonds*. No further archives will (one assumes) be added to the existing grouping, allowing the archivist to manage the extant materials as a 'whole'.

Because the arrangement and description in a custodial approach hinges on linking the identification of the creator of the archives with the archives themselves, any description ends up being entirely self-contained. The 'who, what, where, when, why and how' are intertwined, as shown in Table 11.2. Because information about the creator and the archives are captured together, the entire description, and any subordinate descriptions, may need to be revised when new archives are discovered and a new arrangement or description carried out.

Functional arrangement and description

A functional approach, which as discussed is central to a post-custodial vision of archival care, delinks the creating agency from the records, focusing on the function and series instead. This approach allows the archivist to manage discrete units of evidence and link them to creating agencies without presuming the records form part of a larger 'whole', now or later. It also allows her to gather information about agents and functions and map that information to different series of records later, when new materials appear.

The functional approach identifies three distinct entities: the function, the record series and the agency. Functions, which may be divided into subordinate functions as needed, are conceptual categories to capture information about the activities and tasks performed to accomplish a particular goal or objective. The record series refers to the documentary evidence generated to support the particular function, sub-functions, activities or tasks. The agency is the administrative unit, individual or other distinct entity: a unit that, ideally, has a measure of independence and autonomy and is responsible for executing the functions and, thereby, creating or managing records.

The Australian descriptive standard *Describing Archives in Context: a guide to the Australasian practice* (2007), also known as *DAC*, follows this functional approach: descriptive elements would be captured separately to represent each of the three entities. Then the information can be brought together through links between the different descriptions. Summaries of the different entities are shown in Tables 11.3, 11.4 and 11.5.

Table 11.3 *Definitions of functions and sub-functions*

Element	Definition of element	Information captured in relation to?
Function	A narrative description of the precise function in question, with one entry for each term. Narrow, broader, or related terms are also identified and defined separately.	*What* (activities or tasks)
Sub-function	A narrative description of the precise sub-function in question, with one entry for each term. Again, related terms are identified and defined separately.	*What* (activities or tasks)

Table 11.4 *Core descriptive elements for the records entity*

Descriptive element	Definition of element	Information captured in relation to?
Title	The name of the grouping of records based, such as a series or item.	*What* (archives)
Dates of creation	It is most likely that inclusive dates will be used, but sometimes single dates may also be used if the series represents materials from only one day or year.	*When* (archives)
Scope and content	A description of the contents of the series or a description of the item.	*What* (archives) + *Where* (archives) + *How* (archives)
Extent and physical description	The physical extent of the archives, usually following a standard metric measurement, with a description of the materials, which includes information about the different media in the archives being described.	*What* (archives)

The description of the series or item does not include an administrative history or biographical sketch. That information would be captured separately, in relation to the agent, as shown in Table 11.5 below.

Even in a three-pronged functional approach, other descriptive elements might also be included in any final output for the user, to make the description as detailed as possible. Such information might include restrictions on access, terms of use, whether accruals are expected and whether a more detailed description (such as a narrative finding aid) is available.

Table 11.5 *Core descriptive elements for the agency entity*

Descriptive element	Definition of element	Information captured in relation to?
Name	The name of the agency.	*Who* (creator)
Dates of existence	The inclusive dates in which the agency operated (or the individual lived).	*When* (creator)
Function	A description of the functions or activities of the agency.	*What* (creator)
Administrative history or biography	When describing the archives of a corporate entity such as a business or government, core historical information is captured, including the dates of founding and dissolution, mandate and sphere of responsibility, administrative relationships and structure, names of the corporate bodies, name(s) of chief officers, and other significant information. When describing the archives of a person or family, the following historical information is captured as a minimum: names and vital events; place of residence; education; occupation, life and activities; and other significant information. The importance of the individual or family in relation to the mandate of the archival institution could also be identified, if appropriate.	*Who* (creator) + *What* (creator) + *Where* (creator) + *When* (creator) + *Why* (creator) + *How* (creator)
Predecessor agencies	Identification of any agencies in existence before this one. Only summary information would be given in here to support cross-referencing; a full description of the other agent would be prepared separately.	*Who* (other agent) + *When* (other agent)
Successor agencies	Identification of any agencies created after this one. Only summary information would be given in here to support cross-referencing; a full description of the other agent would be prepared separately.	*Who* (other agent) + *When* (other agent)

Bridging the gap

In 2012, the ICA established the Expert Group on Archival Description (EGAD). EGAD's remit is to develop a standard for archival description that integrates and reconciles a range of existing ICA standards, including the core descriptive standard *ISAD(G)* as well as standards for controlling the terms used to describe persons, families or corporate bodies (*ISAAR(CPF)*); the standard for identifying archival institutions (*ISDIAH*); and the standard for describing functions (*ISDF*). (These standards are discussed in more detail in the section on controlling language, later in this chapter.)

In September 2016, EGAD produced a draft standard called *Records in Contexts: a conceptual model for archival description* (*RiC*), which was circulated for consultation and review. In this draft, the developers of *RiC* claim that the model is designed to help archivists move away from a focus on one particular 'unit of description' and recognize instead that individual records and aggregations of records are distinct and need to be described differently.

RiC also aims to move description away from a focus on levels, opting instead for what the authors refer to as multidimensional description.

This multidimensional approach perceives of description not as an effort to represent a hierarchy, moving from top to bottom, but rather as a network of descriptive elements that can be linked together in an abundance of combinations. To support this multidimensional framework, *RiC* defines 14 primary description entities:

1. record
2. record component
3. record set
4. agent
5. occupation
6. position
7. function
8. function (abstract)
9. activity
10. mandate
11. documentary form
12. date
13. place
14. concept or thing.

While *RiC* moves away from the *fonds* orientation used in earlier standards, it does not focus explicitly on series or function. Instead, the core entities – the materials being arranged and described – are identified as 'record', 'record component' and 'record set'. The *record* is the discrete representation of information in physical or digital form, such as a deed, e-mail or map. The *record component* might be a part of the record, such as the e-mail on the one hand and the digital photograph attached to the e-mail on the other hand. The *record set* is the group of records (and therefore record components) intellectually brought together by an agent at some date for some reason (a concept that seems very close to the series).

After defining each of the primary descriptive entities, *RiC* identifies and explains additional information to be captured in order to set out the properties of each entity. For instance, the description of the 'record' entity might include information about its authenticity and integrity, type (or record form), the time covered, the subject matter addressed, or other contextual information.

Similarly, the entity of occupation would be defined by describing the properties of a particular type of occupation. Here a controlled term such as 'accountant' or 'lawyer' or 'activist' would be used, based, one assumes, on a standardized thesaurus of functions. The description would also include a 'free-form' narrative of the background, origins and history of the occupation, along with details about how the function relates to the agent or agents associated with the archives.

Given that the *RiC* conceptual model was still in draft form at the time I was finishing this book in early 2017, I cannot say whether this model will retain its form and scope once it has been reviewed and revised. No one knows, either, if the standard will actually be adopted by the international archival community, replacing *ISAD(G)* and other ICA standards. One can only wait and watch.

Having it both ways

It seems to me that the custodial approach and the functional approach do *not* need to be mutually exclusive. An institution may choose to adopt a functional approach to arranging and describing records that reflect a continuing organizational function, such as the archives of government ministries or departments. The same institution may also, quite reasonably, describe archives in custody, such as personal papers, by capturing information about all of the materials in hand.

For instance, the archives of a long-deceased local historian may be as complete and 'whole' as they are ever going to be. Investing too much energy in contextualizing functions and agents to describe that archival collection, when no more materials are likely to arrive, may not be the best use of time.

The problem, as discussed later in the chapter, comes with figuring out how to use parallel approaches efficiently and then present the resulting descriptive information for the researcher without having to build a multitude of different descriptive tools, each of which might demand that the archivist present information in different ways.

Controlling language

Regardless of which approach the archivist takes to arrangement and description, the language used to present information in the description needs to be as consistent as possible. The terms chosen to lead a user into archives, which are called access points, need to be standardized to support consistency and to facilitate access. The archivist needs to choose among variations of terms when providing personal, corporate or geographic names or identifying different subjects.

Selecting terms

Standards exist to help the archivist decide which names and terms to use. Actual thesauri or authority lists can be used, such as a glossary of accounting terms or a thesaurus of geographic names. The first job, though, is not just to start picking terms out of different books but instead to establish the principles under which different words or names will be chosen.

What if a person is known by more than one name? Should the archivist use the common name or the legal name? Lewis Carroll or Charles Lutwidge Dodgson? What about a corporate name? UNESCO or United Nations Educational, Scientific, and Cultural Organization? What if a city is known as both Florence and Firenze? The answers, according to most current authority standards for archival description, would be Lewis Carroll, UNESCO and Florence in England but Firenze in Italy. So it is not a matter of choosing a term in one instance but in defining a principle, then using the term that meets that principle.

The standards that help the archivist with establishing these principles (some of which were mentioned earlier in the discussion of *RiC*) include *ISAAR(CPF)*, which is the *International Standard Archival Authority Record for Corporate Bodies, Persons, and Families* (first published in 1996 and revised in 2004), Part II of *RAD* and Part II of *DACS*. The American standard *Encoded Archival Context* (*EAC*), produced in 2009, also provides guidance about the management of contextual information from archives.

The ICA's *International Standard for Describing Institutions with Archival Holdings* (*ISDIAH*), published in 2008, was developed to control the process of naming archival repositories. And the *International Standard for Describing Functions* (*ISDF*), published in 2011, helps with the consistent identification of functions. As noted, one of the goals of *RiC* is to 'reconcile, integrate and build on' these ICA standards to create one descriptive tool. Whether that effort will be successful remains to be seen.

To standardize the name of geographic locations such as towns, cities, roads or mountains, the archivist can choose among a range of standards published by the International Organization for Standardization (ISO), many of which are identified at the end of the book. Or the archivist can establish a principle that she will always use tools such as the National Geospatial-Intelligence Agency's GEOnet Names Server or the *Getty Thesaurus of Geographic Names*.

To standardize subject terms, the *UNESCO Thesaurus* can be useful, though it is common for archival institutions to develop a list of subject terms appropriate to their region or discipline. For example, a group of municipal archives may create a shared thesaurus of local government terms, while a group of archival institutions devoted to sports, medicine or theatre may work together to create a list of subject terms common to their particular areas of interest.

It is important to add an important caveat to the process of providing access points. The archivist should *not* identify a subject, name or event if that word or phrase does not show up in the archival description. If Joe Bloggs is a prominent name in the archives, the archivist should include his name in the archival description, and she might have to explain who Joe Bloggs was. If the name Joe Bloggs is just added to a list of access terms and not identified in the archival description, the researcher – who goes from the access term to the description to the archives – is halted partway along his route. That leaves the researcher on a dead end road, and that is not quality archival service.

The politics of language

Despite the structure provided by standards, the archivist needs to take into account the politics associated with language. In Canada, for instance, there has been an active process under way to replace western place names with aboriginal terms, such as Haida Gwaii for the Queen Charlotte Islands, Dehcho for the Mackenzie River or Iqaluit for Frobisher Bay. The city of Kitchener, Ontario, changed its name from Berlin in 1916 as a direct result of Canadian hostility toward Germans during the First World War. Internationally, Madras is now also known as Chennai; Kingstown, Ireland, is known as Dún Laoghaire; Salisbury, Zimbabwe, is called Harare; and Saigon is better known as Ho Chi Minh City.

The records generated when those places had their now-superseded names reflect the naming conventions at the time, so those original names will be used in the archives; they are part of the authenticity of the record. The overwhelming guidance from archival standards is that, in order to maintain authenticity and reliability, the archivist should use the term employed *at the time the records were created.* The archivist should then provide cross-references to later or alternate names.

Choosing the terminology for subjects can be even more fraught. The words used to depict historical events, economic issues, social perspectives or theoretical concepts can be highly personal and extremely political. The English tend to refer to the Second World War; the Americans to World War II. In Canada, aboriginal people might be referred to as First Nations, natives, Indians or Inuit. In Australia the term aborigines is used. To refer to someone as 'black' or 'coloured' means one thing in the USA or Canada but something completely different in South Africa, India or Poland.

In order to present information about archives as evidence, the archivist needs to respect the situation in effect when those records were first created and used, however distasteful that may feel to her today. Otherwise, the archivist is misrepresenting history, which is the last thing an archivist, of all people, should do. Again, using original language and then guiding the user into archives by creating cross-references from currently preferred terms to language used at the time will help steer users in the right direction while acknowledging that, like anything, language is fluid.

The challenge of over-prescription

As the functional approach grows more popular, archivists around the world are developing thesauri and authority lists to control the terms used to describe different activities in work and life. ICA's *ISDF* provides guidance on how to prepare descriptions of functions, and these descriptions may also identify business processes, activities, tasks, transactions or other actions. A detailed thesaurus of terms is the *Australian Governments' Interactive Functions Thesaurus* (AGIFT). The Society of American Archivists has developed the *Functions and Activities Thesaurus for Business, Academic, Not-for-Profit, and Government Entities* (2010), which is available online.[4] However, as discussed in Chapter 3, rigidly defining functions or agents presumes a level of certitude and precision that does not relate with the messiness of real life, personal or corporate. Over-prescription may help fit functions, agents and records into boxes, but who wants to live in a box?

The practicalities of arrangement

Once the archivist has taken into consideration the theories and standards in place for arrangement and description, she has to face the body of archives itself, whether the materials are in her custody or are records she controls administratively that live somewhere else. Her job now is – to use highly technical language – to 'figure out the stuff'. When working with materials in hand, it is illogical to describe something without first knowing what is in the boxes or on the computer drives. And as discussed in Chapter 3, it is also dangerous, when working with conceptual functions and linking them to agents and series of records, to assume that what *ought* to be there is there and that who *ought* to have performed a function did actually do so. Thus, in reality, arrangement does not really mean arrangement. Arrangement means *making sense* of the contents, context and structure of archives. The following guidelines are intended to help the archivist work through the intellectual and physical stages of arrangement in a sensible fashion.

Initially the archivist needs to review the materials, whether physical pieces of paper or digital bits of information in a computer file, before arranging or rearranging anything. The archivist may choose to create an intellectual order only, outlining or mapping a logical structure that can then represent the materials even though they are not moved around in boxes. Or she may settle on a preferred arrangement by working with notes and lists and hierarchies, then apply the chosen order to the materials by actually sorting and moving them around. The level of work performed will depend on the state of the materials, the priorities for physical over virtual arrangement and the time and resources available. The following points should be considered:

- Before examining the archives in any detail, and certainly before making any physical changes, the archivist should gather as much information as possible about the archives and the agency or agencies responsible for them, including historical and background information, archival appraisal reports or analyses, relevant reports or publications, or information gleaned from conversations with the donor or creator. This research is vital to contextualizing the archives.
- The archivist next examines everything received with the acquisition or accession before disturbing the current order in any way. She looks for an inherent order but does not assume that if the order does not make immediate sense, it does not exist. She documents the materials as they are now, by summarizing the nature and scope of the materials, listing different file titles and identifying any materials in unexpected locations. The goal is to build up an increasingly comprehensive picture of the nature, scope and evolution of the archives.
- During the examination, the archivist will benefit from identifying any unwanted material such as obvious duplicates or blank stationery, as well as items needing conservation treatments or special handling. She can also identify items with specific storage needs, such as audiovisual materials, oversized maps, artefacts or electronic records.
- Remember that, intellectually, the end product of the arrangement process is a final chosen order. This order may be implemented by physically placing items in sequence in folders and boxes or it may be represented by a written statement on arrangement: a listing of files or a summary of different documents in a digital folder. An essential task, then, is for the archivists to document the original order as received. This statement of original order serves as the baseline, showing how materials were on arrival, even if the decision is to change that order later.
- Particularly when examining personal papers, the archivist needs to remember that the 'original order' may be haphazard at best. Patience is

critical. If a logical solution does not present itself immediately, it is sometimes best to leave the materials as they are and focus instead on learning more about the creator first. (Think of arrangement as solving a crossword puzzle with documentary materials; sometimes leaving the puzzle on the desk and coming back later helps solve even the most complicated clue.)

- During processing, the archivist should keep accurate and detailed notes about the contents and nature of the archives, the people or organizations identified in the materials or the physical condition of different items. These notes will be invaluable when the time comes to prepare the archival description and create access points.
- Once a framework for arrangement is established, and if time allows, the archivist can organize the archives physically in keeping with the chosen structure. A rigid physical arrangement based on hierarchies is not necessary. Sometimes it is reasonable to document the chosen order in archival descriptions but store materials according to their size, shape or preservation requirements. Archives are rarely if ever made available on a 'self-serve' basis, and the user will always need to use descriptive tools as an intermediary step in locating relevant resources. All the archivist really needs to be able to do is link descriptions with location information so that materials can be retrieved easily. At a minimum, she needs to know what *is* there, what *should be* there and, in the event of loss or damage, what *is no longer* there.
- If choosing to reorganize materials into a chosen order (especially with paper and analogue materials), it is wise to organize everything at a general level before moving to more specific work. For instance, it may be possible to confirm that files and folders are in their original series, but the archivist may not have time to review every folder and see if documents are flat or if staples or clips need to be removed. It is a poor use of time to work through individual folders, flattening items or replacing clips, before the archival unit as a whole is in good enough physical order that it can be made available for research use.
- Similarly with digital records, it may be appropriate first to group a large number of digital photographs by event (holiday to Spain, attendance at the company Christmas party in 1976), and leave detailed organization until later, which in the digital world likely entails describing each item.
- As arrangement proceeds, items that should be stored elsewhere can be removed if appropriate. For example, fragile or oversized items may need to be stored separately. These items should be replaced with a 'separation sheet', ideally acid-free paper, that identifies the item(s) that

have been removed, and indicates why they have been moved and where they are presently located. One copy of the sheet is put where the original belongs intellectually, and another copy is put with the actual item in its new location, so that its relationship with the larger body of archives is maintained. The location information is also captured in the descriptive tools. (Think of Jenkinson's elephant and label. A separation sheet would have solved his conundrum easily.)

The practicalities of description

As the archival materials are arranged, whether physically or intellectually, the archivist begins the process of description. The purpose of description is to create a representation of the archives (an explanation of the content, structure and context) so that the materials can be located and used by anyone, for any purpose, while still remaining authentic evidence of the work and life of the creator. The process of archival description involves four steps:

1 The archivist will research and write an account of the nature and scope of the archives, whether approached as a totality of archives in hand or as a series of records representing a function. She will also research and write an account of the life and work of the person, family, organization or business responsible for the creation and use of the archives: the agent or records creator.

2 Depending on the descriptive standards she decides to use, the archivist will then capture other descriptive information such as dates, extent, physical condition, access restrictions and so on, so that she can present a full package of descriptive information to researchers and the public.

3 She will then create standardized access points or intellectual points of entry into the archives, such as names, subjects, dates or events, to help researchers determine which archives are relevant to their research.

4 Finally, she will present all the information she has prepared in various descriptive tools, such as descriptive databases, narrative finding aids, indexes or box, file or item lists, so that users can know about the existence of the archives and understand their content, context, structure, scope and nature.

The options for presenting descriptive information are discussed in the next section. But before going there, it is necessary to wrap up a discussion of practicalities by emphasizing that, yet again, the archivist must establish priorities for her work. The best and wisest course of action is to follow the order of action suggested below:

1   Accession all new acquisitions and any backlogged material before turning to archival description. Administrative control is a more critical priority than intellectual control.

2   Before embarking on a descriptive programme, ensure that the tools and technologies chosen conform with institutional policies and priorities and any requirements for information sharing and networking. For instance, many web-based archival information tools require contributors to follow specific descriptive standards. The archivist should confirm which standards to follow – such as *RAD* versus *ISAD(G)* versus *DACS* versus *DAC* – before embarking on complex descriptive projects.

3   When preparing descriptions, again it is best to work from the general to the specific: create summary descriptions for each whole body of archives before preparing detailed descriptions of specific series or items. Otherwise backlogged materials remain entirely inaccessible while the archivist is immersed in a small subset of holdings.

4   Develop a consistent and documented approach to creating access points, based on chosen standards for the use of language. Be sure to identify any issues of access or privacy when preparing any tools for online use. When preparing indexes of personal names, for instance, the archivist may need to clarify any concerns about confidentiality.

5   Once backlogged materials are adequately processed and described, establish priorities for description based on criteria such as the potential level of use of archives. If a particular set of archival materials will be in high demand, the archivist may well save time and improve access by preparing a detailed archival description of those materials, and perhaps by digitizing selections for online access. She can then make those materials available easily, which may satisfy many researchers' needs and leave her more time to tackle other projects.

6   Actively monitor the use of all the institution's finding aids and descriptive tools. Ask users if they find tools understandable and usable and make changes if needed. Review the descriptive programme frequently so that it remains effective and informative. Do not be afraid to change the way archives are described; if the present approach seems problematic, consider other options. But avoid changing so often that the user who arrives in March cannot find the same descriptions when he returns in May.

Presenting descriptive information

Once the archivist has captured all the content that may be included in an archival description, and she has identified access terms to support reference and use, the next step is to present that information in an easily understood form for researchers and the public. The final archival descriptive tool may be a paper or electronic document. The choice of presentation format may depend on the type of material being described, the nature and research interests of the intended audience, the technological capacity of the institution or other factors, as discussed in this section.

The evolution of descriptive tools

It is worth reminding ourselves that digital databases dedicated to archival description (as opposed to bibliographic tools such as *MARC*, which were created for library use and adapted for archival use) have only been around for a quarter of a century or so. Until the 1990s, many archivists still actively produced paper-based finding aids: typed or word-processed descriptions or printed books and pamphlets. A particularly popular activity was the production of thematic or repository guides, which described all of an institution's holdings or identified archives within the institution (or across a region or country) related to a particular topic, such as sports, women, architecture or literary studies.

The next innovation in description was the creation of mechanisms for replicating in digital form the contents of paper finding aids. The researcher might be presented with a PDF version of an archival inventory, containing all the information found in the original print document. In the USA, a standard called *Encoded Archival Description* (*EAD*) was developed in 1993, with the goal of providing a consistent way of marking up or encoding traditional archival finding aids for electronic exchange and presentation. (*EAD3* was released in 2015.) The greatest strength of *EAD* was that it did not just present a digital copy of a PDF file but instead incorporated hyperlinks so that users could open an *EAD*-formatted descriptive tool, see the high-level description of the archival materials on the computer screen, then click on the link to move to a more detailed description of a series, then to another description of a file and so on.

Today, descriptive tools can be categorized in relation to their purpose and structure. While more and more take digital form, paper-based finding aids are still created, especially detailed narratives, which can help contextualize a complex body of archives. These are different genres of descriptive tool often created today:

- *Accession registers or databases* are administrative tools that also serve as the 'first' finding aid. They allow the archivist to identify every accession received and document the location of materials even before detailed finding aids are prepared.

- *Descriptive databases* or networked information resources provide summary information about all groups of material (whether *fonds*, series, item or other) within the custody or control of the institution.
- *Descriptive inventories,* also called 'archival descriptions', 'finding aids' or 'lists', describe the contents of different groups of archives.
- *Guides* provide a brief description of a large group of holdings, such as all the archives held by the institution or all the acquisitions received in the last number of years (a repository guide) or all the holdings of one or more institutions that relate to a particular subject, time, place or event (a thematic guide). Today, repository guides and thematic guides are being replaced by online subject-oriented tools, which allow users around the world to seek out relevant archival materials without having to acquire a printed publication, which is often out of date as soon as it is published.
- *Location files* (or lists or digital databases) are critical administrative finding aids that identify where in the repository certain archival holdings have been stored, so that materials may be retrieved and replaced easily and consistently.
- *Indexes* identify subjects, places, names or other identifiers found in a specific body of archives or across the holdings of an institution. (Increasingly indexing functions are built into online descriptive tools, creating a list of index terms for archives in custody and a thesaurus of terms to use when describing new archives.)

Digital tools

Many institutions are relying more and more on digital tools and software applications to support description. Commercial and open-source software tools make the data entry job much easier, and well-designed tools also support the easy application of descriptive standards, resulting in a consistent presentation of content. Some digital tools go beyond description, providing software support for a number of archival activities, from acquisition and accessioning, to documenting conservation needs or environmental conditions, to capturing archival descriptions, registering and monitoring users and even managing the movement, storage and location of archives throughout the repository.

It is not possible to identify all the software tools available today, and it is unfair to software developers to declare that one tool is the last word and another is completely inappropriate. It is not unreasonable, though, to identify two particular tools, because they have been designed specifically for archival purposes, they are actively used in various places around the world and they are both open source, so are – with all the caveats that come with the word – 'free'.

One tool is *AtoM*, a web-based, open-source software application originally designed with partial support from the ICA. *AtoM* allows the archivist to insert descriptive information into templates. The templates have been designed to match different elements in various descriptive standards, including *ISAD(G), ISAAR(CPF), ISDIAH, ISDF, RAD, DACS, Dublin Core* and the Library of Congress' *Metadata Object Description Schema* (*MODS*), a standard for capturing metadata. By using a tool such as *AtoM*, the archivist can create descriptions according to the standards she has chosen for her institution, by entering information into the chosen template, and then she can upload the completed description to her own institutional database or to a website within an archival network.

Another open-source tool, developed in the USA, is *ArchivesSpace*, which supersedes the popular *Archivist's Toolkit*. *ArchivesSpace* is a web application for managing information about archives and supporting core functions such as accessioning, arrangement and description, authority control, the management of rights, reference service, and the creation of administrative reports. *ArchivesSpace* also supports the creation and capture of metadata and works with data formatted using tools and standards such as *EAD, MARC, MODS, Dublin Core* and *METS*.

Since these and other software applications are constantly changing, the best way to find out current information is to contact the professional archival association or national archives in a particular jurisdiction. The resources section offers some guidance. However, because information about these tools can easily be found on the internet, a first step is to look at their websites to learn more and particularly to download demonstration packages to test out. This way it is possible to research archival software without investing anything more than a little time and effort.[5]

Sample descriptive output

Given the different approaches to archival description, and the move away from printed, paper-based 'finding aids' to online summaries, providing examples of finished archival descriptions in a book like this is challenging, to say the least. However, because illustrations can teach more than words, I am including two samples of descriptive output, one for a body of archives in custody and one to represent a functional approach. In the first instance (Figures 11.1, 11.2 and 11.3) I show how a hierarchical description would be constructed, and in the second (Figures 11.4, 11.5 and 11.6) I show how different descriptions for functions, agents and records would be put together.

The purpose of presenting these examples is not to demand that the archivist create exact replicas of one or the other model. Rather, I want to show what descriptive output might look like in these two different situations, which have formed such a central part of the discussion of archival theory and practice throughout this book. As will be evident, a simple layout of the core descriptive elements results in a display that mirrors the levels or entities presented in different descriptive standards.

Custody-oriented archival descriptions

Figures 11.1, 11.2 and 11.3 show *fonds*, series, and item-level descriptions for a (highly fictitious) Canadian politician and photographer named James Carstairs, whose papers have found their way into the custody of an (even more fictitious) Canadian archival institution. Also included are index terms for people or subjects represented in the archives, which are necessary to lead the researcher interested in different topics into these archives.

Function-oriented archival descriptions

Figures 11.4, 11.5 and 11.6 show function, agency and record descriptions for a (fictitious) environmental management function, the records of which are housed in another (non-existent) Canadian archival repository. Index terms have not been displayed, in part because there is an underlying assumption with the functional approach that the researcher will start his search by looking for functions or agents relevant to his research interest in order to locate particular archives. Since those functions or agents are standardized, and access points lead users from alternate terms to preferred terms, creating separate index points is often a task undertaken later, if at all. That said, the archivist may need to create index terms for specific content within the archives. For instance, access points for the archives described below might be created for the names of the different locations where waste management work was carried out. Note also that this structure presumes that the information is presented in an online format and that the user can click on links to access each part of the three-part description.

Repository identification code	CA GRA
Name of repository	Great River Archives, Great River, Alberta, Canada
Archives code	F1985–006
Title	James Carstairs Archives
Dates of creation	1989–1985 (predominant 1939–1985)
Extent and physical description	14.5 m of textual records and other materials. Includes ca. 14.5 m of textual records, 950 photographs: b&w and col., 3 photograph albums (300 photographs), 125 photographic negatives, 4 audio reels, 2 audio cassettes, 20 maps, 11 objects.
Biography	James Carstairs was born James Cuthbertson Carstairs in Great River, Alberta, on April 27, 1919. He took his early education in Great River, graduating from Great River High School in 1937. Carstairs served with the Canadian Armed Forces in the Second World War between 1937 and 1944. Prior to and after his military service, Carstairs attended the University of Alberta where he obtained a Bachelor of Laws degree. Carstairs practised law with the firm Carstairs and Cartwright, Attorneys-at-Law in Calgary from 1945 until 1950, when he was elected Mayor of Aikensville, Alberta. He served as mayor until 1960 when he entered federal politics. Carstairs was elected as the Liberal Party Member of Parliament for Aikensville in 1960 and held the riding until 1966. From 1962 to 1966, Carstairs served as federal Minister of Fisheries. After his retirement from politics in 1966, Carstairs focused on his personal hobby of photography. He and his wife, Eleanor, relocated to Great River in 1975, where he taught photography courses at Calestoga College. Carstairs was also active in the Great River community, serving on the executives of the Great River Rotary Club, the Great River Chamber of Commerce and the Great River Curling Club between 1975 and 1985. James Carstairs died in Great River on May 22, 1985. James Carstairs married Eleanor Marie Higgs on December 31, 1944. They had four children: Melanie Rose (b. 1946), James Edwin (b. 1948), Sarah Catherine (b. 1952) and Joseph Albert (b. 1958).
Scope and content	The James Carstairs Papers consists of records created, accumulated and used by James Carstairs of Great River, Alberta, between 1919 and 1985. The papers include records pertaining to his family; military service; professional career as a lawyer and politician; vocation of photography and work as a photography instructor; and his personal pursuits and volunteer activities. Record types in the papers include: correspondence; photographs; administrative records; financial records; photocopies of newspaper clippings; speaking notes; scrapbooks; publications; brochures; pamphlets; certificates; maps; audio recordings; and objects.
Custodial history	These archives were donated by Eleanor Carstairs, widow of James Carstairs, to the Great River Archives in one accession in 1987: 1987–222 (February 15, 1987).
Source of supplied title	Title based on contents of the archives.
Notes on arrangement	The materials were received in no discernible order, and the archivist imposed an order based upon an analysis of life and work of James Carstairs, discussions with Eleanor Carstairs and a review of the archival materials in hand.

Figure 11.1 *Presentation of fonds in a custody-oriented description*

Restrictions	Access to the archives for research purposes is not restricted. Individuals wishing to reproduce materials for publication are reminded of the need to obtain permission from copyright holders prior to any publication or dissemination.
Accruals	No further accruals are expected.
Access points	• Aikensville, Alberta – government • Calestoga College, Great River, Alberta • Calgary, Alberta • Carstairs and Cartwright, Attorneys-at-Law (Calgary, Alberta) • Carstairs, James Cuthbertson • Carstairs, Eleanor (née Higgs) • Clubs and organizations – Great River Chamber of Commerce • Clubs and organizations – Great River Curling Club • Clubs and organizations – Great River Rotary Club • Fishing and fisheries • Great River, Alberta • Photography • Politics and government – federal • Politics and government – municipal – Edmonton • Liberal Party of Canada • Second World War • Travel

Figure 11.1 *Continued*

Archives group title	James Carstairs Archives
Series	Political Career
Series no	F1985–006, Series 3
Dates	[192–?]–[196–?]
Extent and physical description	ca. 6.7 m of textual records and other materials, including 4 audio reels, 2 audio cassettes, 8 maps.
Biographical sketch	See *fonds* description.
Scope and content	This series consists of records created, accumulated and used by James Carstairs in his political career between approximately 1950 and approximately 1966. It includes records of Carstairs as Mayor of Aikensville, Liberal Party Member of Parliament for Aikensville and federal Minister of Fisheries. Record types in the series include correspondence; memoranda; speaking notes; campaign and promotional materials; publications; scrapbooks; audio recordings; and maps. This series has been arranged into two sub-series: Municipal Politics: Edmonton; and Federal Politics.
Source of supplied title	Title based on contents of the archives.
Arrangement notes	The materials in this series were presented in two groups, one related to municipal politics and another to federal politics. Eleanor Carstairs indicated in interviews that this was the order used by James Carstairs, and the archivist retained this order when arranging the materials.
Restrictions	Access to the archives for research purposes is not restricted. Individuals wishing to reproduce materials for publication are reminded of the need to obtain permission from copyright holders prior to any publication or dissemination.
Accruals	No further accruals are expected.

Figure 11.2 *Presentation of series in a custody-oriented description*

Item number	F1985–006 – PH 1477–17
Title	[James Carstairs and his curling team at the final day of play at the 1977 Great River Curling Club Bonspiel]
Dates	February 18, 1977
Scope and content	Inscription on verso of photograph reads 'To the top curler in 1977 – Congratulations, Jimmy!'
Note	James Carstairs is the only person identified in the photograph; the other three men remain unidentified.
Physical description	1 photograph: silver gelatin print ; 16 x 27 cm.
Physical condition	Emulsion is cracked in the upper left corner.
Part of	James Carstairs Archives, Archives Group No: F1985–006
Photograph geographic location	Great River, Alberta
Photograph subject term(s):	Great River, Alberta; Great River Curling Club; Curling
Copyright status	Photograph still protected by copyright; photographer unknown.
Location	No. 950–B–8 File 16

Figure 11.3 *Presentation of items in a custody-oriented description*

Repository identification code	CA PALA
Name of repository	Provincial Archives and Library of Alberta, Canada
Title	Regional waste management disposal files
Dates of creation	1956–2014 (series)
Scope and content	Records accumulated and used by regional offices responsible for environmental assessment, used to assess, monitor and report on waste management disposal activities. Series may contain applications for the establishment of a waste disposal site, site review reports and recommendations, copies of certificates of approval, maps and plans of sites, technical and environmental data and statistics, correspondence and photographs.
Extent and physical description	45 m of textual records and other materials, including photographs, cartographic records, data files and e-mails.
Administrative history	Click on the links below for more information: Department of Mines and Energy (1956–1977) Department of Environmental Management (1977–1984) Office of the Environmental Control Administration (1985–1987) Department of Energy, Mines and Resources (1987–2003) Department of Environment and Climate Change (2004–2016)
Restrictions on access	Access to records 50 years old or less is governed by the Freedom of Access to Information and Protection of Personal Privacy Act, 1997; requests for access must be presented to the Provincial Archives and Library.

Figure 11.4 *Presentation of series in a function-oriented description*

| Copyright | Copyright is held by the Crown. There are no restrictions on use for research or private study. Other uses require advance permission; contact the Provincial Archives and Library for guidance. |
| Custodial history | The series was transferred to the custody of the Provincial Archives and Library by the Department of Environment and Climate Change in 2015. |

Figure 11.4 *Continued*

Name	Department of Environmental Management
Dates of existence	1977–1984
Function	The Department of the Environmental Management was responsible for policy development, monitoring and oversight to support environmental protection across the state. Activities included the monitoring of air quality and pollution and reviewing and overseeing land use actions such as mining or forestry, as well as overseeing work associated with waste management and waste disposal in all regions.
Administrative history	The Department of Environmental Management consisted of the Office of the Director, the Office of the Assistant Director, an Administrative Services Directorate, the Air Quality Directorate, the Mining Oversight Office, the Forestry Oversight Office and the Waste Management Agency. The Department received its mandate to operate during the organizational restructuring of the state government in April 1977, as per State Statute 567–4, passed 5 April 1977.
Also known as	Department of Mines and Energy (1956–1977) Office of the Environmental Control Administration (1985–1987) Department of Energy, Mines and Resources (1987–2003) Department of Environment and Climate Change (2004–2016)
Controlling agencies	Click on the link below for information about agencies this department reported to: Ministry of Environment and Resources (1956–1984) Ministry of Environmental Control (1985–2003) Ministry of Climate, Environment, and Sustainable Energy (2004–2016)
Record series	Click on the links below for information about the records series related to this agency: • regional waste management disposal files • environmental policy files • environmental oversight and protection • air pollution monitoring and quality control • lands management files • forestry management files • waste management policy files

Figure 11.5 *Presentation of agencies in a function-oriented description*

Function	Definition
Environmental management (broader term)	The activities and tasks associated with developing policies and strategies for managing the natural and built environment, monitoring and assessing environmental conditions and supporting environmental protection and conservation services.
Environmental impact assessment (narrower term)	The activities and tasks associated with evaluating the effects of the human use of or inputs onto the natural environment. The work includes assessing, monitoring and reporting on environmental activities such as waste management and disposal, infrastructure projects and commercial or residential developments.
Pollution mitigation (narrower term)	The activities and tasks associated with developing standards and specific initiatives to reduce air, land, and water pollution; to mitigate the negative outcomes of pollutants; to increase public awareness of the impact of pollution and the actions associated with pollution reduction; and to promote environmentally and economically sustainable alternatives to activities that generate pollution.

Figure 11.6 *Presentation of functions in a function-oriented description*

While many archivists argue (sometimes heatedly) about *fonds* versus function, a more appropriate discussion might be around when it is appropriate to arrange and describe stable, long-closed, unchanging archives one way and when it is better to describe a complex, dynamic, still growing body of records another way. One can, perhaps, have it both ways. Sometimes. It is also worth remembering that nothing stays the same. As digital archival materials become more ubiquitous, and as those in positions of authority are too often reluctant to accept rigorous record-keeping requirements, archivists are now becoming more and more involved in archival activism, rescuing and managing archives outside formal, traditional institutional frameworks. The validity of this approach is a matter of debate, but it is an increasingly common scenario, and there will be consequences for all aspects of archival practice, including arrangement and description. The archivist ten years from now may have no 'institution' to hold archival materials; she may be working with a consortium of like-minded individuals to manage digital copies of records that have been extracted from other records systems and preserved because this group of archivists feels that otherwise the archives would be lost or damaged. What happens to custodial or post-custodial approaches then, when archival service is no longer bound by either custody or control?

Having ended on that speculative note, I will put my deck of archival tarot cards away and turn to the next and last topic in the book. Once archives have been arranged and descriptive tools have been prepared, the archivist's next responsibility is to help the public use the documentary resources in her institution. The next chapter examines issues related to providing reference and to engaging with actual and potential users of archives.

Notes

1 Some attempts have been made to develop standards specifically for archival arrangement, but the rapid pace of technological change suggests that expending too much effort on outlining hierarchies or levels of control will be for naught when digital objects can be associated with numerous creating agencies, users, stakeholders, functions, activities or events, all at the same time. A place for everything and everything in its place is a very analogue concept.

2 In 2010, the Library of Congress replaced the *Anglo-American Cataloguing Rules* Second Edition, with *Resource Description and Access* (*RDA*), which addresses principles of bibliographic control for libraries and allied cultural institutions such as museums and archives.

3 Note that the levels of repository or country are not included in these tables, but identifying these two pieces of information is important if users outside the repository are going to access descriptions. A repository code can be created, such as SMI for the Smitherman County Archives or VAN for the Vancouver Community Archives. Or existing codes can be used: lists of repository codes have been developed in various jurisdictions, including the Library of Congress in the USA and The National Archives in the UK. Country names can also be codified using standards such as ISO 3166: *Codes for the Representation of Names of Countries and their Subdivisions*. This standard provides accepted codes for countries, which would show, for instance, FI for Finland and ZA for South Africa.

4 The Australian thesaurus is available at www.naa.gov.au/agift/00700013.htm. The American tool is at www2.archivists.org/sites/all/files/FunctionsThesaurus2010.pdf.

5 For more on *AtoM*, see https://www.archivematica.org/en/; for more on *ArchivesSpace*, see http://archivesspace.org/.

12

Making archives available

To oblige persons often costs little and helps much.
Baltasar Gracián (1601–58) *The Art of Worldly Wisdom*, 1647

Finally, we have reached what some consider the ultimate archival activity: making archives available for use. Once the archivist has acquired, arranged and described archival materials, and stored them so they are safe from harm, she can, and *should*, open the doors and invite the public in.

Traditionally, that is what archivists did. They opened the doors and invited the public, or a select few, into a reference room, where the users sat, in scholarly silence, waiting for boxes and folders to emerge, like treasures on a platter, from the storage vaults. The medieval archivist in the heart of England did not cart the town's archival treasures around in a wagon and set up roadside exhibits of scrolls and parchments. Original archival materials were kept in locked containers, brought out for the privileged few who were permitted access to the archival *sanctum sanctorum*.

Today, when people can access information through the internet 24 hours a day, archivists still preserve and protect physical, tangible goods, not only paper archives or audiovisual recordings or photographs but also very physical and very expensive computer servers and storage devices used to store and make available irreplaceable electronic archives. But while the physical space for holding archives will not go away, people no longer have to go to the archival reference room for answers to all their questions. Not every item in archival custody will ever be digitized, and helping the researcher in person will still be necessary and valuable, but archivists can make more and more information available online, through databases, websites, digital information networks and social media.

But while computers have made the act of gaining access easier, they have made the process of providing it much harder. The archivist today faces the challenge of balancing access and privacy, respecting individual rights and protecting both physical and digital holdings from loss or harm, problems which were much easier to manage when everyone wanting access stood in line in front of a reference desk.

The archivist also faces increased pressure to make holdings available instantaneously. Archival access and outreach – once overlooked and neglected components of archival service – are now a priority for funders and decision makers, who often have a mistaken idea about how easy it is to digitize archives and make them available online.

The archivist's first reference responsibility, though, does not change. Once she has gained legal, physical and intellectual control of the holdings in her institution, she needs to make them available for use, in keeping with necessary conditions on access. At a bare minimum, the archivist needs to provide the space and services necessary to allow people to come into her institution and access archives in person.

It is not enough to set aside a corner of the archivist's desk as a 'reference' facility available only when the archivist is not sitting there. Nor is it appropriate to vet researchers to decide if their topic is 'worthy' enough to allow entrée to the archives. If the archival institution exists to support the acquisition and preservation of archives in order to make them available, then they should be made available. But – and there is always a 'but' – reference is a balancing act, as discussed below.

Providing equitable access

In theory, anyone should be welcome in the archival institution. This is particularly true if the facility is supported through public funds and preserves archives for public use. If someone wishes to use the holdings of the repository, and if the materials in question are not restricted, the archivist should not limit use.

In some parts of the world, access to archival facilities and holdings is highly restricted, if not truly onerous. In certain countries, researchers must apply in writing months in advance to obtain permission to visit the institution. In other places, only citizens of that country may access the government's archives. Foreign nationals might not even be allowed into the building. In reality, no archivist can overturn the legal or administrative requirements of her own sponsor agency or government by herself. She is bound by her terms of employment to follow existing laws and regulations. Still, the archivist has a responsibility as a member of her profession to do the utmost to acquire, preserve and *make available* the materials in her care, with respect for the rights of records creators, other citizens and future users.

Conditions on access

On behalf of her institution, the archivist can establish some reasonable conditions on access, to protect the holdings and ensure the rights of researchers and the public are respected. It is common and sensible, for instance, to ask all researchers to register and provide identification before being admitted to the reference room. Does the user need to provide academic credentials? Does the researcher have to be a citizen of the country? A resident? A taxpayer? Some institutions may welcome children in the reference room, while others may define it as an adults-only space. Some countries may need to limit public service during public holidays or religious festivals, others may be happy to remain open 24/7/365.

Some repositories, such as corporate archives, may only provide access to people within the organization. That may be reasonable. Others, such as community archives, may serve everyone from academic researchers to genealogists to school children. The reference policies of each type of institution will reflect these differences in audience and scope.

Access can also be affected by the nature of the materials. How will the archivist provide access to an extensive but extremely fragile collection of medieval scrolls? How will she provide access to a collection of e-mails stored in the institution's digital repository? In these instances, access depends on resources, from stands to support oversized scrolls to computers for public use in the reference room.

Access and privacy

As discussed in Chapter 7, the archivist needs to consider the privacy rights of the creators and the people named in archives. Decisions about access are made first to respect legal or policy requirements, then to respect the wishes of donors, then to protect the physical material from harm. The archivist should not circumvent any such conditions, which should be documented in descriptive tools.

Beyond the privacy of individuals identified in archives, the archivist must also consider the rights of the users of those materials. People access archives for many reasons, from family history to legal research. Some uses of archives might be highly personal and sensitive. What if a researcher is seeking archives that might confirm he was adopted as a baby? He might not want to explain his research request within earshot of everyone else in the reference room. Another researcher might be researching government records related to mining because he wants to stake a claim. His economic interests could be damaged if his research request is broadcast to other potential prospectors in the building.

The archivist also has to balance competing research demands. How does she provide equitable service to legal researchers on opposing sides of a court case? She needs to do her utmost to provide the same level of assistance to both parties without becoming personally interested in one side or the other, and without violating the privacy of either party.

Respecting diversity and ensuring accessibility

The archivist must also be sensitive to her constituents. If an archival institution serves a bilingual or multicultural population, the archivist needs to consider if and how to address the needs of different members of the community. How can the institution provide the widest possible access to the archives in its care if the records are in different languages? Similarly, archives may illustrate events or activities that are upsetting to some in society. How much responsibility can the archivist take for warning researchers that they may find the materials troubling? More practically, how can the archival institution reasonably support access by people with different abilities or needs? Can she accommodate the needs of researchers with impaired hearing and sight? What is the institution's responsibility for ensuring people using mobility devices like wheelchairs can get into the building?

Establishing a reference and access framework

The archivist needs to formalize policies and processes related to reference and access. These policies explain the institution's responsibility to ensure users can access holdings and benefit from the content in them. Figure 12.1 illustrates a sample reference and access policy for a fictitious community-based archival institution, the Cheswick Historical Society Archives.

The mandate of the Cheswick Historical Society Archives, as governed by the Cheswick Historical Society Constitution and Bylaws, is to acquire, preserve and make available the documentary heritage of the town of Cheswick and the surrounding community, including archives of the Cheswick local government authority as well as private papers from individuals, businesses and organizations related to the community, in order to illuminate and foster understanding of the history, development and identity of the town of Cheswick and its people.

Figure 12.1 *Cheswick Historical Society Archives reference policy*

The materials collected by the Cheswick Historical Society Archives include archival materials in any media that are concerned with the development and history of the community. The Archives and the Cheswick Museum work closely together to co-ordinate the preservation of both archives and artefacts.

To support equal access to its holdings while protecting the materials for current and future use, the Cheswick Historical Society Archives advises visitors to the institution of the following conditions on access and use.

Hours
The archives' reference room is open to researchers Tuesdays to Saturdays from 9 a.m. to 5 p.m.

Registration
All researchers are requested to register, providing their name, address, telephone number and signature, and they are required to present proof of identification, including confirmation of address, contact details and, if possible, an e-mail address. Personal information gathered will only be used for security and communication purposes and for statistical analysis and will not be published or disseminated beyond the archival institution.

Reference room conditions of use
1   Researchers may not bring coats, briefcases, backpacks or personal books into the reference room. Storage cubicles are provided in the reception area and locks and keys are available free of charge from the reference archivist. Researchers are advised to keep their valuables, such as wallets, on their person; the Cheswick Historical Society Archives is not responsible for lost or stolen items.
2   Personal computers, small digital cameras, cellular phones with cameras and dictation or recording equipment for personal note taking or for photographing documents or images are permitted in the reference room. Camera flashes, video cameras, tripods and scanning equipment are not permitted.
3   No internet connectivity is provided for users' own computers, but internet access to the online finding aids of neighbouring archives is available through the computer in the reference room. Researchers wishing to access the internet for e-mail or other purposes are asked to consult the list of nearby internet cafés, available in the reference room.
4   Pens or ink of any kind may not be used in the reference room. The archivist will supply pencils on request.
5   Smoking, eating and drinking are prohibited in the reference room. Researchers may access the staff lunch room to consume their own refreshments. Smoking is only permitted outside the building in the designated smoking area.
6   All archival materials must be handled carefully. When working with paper archives, researchers are requested to open only one folder at a time and to keep items in their existing order. They are advised not to place bound materials face down, nor to lean on materials or write on or trace over materials.
7   When handling analogue materials such as audiovisual recordings, researchers will follow the instructions of reference staff for loading and viewing materials on equipment provided in the audiovisual area. Researchers may not use their own equipment for audiovisual playback or recording.

Figure 12.1 *Continued*

. 8   To access digital holdings, researchers will use the computer set up for digital archives reference. Print facilities are provided for a fee. Researchers must obtain an access code from the archivist before they can log into the computer and printer.

9   No archival material may be removed from the reference room. The archivist reserves the right to inspect all containers, bags or folders when researchers leave the room.

10   Researchers who wish to view restricted materials must contact the individual or agency imposing the restrictions. Staff will be happy to provide contact details whenever they are available but cannot permit access to any restricted materials without written authority from the appropriate agency.

Reproduction, copyright and publication

1   Archival materials are fragile and irreplaceable, and they can be damaged by excessive exposure to the light from photocopiers or scanners. Consequently, researchers are strongly urged to allow enough time to conduct necessary research on site at the archival institution and to request reproductions of documents for off-premises study only if absolutely necessary.

2   No materials may be duplicated that are subject to restrictions on reproduction, either from donors or depositors of the archives or by the terms of copyright law, or because materials are restricted for preservation, processing or other reasons.

3   If materials in question are not restricted or protected by copyright conditions, the Cheswick Historical Society Archives will provide print or digital copies of archival materials for a fee. A schedule of fees is available in the reference room.

4   Researchers requesting copies of items from the archives must sign a request for reproductions form confirming that the materials are for personal or reference use only and will not be published or distributed for any other purpose.

5   The Archives cannot guarantee copies will be made immediately and will advise users of the estimated time required to complete copying requests. Rush orders will only be accepted at the discretion of the archivist and may be subject to additional fees.

6   Researchers may photograph archival materials using small digital cameras or cameras in their cell phones. However, they must sign a request for reproductions form before beginning to make copies and they are expected to abide by the terms and conditions outlined in that form.

7   It is the responsibility of researchers to obtain copyright clearance to publish or distribute any archival material. Whenever possible, the archivist will provide contact information for copyright holders to facilitate the copyright clearance process, but the archivist will not undertake the clearance process on behalf of any researcher.

8   If a researcher wishes to publish material from archival collections and has obtained the necessary permissions, the researcher is asked to credit the archival institution as follows: Cheswick Historical Society Archives, archives title and number, series, volume or file number, title or identification of document and dates of the document. For example:

Cheswick Historical Society Archives, Cheswick Community Festival Society Archives, No. 2006–22, Series 13, File 19, Annual Report on Festivals, 1959, December 12, 1956.

Figure 12.1 *Continued*

Support for users

The Cheswick Historical Society Archives is committed to providing equitable access to archival holdings to everyone, including people with disabilities. As much as possible, the Archives will strive to provide services and resources in a manner that supports access and use regardless of ability, including providing archival descriptions available in different formats and making copies of original material to permit alternate methods of handling and use. The Archives also maintains a list of community service agencies that researchers may consult for assistance with such research.

The staff of the archives will be pleased to assist and advise researchers who visit the archives in person, but given the limited resources available the Cheswick Historical Society Archives can only provide remote research support of no more than one hour every three months to external researchers who cannot visit the institution in person. All requests must be approved in advance. Cases of legal or humanitarian urgency may justify the provision of additional research services, at the Archives' discretion. The Archives maintains a list of professional researchers who can be hired to provide further assistance. However, the Archives does not endorse the people on the list and does not assume any responsibility for the quality of their work.

The Cheswick Historical Society Archives supports remote access to information from and about its holdings by contributing archival descriptions to the national archival descriptive network and by publishing information on its website. For more information, go to www.CheswickHistory.edu.uk.

Further information

Anyone is welcome to contact the Archivist if they have questions or need further information. Contact details are provided below:

Cheswick Historical Society Archives
4556 Stewardson Way
Cheswick, Cambridgeshire CB0 1AW
UK
Tel: 01223 566555
Fax: 01223 566556
Website: www.CheswickHistory.edu.uk
Email: info@CheswickHistory.edu.uk

Figure 12.1 *Continued*

Providing reference services

No matter who comes into the reference room, the archivist needs to create a supportive service environment by investing in resources such as information technology, reference publications, office equipment and general supplies. The basics of a safe and comfortable environment must be a given: desks and chairs, light and heat, access to nearby refreshment facilities and so on. The institution's descriptive tools, print and electronic, should be available for easy use in the reference area. A collection of standard reference materials such as atlases, dictionaries, encyclopaedias, local histories and relevant periodicals or journals is helpful. Beyond those necessities, the archivist needs to consider the following questions:

- Will users be able to access the internet in the reference room to use web-based reference tools? What security issues need to be considered? What are the costs of acquiring, maintaining and upgrading the equipment? How will the archivist address the inevitable problem of researchers misusing the technology or overstaying their welcome at the only computer in the reference room?
- Does the archives collect microfilm, sound recordings, video tapes or other media-dependent materials? If so, how will users access these materials? The institution may need to invest in microfilm readers and printers, tape players, video machines or DVD players.
- Will the institution provide photocopies? Under what conditions? The archivist needs to develop policies about what will or will not be copied, how much users will be charged, how and when copies will be made and how users will be advised of copyright concerns. And the institution will need reliable access to a photocopier.

The archivist also needs to clarify if the institution will set any specific conditions on activities within the reference room. Under what conditions will researchers be allowed to bring computers or cell phones into the room? Will they be allowed to photograph archival materials using their own cameras or cell phones? Permitting researchers to take their own photographs of documents or images can be a great time saver, especially compared with transcribing archives by hand. But immediate and ad hoc reproduction opens the door to potential copyright violations.

The archivist also has to decide if the institution can support the use of personal electronics. She needs to consider if there are enough outlets to allow users to plug in their computers or charge up their cell phones. She needs to set parameters around how and where and when researchers can photograph documents so they do not disturb others in the room. She needs to assess the security measures needed to prevent unauthorized use of the institution's own computer networks.

Individual support for users

To provide quality reference services, the archivist must know her institution's collections and services well. She also needs to understand the different types of visitors who come to the institution. No aspect of archival work is more people oriented than reference. The archivist needs to be comfortable with explaining, often many times over, how the institution operates, what materials it holds and how to use reference tools. Even the most informative website or orientation guide will not replace human answers to human questions. (In truth, a really good reference archivist is often more interested in the visitor than in the archives.)

If the reference archivist is communicating the same information multiple times, it may be helpful to prepare print or digital reference guides that answer frequently asked questions. Some institutions produce introductory films, available in the lobby and on the institution's web page, explaining the facility and its holdings and services. Leaflets in the reference room can explain to researchers how to access genealogical records or documents related to the history of their house. The investment in good quality reference tools is not inconsiderable, but the savings in time, and the increased public understanding of archives, are often well worth the effort.

Reference interviews

The archivist might conduct an in-depth reference interview to help identify a researcher's particular interests and steer him in the direction of suitable materials. Sometimes this interview is helpful for both parties, but if it becomes obligatory it can become just another bureaucratic hoop. A seasoned academic researcher may only be interested in knowing about recent changes in holdings or services and needs no additional guidance from the reference archivist. But a local citizen investigating his family history may have never visited an archival institution before. He may benefit greatly from a face-to-face conversation with an archivist, who can steer him through the nuances of research and also, perhaps reassure him of the importance of his work and the fact that the institution exists for him too, not just for lawyers or professors or doctoral students.

Online reference

It is rare in the first decades of the 21st century to find an archival institution that does not have some sort of internet presence. Some have basic websites or pages within their sponsor agency's website. Others make all their summary descriptions available online through dedicated archival software, linking digital objects such as photographs or documents to the descriptions, giving the remote researcher comprehensive access to a wide range of virtual content.

A forward-thinking archivist will embrace digital technologies to support reference services as much as the technological infrastructure in her jurisdiction allows. She must be careful, though, not to let the lure of shiny new digital devices or systems pre-empt core archival responsibilities for accountability, transparency and efficiency in all operations. For instance, there is little benefit to making all descriptive information available in a database but not have an internet connection. Users then have to come into the institution to use a computer in the reference room to find out about holdings, defeating the benefit of digital technologies. And when the researchers come, what happens if they all have to line up to use the only computer in the office? If internet capacity is not possible, it would be better to invest in more computers or to create parallel paper finding aids, at least until the institution has the capacity to become fully digital.

Still, the 21st-century world *is* digital. The archivist needs to assess whether and how she can provide the following web-based resources:

- *Institutional websites.* An institution should have a basic website or a dedicated page within the website of its sponsor agency. Basic information on the site might include mandate statements, policies, acquisition areas, opening hours and contact information. If the institution has responsibility for organizational records as well as archives, the website might be divided into sections for members of the agency (such as records management advice) and members of the public (about accessing and using the archives). If the institution caters to specific groups it might also provide information relevant to their interests, such as genealogy and family history or the history of events, activities or people from the area, such as military bases, religious groups, sports activities, milestone dates, aboriginal communities, political figures and so on. Links can be provided to resources such as how to plan a visit, understanding copyright conditions and fees for reproduction or research, guidelines for potential donors, educational programs offered by the archives and answers to frequently asked questions. A section for current news and another to invite public feedback should also be included.
- *Online descriptive databases.* A database of archival descriptions, with actual digital objects attached as appropriate, can support remote reference. Such a database is often nested within the institution's website. It needs to be maintained continuously and updated regularly. Whenever it needs to be taken offline for servicing or upgrading, an announcement should be posted on the institution's website so users are aware of the situation.
- *Online photographic databases.* Some institutions develop a separate database specifically to hold descriptions and digital copies of

photographs, which are often an institution's most-used holdings. Again, the database needs to be kept up to date and monitored regularly to ensure it is fully operational.

- *Information in archival networks.* Contributing descriptive information about the archives' holdings to regional, national and international archival networks can support reference by making information easily available beyond the institution's own website. It is essential that the archivist adhere to the standards and controls set by the network, and that she ensure descriptions are up to date. Archival networks are becoming more popular in many countries; the websites of national archives and archival associations usually include more information or links to the sites.

- *Digital reference resources.* The institution might also develop self-service tools such as 'how to find your ancestors' or 'researching the Great Flood of 1976'. Lists of mayors in the town over two centuries might be useful information in a municipal archives, while a list of the names of all authors represented in the archives might be useful in an institution devoted to literary history.

Any website or other digital tool used to support any of the institution's services needs to be maintained. The archivist must allocate resources and time to ensuring the information on the site does not go 'stale' and the technology remains as up to date as possible.

Digitization as a reference tool

The digitization of archival materials was introduced in Chapter 9 in relation to preservation. But digitization is also a valuable tool for increasing access to archives. Therefore it can be an important aspect of a reference programme. Digitization can provide remote access to holdings and help support exhibits and outreach.

One of the most disturbing 'unintended consequences' of the internet age is that today too many people assume that if they cannot find something through a Google search, what they seek does not exist. The archivist can enhance access to archives through digitization, but she also has a responsibility to select items for digitization thoughtfully and deliberately, and she must make clear that the items chosen represent only a small portion of all the holdings available.

The archivist also has a moral responsibility to explain why some materials were or were not digitized. Many valuable materials may be protected by copyright and so cannot be digitized. But if institutions only digitize materials in the public domain and do not explain why, users will not realize why they are seeing what might be a skewed sampling of information. The user needs to know what he is seeing and *not* seeing when he views a virtual exhibit or accesses an online database of digital images.

Documenting reference services

All the work performed and all interactions with researchers, physical or virtual, should be documented in some form, for security and statistical purposes. For instance, all researchers should sign a register each time they visit the institution, including the date and their name, address and signature. The register may also include a space where the researcher can identify his particular topic of interest: this information can provide helpful anecdotal evidence of the types of research being done in the institution, and the statistics can be analysed to show patterns in reference activities.

As already mentioned, this register is also a useful tracking device, allowing the archivist to know which researchers were in the reference room on which day, to locate everyone in an emergency. The tool can also help identify who was using materials, and when, in case archives are not found where they ought to be at the end of the day. If a computerized register is used instead of a paper tool, the data should be backed up several times a day and processes should be established to ensure the information can be accessed remotely in an emergency.

When answering reference questions via e-mail or telephone, the archivist should also keep statistics: date and time of contact; nature of the research question; and name and contact details of the person requesting information. Copies of written responses to letters or e-mails should be indexed as part of the archives' own records. These documents may be helpful later to answer a similar question.

Statistics should also be maintained on the use of all web-based and social media resources. How many people accessed which pages in a website? How many Twitter followers does the institution have? How often are descriptions downloaded from the database? The data will show whether changes in tools or resources have changed reference and public use: fewer phone calls and more hits on the website; a decrease in visitors to the institution but an increase in visits to the virtual exhibit? The archivist can then consider if these changes are good, and if the archivist needs to adjust any services. An increase in website traffic, for instance, might mean it is a good investment to update the website more regularly.

Statistics are also essential for presenting a business case for change to the sponsor agency. Resource allocators are more easily persuaded to increase or reallocate budgets when presented with hard data. If the number of online users has doubled in a year, the archivist can lobby for more staff to support web-based services. If the greatest number of public complaints relates to the absence of weekend reference services, the archivist can argue persuasively the logic behind closing to the public on Mondays and opening on Saturdays instead.

Outreach and community engagement

Archives used to be fortresses, and the public – which we have already agreed was a very small public back then – came to the gates and asked for permission to enter. The medieval archivist did not hire the town crier to advertise the existence of the king's archives and urge everyone to come to a family history day at the castle.

Today, outreach and community engagement are central to making the public aware of the resources of the archival institution. Outreach can also foster a greater understanding of the value and purpose of archives in general, which can increase support not just for one particular institution but for archives as a whole. It is tempting, though, for all archivists to embrace the latest and greatest new marketing and outreach techniques and end up being distracted from other core archival responsibilities. Balance, balance, balance.

No matter what other outreach initiatives the archivist considers, she has an obligation first to communicate information to the public concerning the holdings and services of her institution. This is a reference responsibility. Beyond that, the archivist can also create virtual or physical exhibits that illuminate holdings in the collection or highlight issues of relevance to the community. Exhibits and displays can also explain how archives work, what the institution does or does not acquire and how people can engage with their community's archives. The archivist is not a publicist, but she can and should be an advocate. Promoting the value of archives and the wealth of the repository's holdings is an essential part of providing accountable and effective archival service.

Outreach must be planned, like anything else. The first task is to understand the social and cultural milieu in which the archival institution operates. The archivist in a corporate repository that is open to employees only will craft a very different outreach strategy from the archivist in a local historical society archives. A community museum may develop in-house programmes for school children, but a state institution may decide to create a travelling exhibit to reach citizens across a large region. A digital exhibit may be perfect in a university archives, catering to students, faculty and staff who spend hours at their computers. A similar initiative may be ignored in communities where access to the internet is inconsistent at best.

Still, the potential scope for outreach activities is limitless. A few engagement activities might include the following:

- genealogical workshops
- seminars on the management of personal archives
- on-site or travelling exhibits and displays
- print or digital publications such as guides, brochures and souvenir books
- newspaper or magazine articles
- screenings of archival films in a local auditorium
- local history tours
- open houses or 'visit the archives' events
- local television or radio advertisements or programmes.

The best choices will be made when the archivist consults with her users, so that she can meet the needs and priorities of her particular community.

Web-based and social media tools

The archivist will also want to consider whether the institution will use web-based or social media tools for outreach. Web-based tools are made available through the institution's official website; usually no restrictions are placed on access: anyone who can open up the website can access the information therein. On the other hand, social media tools are computer-based technologies that allow people to create and share information, ideas and content through digital networks, but social media often requires that people become part of a 'virtual community'. They need to register with the social media application on their computer or smart phone, after which they can receive and share information with others in that community through the tool.

Examples of web-based and social-media-oriented outreach activities and tools are discussed below.

Blogs

An archivist might create a blog to discuss archival projects or to provide an account of a visit to another archival repository. She may share news about upcoming events or stories behind items in the archives. As with any other outreach tool, a blog needs to be suitable for public consumption. Sensitive, confidential or other inappropriate information should not be included. Anyone can read a blog if it is made available through a publicly accessible section of a website, and they can usually add comments, but they cannot change the content.

Wikis

Wikis are websites that allow anyone with full access to the wiki to read, add, edit or remove content. The goal of a wiki is to allow a group of people to share their knowledge about some event, issue or question. The archivist could create a wiki as she describes a body of archives, posing questions about the history of the period or posting digital copies of images so that members of the group can add comments about the people in a photograph or the context of a report. This 'crowd-sourced' information, while not always accurate, adds to the body of knowledge about archives. It can also help engage the public in the effort to arrange, describe and make available documentary resources.

Podcasts

Podcasts are digital audio files that can be downloaded from the internet so people can listen to them on a computer or mobile device such as a smartphone. The archivist could create podcasts of a monthly historical lecture series or oral history interviews from decades in the past. Podcasts can be produced individually or in series. Companies such as iTunes provide access to a vast range of podcasts, some free and some for a charge, but the archivist can establish processes to allow people to subscribe to podcasts directly through the institution's website.

RSS feeds

An RSS (rich site summary) feed is a format for delivering regularly changing web content. It is similar to a syndicated television or radio broadcast, with the next instalment available regularly to whoever wants to receive it. People can sign up for an RSS feed and have guaranteed access to updated blogs, newsletters or other dynamic information. The archivist can encourage people to sign up through the institution's RSS feed so that they automatically receive this regularly changing content. But the archivist who sets up an RSS feed needs to maintain it; a regularly scheduled update needs to appear as scheduled.

Facebook

Facebook is an American web-based social networking tool that can be accessed on computers and on devices such as smart phones or tablets. To join Facebook, a person registers to use the site, after which they create a user profile, adding information such as their name, occupation, education, age, location, interests and so on. They can then become 'friends' with other users, allowing them to exchange messages or post updates about their activities. An archivist who creates an institutional Facebook page can open the page to anyone who wants to join, and the archivist can then use Facebook to post announcements about upcoming special events, recent acquisitions or other news. One critical challenge with Facebook is that anyone wanting to communicate through Facebook needs to register and have an account with the corporation. Another serious challenge is that, according to many legal interpretations of Facebook's terms of use, the corporation can claim to own all the content on any Facebook page. There have been instances where the relatives of people who have died cannot access their loved one's personal photographs or communications, as they cannot claim to 'be' that person or have rights to that person's digital estate. The archivist deciding to use Facebook is well advised to ensure that it is not the *only* social media tool for sharing information with the public, and that the terms and conditions imposed by the corporation do not negatively influence the archival institution, its sponsor agency or its user community.

Flickr

Flickr is a social media tool that stores still and moving images and allows users to share them with other people, creating an online community of users with common interests. People can see some content on Flickr without creating an account, but they do not receive widespread access to content, nor can they add their own images or videos, until they have created their own account. The archivist can post archival photographs or videos on Flickr for public access, providing a way for the public to see some of the institution's holdings. Copyright conditions are, as always, a challenge: it is wise only to include content free of intellectual property controls or other restrictions.

Pinterest

Like Flickr, Pinterest stores images, but in this case users can 'pin' images they like to a 'board' for later reference. Many people use Pinterest to collect images they find in other sources, whether commercial or personal, like a bulletin board with family photographs or a binder with ideas for decorating the kitchen. The archivist can use Pinterest to create boards for topics such as sports, buildings, parks and so on, pinning digital copies of historical photographs onto the different boards, thus increasing exposure to the institution's holdings.

YouTube

YouTube is a video sharing website where users can upload, view and share video content. Anyone can search for and see content on YouTube but people have to create an account if they want to upload their own videos. The archivist can upload historical films to YouTube to facilitate access, or she can also share recordings of recent events, such as conference speeches, guest lectures or practical demonstrations. The archivist might also produce instructional videos about topics such as how to undertake archival research, trace ancestors or complete a reproduction request. Posting these videos on YouTube creates an online set of self-service reference tools.

Twitter

Twitter is an online social networking and news sharing service. Users have to create an account, then they can post messages, called 'tweets' (which are restricted to 140 characters) about anything they like. Users interested in different people or organizations can 'follow' them on Twitter so that they always receive new messages posted by that person or group. The archivist can use Twitter to promote events or share news. For instance, a tweet can announce an upcoming lecture series and include a link to the registration page, or advise that the computer servers in the reference room are going to be offline for the morning while an upgrade is being performed. Twitter is an extremely fast and nimble way of sharing immediate news, but it is not a useful forum for complex debates. The archivist using Twitter would be wise to establish ground rules around how the institution will use the tool, or else the person in charge of Twitter for the institution could end up caught in arguments with users about anything from changed reference room hours to decisions about public funding. Those are difficult arguments to have with only 140 characters to spare.

Incorporating archival information into web resources

In addition to these web-based and social media tools (and many others, such as Instagram, Snapchat, Vine, Tumblr . . . the list goes on), the archivist should consider incorporating information from and about archives into publicly available web-based resources.

A prime candidate for archival input is the online encyclopedia Wikipedia, which includes entries on over 5 million separate topics and is viewed by as many as 15 billion people each month. Many archivists around the world regularly add information about archival collections to relevant Wikipedia pages, such as the biographies of people whose archives are in their institutions, along with links to their institutional web pages or to other descriptive tools.[1]

The potential for disseminating archival information through Wikipedia is tremendous, allowing the archivist to bypass archives-specific descriptive networks entirely in the quest to inform the public about holdings. But a mention in Wikipedia does not replace a good description of archival materials. And the archivist deciding to add content to Wikipedia needs to review the guidelines for adding content and ensure the terms and conditions suit her institutional requirements.

Social media pros and cons

Facebook, Twitter, Wikipedia and other web-based and social media tools can help break down the borders between the institution and the public. The very use of such tools by an archival institution is a signal to the public that the institution is not stuck in the past. Some have argued that archival institutions can reach a younger demographic by remaining technologically current. Anecdotal evidence suggests that the use of Facebook, Twitter or other technologies has resulted in increased hits on institutional websites, more visits to the facility and more donations and financial contributions.

The web environment also fosters collaboration, allowing the user to become an active contributor to the archives, not just a passive recipient of archival services. Engaging citizens in deciphering and decoding their history can generate a wealth of information and promote a sense of community. Web-based and social media tools help to break down the barriers between 'experts' and the 'common folk'.

There is a danger, though, of becoming swept up in technology. Before she commits the institution to the latest and greatest digital innovation the archivist needs to have satisfactory answers to the following sort of questions:

- Will the tools support the institution's core goals?
- What are the hard and soft costs of investing in these technologies?
- What equipment and resources will be needed, and what training will staff need to use the tools effectively?
- Can the institution commit to updating Facebook or web pages weekly, or more frequently, to ensure content remains fresh?
- Does the institution have enough 'new' news to disseminate?
- Will using tools such as Facebook or Twitter put the institution's holdings, information or staff – or the public – at risk?
- What controls must be established to protect the individual privacy of people accessing web resources?
- What protections are needed against possible copyright violations or other infringements?
- Will the communications created using social media be records? If so, how will they be captured and saved, and how long should they be kept?

Whatever technologies she chooses, the archivist must ensure they are sustainable *and* sustained. A broken link to a website is not just frustrating: for someone desperately trying to seek archival evidence that supports a lawsuit or a family search, hitting a dead end on an archives' website can be heartbreaking.

Some archivists vigorously support the use of new technologies and the creation of more collaborative approaches. Others are concerned about the role of the archival institution as a place of evidence and look askance at the idea of inviting the public to help co-create archival tools and resources. Regardless of whether or not archivists like it, though, digital technologies are not going away. Different social media tools and platforms will emerge and others will disappear. But the internet is not a transitory contrivance. The archivist needs to consider strategies for participating in the world of social networking, while still protecting the irreplaceable archival materials in her care.

Having addressed the last piece of the archival puzzle, providing access to archives and encouraging public engagement and use, the only task left in this book is to conclude with a brief speculation on the future of archives . . . and archivists.

Note

1   Professional archival associations are now starting to hold Wikipedia 'edit-a-thons': scheduled virtual meetings of archivists who come together to edit Wikipedia pages to add archival information. By working together, more experienced archivists can help newcomers understand how Wikipedia works, and by working as a group, archivists can focus on chosen topics, such as editing all entries related to 19th-century political figures in their country or all entries related to science and industry.

Conclusion

> There will always be a frontier when there is an open mind and a willing hand.
>
> Charles Kettering (1876–1958), inventor and engineer

As I get older and I occasionally luxuriate in the thought that I *must* be getting wiser, I understand better what my psychiatrist father meant when he warned me, as a teenager, of the dangers of what he called 'temporal chauvinism'. This, he argued, was the mistaken belief that we, in our current time and place, are the latest and greatest and best of our generation, and that our creations, inventions and ideas are right and true and good, better than anything that came before. All societies, he claimed – particularly their younger members – are prone to embrace the conceited, erroneous notion that they and theirs are better than anyone or anything that came before. (My mother, a jazz singer, was more lyrical. 'Listen, Missy,' she would laugh. 'Don't forget, a lot of things happened before you were born.')

A lot of things did happen before we were born, and a lot of things are going to happen after we move on to a new frontier. And perhaps more than many other disciplines, the work of managing the documentary evidence of a society – its archives – demands the greatest respect for this temporal reality. Every change in the technology used to *create* information, from a clay tablet to a piece of sheepskin to a biometric chip, changes the way in which we need to *manage* that information. Helping society accomplish this task of *creating* and *managing* authentic evidence is the job of the archivist. Ergo, staying on top of the changes brought by time, not thinking we have got it all figured out today, is fundamental to the success of archival work. Change is our business.

Thus, archivists need to remain nimble, agile and humble. Clinging to theories when reality slaps us in the face is just as futile as following an old habit when science proves it wrong. There was a time when archives were defined as old and linear. No more. There was a time when the archivist could wait for stuff to come to her instead of going out and finding it. No more. There was a time when records stayed safe in a closet until the archivist could get around to sorting them. *No more.*

Principles and theories provide a valuable map, helping us find our way to some destination. But that is all they are: the map, not the destination. Captain James Cook did not *use* maps to sail his way around the world. He sailed around the world in order to *make* maps. And along the way, Cook and his crew gathered volumes of data, collected thousands of botanical specimens, encountered diverse civilizations and charted vast oceans.

And when they came home, Cook and his companions brought back ships' logs, charts, drawings, reports, diaries and maps, showing where they had been and what they had seen. Their archives became part of society's documentary memory, allowing those who came after to crack open the smallest sliver of light on the experiences of Cook and other explorers from centuries before. Some people lament the travels of Cook and his type, suggesting they should have stayed well enough at home. To argue thus is to argue with history. To put a temporal spin on an old cliché, it *was* what it *was.*

The task of a society, and therefore a particular responsibility for the archival profession, is not to try to reverse times past, on the assumption that *of course* we know better now. The real task is to learn about that past, accepting the reality of events but not assuming they must be repeated. In keeping with the adage about repeating the past if we ignore it, societies that seek to be civilized, respectful and mature have an obligation to preserve the evidence of the past – the *real* facts, not some bizarre set of alternative facts – and to learn from those facts in order to consider new directions and, perhaps, make better decisions.

Societies then have to document today's actions, transactions and decisions, creating and preserving their own charts and plans and maps. They then need to leave that evidence behind so that generations to come will be able to do the same over again: learn and understand and reflect, using the original facts whenever they need evidence for a course correction.

In Kettering's words, the archivist's job is to be the willing hand that supports the job of documenting society, so that the society is left with authentic evidence. To accomplish that job, those responsible for record keeping, above all others in society, must come to our work with open minds. We hold too much power not to be humble. We cannot be so bound by habit that we refuse to consider different approaches, and we cannot be so constrained by theory that we lose sight of the purpose of our work in the first place. And we must never, ever, lose sight of the goal: to protect authentic evidence to support accountability, protect memory and foster identity.

Archivists do not preserve documents in acid-free containers because we want to keep the manufacturers of acid-free containers in business. We do so because research into archival preservation tells us that such containers support the stability of paper records. We do not apply descriptive standards to prove to other archivists that we have followed the rules. We apply them because adopting common practices helps support the goal of making archives understandable and usable.

Archivists do not define archives as *fonds* because that is the only way to conceive of an organic unity of documentary evidence. We do so because the *fonds* seemed like a mighty logical concept at one time. When evidence tells us it is time to change, we should change. As soon as the *fonds* is no longer a useful concept (and I for one am ready to vote it off the island), surely we should stop using it. To do otherwise, as my father would say, is the ultimate in neurosis.

Cook explored the oceans. Neil Armstrong explored the stars. Someday, some explorer in the dark matter of outer space might meet one of those elusive alien civilizations and find out that a Vulcan mind meld is really, truly possible. Then no one will have to write down anything. We can just 'think' everything into a big box and keep it forever. Big data indeed.

In the meantime, back on earth and in our homes, the Internet of Things means that our refrigerators and cars and furnaces are going to start talking to us. It will not be long before we never have to wonder if we should cut the end off our roast. Equipped with the latest in artificial intelligence technologies, our stove will weigh the meat, decide the temperature, set the timer and let us know when the roast is done. (Now if only it would set the table and do the dishes.)

When I was a teenager, and telephones were stuck on a table in the front hall, my mother could hear every word of my hours-long gossip sessions with my friends, mostly about how much more we understood about life than our creaky old parents. As I moaned that I had no privacy, I had no idea that one day I would carry my phone around in my pocket. Or that I would rarely use my phone as a phone. Or that my privacy would be imperilled every day, a risk I have to balance against the joy that comes from using my smartphone as dictionary, calculator, camera, newspaper, clock, calendar, map, instant messenger and, very occasionally, as a phone. I wonder if Cook would have bothered to explore the South Pacific if he had had an iPhone in his pocket. What would have happened to the world then?

If Cook had not mustered himself out of his chair and explored the world in order to *make* maps, I suspect we would not have iPhones today, or people walking on the moon, or refrigerators that tell us when we are out of milk. We cannot grow as humans and as societies if we do not explore new frontiers. And we cannot grow wiser and more mature if we do not document our explorations, so that the next generation will know what has gone before. We have an obligation to leave behind the evidence, the facts, in large part as an antidote to temporal chauvinism.

To be the willing hands that help our society leave this evidence behind, archivists need to remember that anything we devise to 'solve' the 'problems' of records and archives today is not going to be the last word. We must always balance theory and practice, never becoming so wedded to either that we lose sight of our ultimate goal. Our job is to help our societies create and manage documentary sources of evidence that support accountability, protect memory and foster identity. As the tools and technologies used to create and manage that evidence keep changing, so must we. *Change is our business.*

I have written this book at a time of tremendous change, not only in technologies but also in governments and societies. The British have voted to leave the European Union. The Americans have elected a president who believes that the media create 'fake news' and has called for foreign powers to hack into American government computer systems. In Canada, the premiers of more than one province have been accused of deleting e-mails and other official records without permission from the departments responsible for accountable records care. People crossing international borders are being asked to surrender the passwords to their social media accounts so that border guards can see if they pose a threat to security. Privacy is being violated daily; records are being mismanaged; and the need for accountable evidence is greater than ever.

I would love to go back to the days when the archivist's job was to help preserve historical photographs of community events, so that local citizens could attend Heritage Day fairs and enjoy reminiscing about their youth. I hope we can maintain that personal connection with archives and help create communities that are civilized, respectful and mature. In the meantime, we have to focus on evidence and accountability these days, no matter how frustrating the effort can be as we are thwarted time and again in our work. And we have to remember that everything will keep changing: that we must balance our understanding of archival theory and practice with the reality of how to achieve archival goals in a world that will not stay still.

I hope this book has helped introduce you to the principles and practices surrounding archival work today, while opening your mind to the possibilities that might come if we all work together to strike a sensible balance between theory and reality, in order to be the stewards of our society's precious documentary resources. I wish you every success with your critically important work.

To learn more

The first edition of this book contained an extensive list of resources on all manner of archival topics. In this edition, the list has been pared down to the bare essentials, for three reasons:

- The most up-to-date information on current archival practices comes not in manuals but in journal articles. It is much easier to direct you to those journals than try to list every specific article that might relate to different archival topics.
- Many archival institutions are embracing a welcome leadership role in archives by disseminating valuable and timely information about archival practice through their websites and social media networks. Directing you to those institutional websites will ensure that you can find the most up-to-date information.
- Since the first edition of this book was published, the topic of 'archives' has blossomed. When people are writing not only about the preservation of medieval charters but also on the tattoo as archive, a short bibliography cannot even pretend to cover this ever-growing literature. You are encouraged to consider if the core resources meet your needs first, then to look at the new content coming out in journals and websites, so you can decide what to read next given your particular interests.

So, rather than trying to pin this jelly of constantly changing sources to the wall of a printed bibliography, I have focused on highlighting a few core readings and recent titles, almost all published since 2000. I also include some useful web resources. I begin by listing the notable journals on archives and record-keeping issues around the world. Then I list some of the national or state archival institutions that provide useful guidance for records and archives issues or that offer a valuable example of different aspects of archival service. I also include a list of major associations involved with records, archives, information or cultural issues. Finally, I provide a 'top pick' list of resources related to the different topics addressed in this book, from archival theory to digital preservation.

In each section of that bibliography, I have identified no more than a half-dozen readings I think provide a diversity of perspectives on the topic in question. The works I believe you should consider first are marked with an asterisk. Where appropriate, I also include formal standards and guidelines, such as those published by the International Standards Organization (ISO) and the ICA.

Despite my belief that the integration of records and archives management is necessary and inevitable, I necessarily have to focus here more on the archival end of the spectrum. I have included only a small selection of items relating to records management and record keeping, both traditional and electronic.

Records and archives journals

Much of the cutting-edge literature in archives management is in periodical form. Some more prominent journals in publication today are listed below, with national affiliation and web address included. Most of the journals listed below provide at least some of their content free of charge:

- *African Journal of Library, Archives and Information Science* (www.ajol.info/journals/ajlais)
- *American Archivist* (www.archivists.org/periodicals/aa-toc.asp)
- *Archifacts* (https://www.aranz.org.nz/Site/publications/archifacts/default.aspx)
- *Archival Issues* (www.midwestarchives.org/archival-issues)
- *Archival Science* (www.springerlink.com/content/105703/)
- *Archivaria* (http://archivists.ca/content/e-archivaria)
- *Archives and Manuscripts* (www.archivists.org.au/learning-publications/archives-and-manuscripts)
- *Archives and Records: The Journal of the Archives and Records Association* (www.archives.org.uk/publications/archives-and-records-ara-journal. html)
- *Comma* (www.ica.org/)
- *D-Lib Magazine* (www.dlib.org/)
- *ESARBICA Journal* (www.ajol.info/journal_index.php?jid=207)

- *Information and Culture* (formerly *Libraries and the Cultural Record,* www.infoculturejournal.org/about)
- *Information Management* (http://content.arma.org/IMM/online/InformationManagement.aspx)
- *International Journal of Information Management* (https://www.journals.elsevier.com/international-journal-of-information-management)
- *Journal of Film Preservation* (www.fiafnet.org/pages/Publications/Latest-Issue.html?PHPSESSID=rupf4kmb632bqjov7rig2ar393)
- *Journal of the Association for Information Science and Technology* (http://onlinelibrary.wiley.com/doi/10.1002/asi.2016.67.issue-4/issuetoc)
- *Journal of the Institute for Conservation* (http://icon.org.uk/)
- *Manuscript Studies: A Journal of the Schoenberg Institute for Manuscripts* (http://mss.pennpress.org/current-issue-abstracts/)
- *Provenance: Journal of the Society of Georgia Archivists* (http://digitalcommons.kennesaw.edu/provenance/vol34/iss1/)
- *RBM: a Journal of Rare Books, Manuscripts, and Cultural Heritage* (formerly *Rare Books & Manuscripts Librarianship,* http://rbm.acrl.org/)
- *Records Management Journal* (www.emeraldinsight.com/loi/rmj)
- *The iJournal* (http://theijournal.ca/index.php/ijournal/index)

Records and archives institutions

National and state institutions responsible for the care of records and archives provide a wealth of guidance on their websites and other resources. A highly selective number of English-language institutions are identified here, including those that served as valuable case studies as I crafted the fictitious scenarios in this book. You are encouraged to keep visiting these websites regularly, and to look at the websites for other national, state provincial or local archival institutions, to see what new information is added over time:

- Archives New Zealand: www.archives.govt.nz/
- Archives of Ontario (Canada): www.archives.gov.on.ca/en/index.aspx
- Library and Archives Canada: www.bac-lac.gc.ca/eng/Pages/home.aspx
- Library of Congress (USA): www.loc.gov/index.html
- National Archives and Records Administration (USA): www.archives.gov/index.html
- National Archives of Australia: www.naa.gov.au/
- State Archives and Records of New South Wales (Australia): www.records.nsw.gov.au/

- State Records Office of Western Australia: www.sro.wa.gov.au/
- The National Archives (UK): www.nationalarchives.gov.uk/

Records and archives associations

A number of professional associations and organizations involved with records and archives management provide valuable resources to members and non-members, including posting information on their websites such as guidelines, articles, tools and links to other information resources. Also included below are the websites of allied organizations that provide resources and services useful to archival management:

- Archives and Records Association of New Zealand (ARANZ), https://www.aranz.org.nz/Site/home/default.aspx
- Archives and Records Association UK and Ireland (ARA), www.archives.org.uk/
- Archives Association of British Columbia (AABC), particularly the extremely valuable archivist's toolkit of resources, at http://aabc.ca/resources/archivists-toolkit/
- Association for Information and Image Management (AIIM), www.aiim.org/
- Association of Canadian Archivists (ACA), http://archivists.ca/
- Association of Commonwealth Archivists and Records Managers (ACARM), www.acarm.org/default.asp
- Association of Records Managers and Administrators (ARMA International), www.arma.org/
- Australian Society of Archivists Inc. (ASA), www.archivists.org.au/
- Canadian Conservation Institute (CCI), http://canada.pch.gc.ca/eng/1454704828075
- Co-ordinating Council of Audiovisual Archives Associations (CCAAA), www.ccaaa.org/
- Council on Library and Information Resources (CLIR), www.clir.org/
- International Centre for the Study of the Preservation and Restoration of Cultural Property (ICCROM), www.iccrom.org/
- International Committee of the Blue Shield (ICBS), www.ifla.org/blueshield.htm
- International Conference on the History of Records and Archives (I-CHORA) (a regular conference held around the world since 2003); for information on the most recent conference in 2015 see http://ichora.org/
- International Council on Archives (ICA), www.ica.org/

- International Organization for Standardization (ISO), www.iso.org/iso/home.htm
- International Records Management Trust (IRMT), www.irmt.org
- Joint Information Systems Committee (JISC), www.jisc.ac.uk/
- Northeast Document Conservation Center (NEDCC), https://www.nedcc.org/
- Society of American Archivists (SAA), www.archivists.org/
- United Nations Educational Scientific and Cultural Organization (UNESCO), www.unesco.org/

Additional readings

Below is a list of monographs, book-length works, standards and web-based resources sites selected because they offer a useful introduction to the topic identified. I have not included many publications that do not have a bearing on the principles and practices discussed in this book, however interesting they may be to me. In each section, I have marked with an asterisk no more than two or three works that I believe are 'core' readings; this selection does not diminish the value of the other titles but is intended to help you establish priorities when deciding where to go next in your reading.

As noted, I have also established an (almost) arbitrary cut-off date of 2000: with a handful of exceptions, I have only included 21st-century publications. Works published before that date that remain useful are gathered together in their own section as 'foundational archival writing'; a small number of older works are included in other sections if they are the only or best sources on the topic.

In preparing this updated resources list, I must acknowledge the wonderful service performed by Canadian archivist David Rajotte, who for six years now has faithfully prepared a weekly list of publications, presentations and other resources on archives and library topics. *Nouvelles du patrimoine documentaire – Documentary Heritage News* is published on the Canadian archival listserv (available through the e-mail address arcan-l@mailman.srv.ualberta.ca) and posted on David's blog at http://documentary-heritage-news.blogspot.ca/p/about-this-blog-propos-de-ce-blogue.html. David does this work entirely outside working hours, and archivists in Canada and around the world owe him a great debt for his dedication and thoroughness. I highly encourage you to make use of this valuable resource.

Given my decision not to include specific articles in this reading list, I also urge you not to ignore the contributions of authors who publish primarily in journals. Below is a list of some of my favourite archival writers, whose ideas

I find insightful, thoughtful or (quite often) provocative. It is a very personal list, heavily populated with Canadians, and I am sure I will hear from many important writers whose names are not included. There is not enough room to list everyone, but there are a few people who I believe are contributing valuable insights into English-language archival literature today: Tom Adami, Chris Hurley, Randall Jimerson, Shadrack Katuu, Eric Ketelaar, Heather MacNeil, Jennifer Meehan, Tom Nesmith, Mpho Ngoebe, Barbara Reed, Elizabeth Shepherd, Ciaran Trace, Frank Upward and Geoffrey Yeo.

The topics covered in the sections below are not organized along the chapters in the book. Instead I have ordered them according to different topics, as shown in the list below:

- overviews, introductory works, handbooks and manuals
- foundational archival writing
- writings on archival history (including works published before 2000 that now provide a historical perspective)
- works on the role and nature of archives, archival institutions and the profession
- writings addressing postmodernism, activism and the role of archives for social justice
- writings about concepts of provenance and the *fonds*
- writings about concepts of the series system, records continuum and functional approaches
- manuals, guidelines and standards for records management
- works on electronic records and archives management
- manuals, guides and standards on digital preservation
- research initiatives in electronic records management and digital preservation
- publications and standards on metadata management
- manuals, guides and standards on preservation and conservation
- manuals and guides on emergency planning and disaster response
- writings on digitization for preservation and access
- writings on the preservation and management of different types of archival materials
- writings on legal and ethical issues for archivists, including access and privacy administration
- works on copyright administration
- works on managing archival institutions, facilities and staff
- writings related to specific types of archival institution
- writings on the acquisition and appraisal of archives

- manuals and guides to archival arrangement and description
- writings on authority control
- standards for archival description, authority control and naming conventions
- writings on archival reference service
- works on archival outreach and public engagement, including the use of social media.

Overviews, introductory works, handbooks and manuals

Bettington, J. et al. (eds) (2008) *Keeping Archives*, 3rd edn, Australian Society of Archivists.

Brown, C. (2013) *Archives and Recordkeeping: theory into practice*, Facet.

Cox, R. (2000) *Managing Records as Evidence and Information*, Quorum Books.

*Eastwood, T. and MacNeil, H. (2017) *Currents of Archival Thinking*, 2nd edn, Libraries Unlimited.

Gilliland, A. J. (2014) *Conceptualizing 21st Century Archives*, Society of American Archivists.

Harris, V. (2000) *Exploring Archives: an introduction to archival ideas and practice in South Africa*, 2nd edn, National Archives of South Africa.

Hunter, G. S. (2003) *Developing and Maintaining Practical Archives: a how-to-do manual*. 2nd edn, Neal-Schuman Publishers Inc.

Jimerson, R. C. (ed.) (2000) *American Archival Studies: readings in theory and practice*, Society of American Archivists.

*O'Toole, J. and Cox, R. (2006) *Understanding Archives and Manuscripts*, Society of American Archivists.

*Williams, C. (2006) *Managing Archives: foundations, principles and practice*, Chandos.

Foundational archival writing

Cook, M. (1999) *The Management of Information from Archives*, 2nd edn, Gower.

Duranti, L. (1998) *Diplomatics: new uses for an old science*, Scarecrow Press.

Hensen, S. L. (comp.) (1989) *Archives, Personal Papers, and Manuscripts: a cataloging manual for archival repositories, historical societies, and manuscript libraries*, Society of American Archivists.

Jenkinson, H. (1922) *A Manual of Archive Administration, including the Problems of War Archives and Archive Making*, Clarendon Press.

Muller, S., Feith, J. A. and Fruin, R. (1898) *Manual for the Arrangement and Description of Archives*, trans. A. H. Leavitt, republished 2003, Society of American Archivists.

Norton, M. C. (1975) *Norton on Archives: the writings of Margaret Cross Norton on archival and records management*, ed. T. W. Mitchell, republished 2003, Society of American Archivists.

Posner, E. (1967) *Archives and the Public Interest: selected essays*, edited by Ken Munden, 2006, Society of American Archivists.

Posner, E. (1972) *Archives in the Ancient World*, Harvard University Press, republished 2003, Society of American Archivists.

Schellenberg, T. R. (1956) *Modern Archives: principles and techniques*, republished 2003, Society of American Archivists.

Working Group on Archival Descriptive Standards (1986) *Toward Descriptive Standards: report and recommendations of the Canadian Working Group on Archival Descriptive Standards*, Bureau of Canadian Archivists.

Yates, J. (1989) *Control through Communication*, Johns Hopkins University Press.

Writings on archival history (including works published before 2000 that now provide a historical perspective)

Brosius, M. (ed.) (2003) *Ancient Archives and Archival Traditions: concepts of record keeping in the ancient world*, Oxford University Press.

Cantwell, J. (1991) *The Public Record Office, 1838–1958*, Her Majesty's Stationery Office.

*Clanchy, M. T. (1993) *From Memory to Written Record: England, 1066–1307*, Basil Blackwell.

Cox, R. (2004) *Lester J. Cappon and the Relationship of History, Archives, and Scholarship in the Golden Age of Archival Theory*, Society of American Archivists.

Ellis, R. and Walne, P. (eds) (1980) *Selected Writings of Sir Hilary Jenkinson*, republished 2003, Society of American Archivists.

*Foscarelli, F. et al. (eds) (2016) *Engaging with Records and Archives: histories and theories*, Facet.

Moore, L. J. (2008) *Restoring Order: the Ecole des Chartes and the organization of archives and libraries in France, 1820–1870*, Litwin Books.

*Procter, M. (forthcoming 2018) *A History of Archival Practice*, Routledge.

Sickinger, J. P. (1999) *Public Records and Archives in Classical Athens*, University of North Carolina Press.

Wosh, P. J. (ed.) (2011) *Waldo Gifford Leland and the Origins of the American Archival Profession*, Society of American Archivists.

Works on the role and nature of archives, archival institutions and the profession

Biber, K. and Luker, T. (eds) (2017) *Evidence and the Archive: ethics, aesthetics and emotion*, Routledge.

*Blouin, F. X. Jr and Rosenberg, W. G. (eds) (2006) *Archives, Documentation, and Institutions of Social Memory: essays from the Sawyer seminar*, University of Michigan Press.

Brown, J. S. and Duguid, P. (2002) *The Social Life of Information*, HBS Press.

Cox, R. (2005) *Archives and Archivists in the Information Age*, Neal-Schuman.

*Hill, J. (ed.) (2010) *The Future of Archives and Recordkeeping: a reader*, Facet.

McKemmish, S. et al. (eds) (2005) *Archives: recordkeeping in society*, Charles Sturt University, Centre for Information Studies.

Shepherd, E. (2009) *Archives and Archivists in 20th Century England*, Ashgate.

Smith Rumsey, A. (2016) *When We Are No More: how digital memory is shaping our future*, Bloomsbury Press.

Taylor, H. A. (2003) *Imagining Archives: essays and reflections*, ed. T. Cook and G. Dodds, Society of American Archivists.

Writings addressing postmodernism, activism and the role of archives for social justice

Cox, R. and Wallace, D. (eds) (2002) *Archives and the Public Good: accountability and records in modern society*, Quorum Books.

Hamilton, C. et al. (eds) (2002) *Refiguring the Archive*, David Philip.

Harris, V. (2007) *Archives and Justice: a South African perspective*, Society of American Archivists.

*Jimerson, R. C. (2009) *Archives Power: memory, accountability, and social justice*, Society of American Archivists.

*Procter, M., Cook, M. and Williams, C. (eds) (2005) *Political Pressure and the Archival Record*, Society of American Archivists.

Thomas, D., Fowler, S. and Johnson, V. (2017) *The Silence of the Archive*, Facet.

Writings about concepts of provenance and the fonds

*Eastwood, T. (ed.) (1992) *The Archival Fonds: from theory to practice*, Bureau of Canadian Archivists.

Lemieux, V. (ed.) (2016) *Building Trust in Information: perspectives on the frontiers of provenance*, Springer.

*Nesmith, T. (ed.) (1993) *Canadian Archival Studies and the Rediscovery of Provenance*, Scarecrow Press.

Swedish National Archives (1994) *The Principle of Provenance: report from the first Stockholm conference on the archival principle of provenance, 2–3 September 1993*, Swedish National Archives.

Writings about concepts of the series system, records continuum and functional approaches

*Biskup, P. et al. (eds) (1995) *Debates and Discourses: selected Australian writings on archival theory, 1951–1990*, Australian Society of Archivists.

Cunningham, A. (ed.) (2010) *The Arrangement and Description of Archives amid Administrative and Technological Change: essays and reflections by and about Peter J. Scott*, Australian Society of Archivists.

Ellis, J. A. (ed.) (2000) *Selected Essays in Electronic Recordkeeping in Australia*, Australian Society of Archivists.

*McKemmish, S. and Piggott, M. (eds) (1994) *The Records Continuum: Ian Maclean and Australian Archives first fifty years*, Ancora Press in association with Australian Archives.

Manuals, guidelines and standards for records management

Coleman, L., Lemieux, V., Stone, R. and Yeo, G. (2011) *Managing Records in Global Financial Markets: ensuring compliance and mitigating risk*, Facet.

Crockett, M. (2015) *The No-nonsense Guide to Archives and Recordkeeping*, Facet.

ISO 16175:2010 *Principles and Functional Requirements for Records in Electronic Office Environments* (3 parts), International Standards Organization.

ISO 15489:2016 *Information and Documentation – records management* (2 parts), International Standards Organization.

*International Records Management Trust (1999) *Management of Public Sector Records*, www.irmt.org/education-and-training.

*Shepherd, E. and Yeo, G. (2003) *Managing Records: a handbook of principles and practice*, Facet.

Smith, K. (2007) *Public Sector Records Management: a practical guide*, Routledge.

Works on electronic records and archives management

Dobreva, M. and Ivacs, G. (forthcoming 2017) *Digital Archives: management, access and use*, Facet.

International Council on Archives, Committee on Current Records in the Electronic Environment (2005) *Electronic Records: a workbook for archivists*.

International Records Management Trust (2004) *The E-Records Readiness Assessment Tool*, www.irmt.org/development-research/assessment-tools.

*International Records Management Trust (2009) *Training in Electronic Records Management*, www.irmt.org/education-and-training/education-and-training-2.

Lee, C. A. (ed.) (2011) *I, Digital: personal collections in the digital era*, Society of American Archivists.

Levy, D. M. (2001) *Scrolling Forward: making sense of documents in the digital age*, Arcade.

*MacLeod, J. and Hare, C. (eds) (2005) *Managing Electronic Records*, Facet.

*Smith, K. (2007) *Planning and Implementing Electronic Records Management: a practical guide*, Facet.

Tapscott, D. and Tapscott, A. (2016) *Blockchain Revolution: how the technology behind Bitcoin is changing money, business, and the world*, Penguin Random House.

Manuals, guides and standards on digital preservation

Bantin, P. C. (2016) *Building Trustworthy Digital Repositories*, Rowman & Littlefield.

*Brown, A. (2013) *Practical Digital Preservation: a how-to guide for organizations of any size*, Facet.

Corrado, E. M. and Sandy, H. M. (2017) *Digital Preservation for Libraries, Archives, and Museums*, 2nd edn, Rowman & Littlefield.

Delve, J. and Anderson, D. (2014) *Preserving Complex Digital Objects*, Facet.

Duranti, L., Eastwood, T. and MacNeil, H. (2003) *Preservation of the Integrity of Electronic Records*, Kluwer.

Foster, A. and Rafferty, P. (2016) *Managing Digital Cultural Objects: analysis, discovery and retrieval*, Facet.

*Giaretta, D. (2011) *Advanced Digital Preservation*, Springer.

Harvey, R. (2011) *Preserving Digital Materials*, De Gruyter.

ISO 13008:2012 *Digital Records Conversion and Migration Process*, International Standards Organization.

ISO 14721:2012 *Space Data and Information Transfer Systems: open archival information system – reference model (OAIS)*, International Standards Organization.

ISO 17068:2012 *Trusted Third Party Repository for Digital Records*, International Standards Organization.

Lavoie, B. F. (2004) *The Open Archival Information System Reference Model: introductory guide*, Digital Preservation Coalition, www.dpconline.org/about/cse-results?q=reference%20model.

Oliver, G. and Harvey, R. (2016) *Digital Curation*, Facet.

*Prom, C. J. (ed.) (2016) *Digital Preservation Essentials*, Society of American Archivists.

Research Libraries Group (2005) *An Audit Checklist for the Certification of Trusted Digital Repositories*, www.worldcat.org/arcviewer/1/OCC/2007/08/08/0000070511/viewer/file2433.html.

Research initiatives in electronic records management and digital preservation

Australasian Digital Record Keeping Initiative (ADRI) (across Australasia), http://adri.gov.au/.

Digital Preservation Strategy (New Zealand), http://archives.govt.nz/advice/government-digital-archive-programme/digital-preservation-strategy/digital-preservation-strat.

FutureProof (New South Wales), http://futureproof.records.nsw.gov.au/about/.

International Centre for Archives and Records Management Research (ICARUS) (University College London), www.ucl.ac.uk/dis/icarus.

InterPARES (University of British Columbia), www.interpares.org/welcome.cfm.

Preserving Digital Records (The National Archives, UK), www.nationalarchives.gov.uk/information-management/manage-information/preserving-digital-records/.

Victorian Electronic Records Strategy (VERS) (Australia), http://prov.vic.gov.au/government/vers.

Publications and standards on metadata management

*Baca, M. (2016) Introduction to Metadata, 3rd edn, Getty Research Institute.

Dappert, A., Guenther, R. S. and Pyrard, S. (eds) Digital Preservation Metadata for Practitioners: implementing PREMIS, Springer.

Gartner, R. (2016) Metadata: shaping knowledge from antiquity to the semantic web, Springer.

ISO 15836:2009 Information and Documentation – the Dublin Core metadata element set, International Standards Organization.

ISO 23081:2011 Information and Documentation – records management processes – metadata for records (3 parts), International Standards Organization.

Library of Congress (2016) Metadata Encoding and Transmission Standard (METS), www.loc.gov/standards/mets/.

Library of Congress (2016) Metadata Object Description Schema (MODS), www.loc.gov/standards/mods/.

Library of Congress (2016) PREMIS: preservation metadata maintenance activity, www.loc.gov/standards/premis/.

Manuals, guides and standards on preservation and conservation

Ankersmit, B. and Stappers, M. (2017) Managing Indoor Climate Risks in Museums, Springer.

Banks, P. N. and Pilette, R. (eds) (2000) Preservation: planning and issues, American Library Association.

Dalley, J. (1995) *The Conservation Assessment Guide for Archives*, Canadian Council for Archives.

*Forde, H. and Rhys-Lewis, J. (2013) *Preserving Archives*, Facet.

Gorman, G. E. and Shep, S. J. (eds) (2006) *Preservation Management for Libraries, Archives and Museums*, Facet.

*Harvey, R. and Mahard, M. R. (2014) *The Preservation Management Handbook: a 21st century guide for libraries, archives and museums*, Rowman & Littlefield.

Ogden, S. (2007) *Preservation of Library and Archival Materials: a manual*, Northeast Document Conservation Center.

*Ritzenthaler, M. (2010) *Preserving Archives and Manuscripts*, Society of American Archivists.

Manuals and guides on emergency planning and disaster response

Ball, C. and Yardley-Jones, A. (eds) (2001) *Help! A survivor's guide to emergency preparedness*, Museums Alberta.

*Dadson, E. (2012) *Emergency Planning and Response for Libraries, Archives and Museums*, Facet.

*Mallery, M. (ed.) (2015) *Technology Disaster Response and Recovery Planning*, Facet.

*Walsh, B. (2003) *Salvage Operations for Water Damaged Archival Collections: a second glance*, Canadian Council of Archives, www.cdncouncilarchives.ca/salvage_en.pdf.

Wellheiser, J. G. (2002) *An Ounce of Prevention: integrated disaster planning for archives, libraries, and record centers*, Scarecrow Press.

Writings on digitization for preservation and access

Hoffman, A. (2016) *Digitizing Your Community's History*, Libraries Unlimited.

ISO 13028:2010 *Implementation Guidelines for Digitization of Records*, International Standards Organization.

*Puglia, S. et al. (2004) *Technical Guidelines for Digitizing Archival Materials for Electronic Access*, National Archives and Records Administration, www.archives.gov/preservation/technical/guidelines.html.

Purcell, A. D. (2016) *Digital Library Programs for Libraries and Archives: developing, managing, and sustaining unique digital collections*, ALA Neal-Schuman.

*Sitts, M. K. (ed.) (2000) *Handbook for Digital Projects: a management tool for preservation and access*, Northeast Document Conservation Center.

Writings on the preservation and management of different types of archival materials

Paper-based archives, including architectural and cartographic materials, books and publications

Aber, S. E. W. and Aber, J. (2016) *Map Librarianship: a guide to geoliteracy, map and GIS resources and services*, Chandos.

*Adcock, E. (1998) *IFLA Principles for the Care and Handling of Library Materials*, International Federation of Library Associations and Institutions.

ANSI Z39.48–1992 (2010) *Permanence of Paper for Publications and Documents in Libraries and Archives*, American National Standards Institute and National Information Standards Organization.

CAN/CGSB-9.70 (2016) *Permanence of Paper for Records, Books and Other Documents*, Standards Council of Canada.

*Ellis, M. H. (2016) *The Care of Prints and Drawings*, 2nd edn, Rowman & Littlefield.

International Council on Archives, Architectural Records Section (2000) *A Guide to the Archival Care of Architectural Records, 19th and 20th Centuries*.

ISO 11108:2015 *Information and Documentation – archival paper – requirements for permanence and durability*, International Standards Organization.

ISO 9706:2015 *Information and Documentation – paper for documents – requirements for permanence*, International Standards Organization.

Lowell, W. and Nelb, T. R. (2006) *Architectural Records: managing design and construction records*, Society of American Archivists.

Millar, L. (2009) *The Story Behind the Book: preserving authors' and publishers' archives*, Simon Fraser University, CCSP Press.

Photographic materials

Baldwin, G. (1991) *Looking at Photographs: a guide to technical terms*, J. Paul Getty Museum.

Burke, P. (2001) *Eyewitnessing: the use of images as historical evidence*, Cornell University Press.

Jürgens, M. C. (2009) *The Digital Print: identification and preservation*, Getty Conservation Institute.

Lavédrine, B. (2003) *A Guide to the Preventive Conservation of Photograph Collections*, trans. Sharon Grevet, Getty Conservation Institute.

*Ritzenthaler, M. L. et al. (2006) *Photographs: archival care and management*, Society of American Archivists.

Schwartz, J. M. (2003) *Picturing Place: photography and the geographical imagination*, I.B. Tauris.

Audiovisual and film archives

Gracy, K. F. (2007) *Film Preservation: competing definitions of value, use and practice*, Society of American Archivists.

*Harrison, H. P. (1997) *Audiovisual Archives: a practical reader*, UNESCO, http://unesdoc.unesco.org/images/0010/001096/109612eo.pdf.

*National Film Preservation Foundation (2004) *The Film Preservation Guide: the basics for archives, libraries, and museums*.

*Smiraglia, R. P., with Beak, J. (2016) *Describing Music Materials: a manual for resource description of printed and recorded music and music videos*, 4th edn, Rowman & Littlefield.

Smither, R. and Surowiec, C. A. (eds) (2002) *This Film is Dangerous: a celebration of nitrate film*, Fédération Internationale des Archives du Film (FIAF).

United Nations Educational, Scientific and Cultural Organization (2003) *Glossary of Terms Related to the Archiving of Audiovisual Materials*, UNESCO.

Fine art

*Schaffner, I. and Winzen, M. (eds) (1998) *Deep Storage: collecting, storing and archiving in art*, Prestel.

Winkler, K. (ed.) (2001) *Their Championship Season: acquiring, processing and using performing arts archives*, Theatre Library Association.

Websites and web archiving

*Brown, A. (2006) *Archiving Websites: a practical guide for information management professionals*, Facet.

Masanès, J. (ed.) (2006) *Web Archiving*, Springer.

Intangible heritage

*Stefano, M. L. and Davis, P. (2017) *The Routledge Companion to Intangible Cultural Heritage*, Routledge.

Writings on legal and ethical issues for archivists, including access and privacy administration

Behrnd-Klodt, M. (2008) *Navigating Legal Issues in Archives*, Society of American Archivists.

Behrnd-Klodt, M. and Wosh, P. J. (eds) (2005) *Privacy and Confidentiality Perspectives: archivists and archival records*, Society of American Archivists.

*Cox, R. (2006) *Ethics, Accountability and Recordkeeping in a Dangerous World*, Facet.

Leta Jones, M. (2016) *The Right to be Forgotten*, NYU Press.

*MacNeil, H. (1992) *Without Consent: the ethics of disclosing personal information in public archives*, Scarecrow Press.

Wright, D. and De Hert, P. (eds) (2016*) Enforcing Privacy: regulatory, legal and technological approaches*, Springer.

Works on copyright administration

Center for the Study of the Public Domain (2005) *Access to Orphan Films: submission to the copyright office*, Duke Law School, https://law.duke.edu/cspd/pdf/cspdorphanfilm.pdf.

Cornish, G. P. (2015) *Copyright: interpreting the law for libraries, archives and information services*, Facet.

Hirtle, P. B., Hudson, E. and Kenyon, A. T. (2009) *Copyright and Cultural Institutions: guidelines for digitization for US libraries, archives, and museums*, Cornell University Library.

Lemmer, C. A. and Wale, C. P. (2016) *Digital Rights Management: the librarian's guide*, Rowman & Littlefield.

*Padfield, T. (2015) *Copyright for Archivists and Records Managers*, Facet.

Secker, J. and Morrison, C. (2016) *Copyright and E-learning: a guide for practitioners*, Facet.

*Society of American Archivists, Intellectual Property Working Group (2009) *Orphan Works: statement of best practices*.

Works on managing archival institutions, facilities and staff

Bastian, J. A. and Webber, D. (2008) *Archival Internships: a guide for faculty, supervisors, and students*, Society of American Archivists.

Campbell, N. J. (1998) *Writing Effective Policies and Procedures*, Association of Records Managers and Administrators.

Deyrup, M. M. (ed.) (2016) *Creating the High-Functioning Library Space: expert advice from librarians, architects, and designers*, Libraries Unlimited.

*Evans, G. E. and Alire, C. (2013) *Management Basics for Information Professionals*, Facet.

*Hallam, A. W. and Dalston, T. R. (2005) *Managing Budgeting and Finances: a how-to-do-it manual for librarians and information professionals*, Neal-Schuman.

Kurtz, M. (2004) *Managing Archival and Manuscript Repositories*, Society of American Archivists.

Lemieux, V. L. (2004) *Managing Risks for Records and Information*, Association of Records Managers and Administrators.

Lowe-Wincensten, D. (ed.) (2016) *Beyond Mentoring: a guide for librarians and information professionals*, Chandos.

McMillan, E. J. (2003) *Not-for-Profit Budgeting and Financial Management*, Wiley.

*Pacifico, M. F. and Wilsted, T. P. (eds) (2009) *Archival and Special Collections Facilities: guidelines for archivists, librarians, architects and engineers*, Society of American Archivists.

Pratchett, T. and Young, G. (2016) *Practical Tips for Developing Your Staff*, Facet.

*Ray, L. and Haunton, M. (forthcoming 2017) *Management Skills for Archivists and Records Managers*, Facet.

Roberts, S. and Rowley, J. (2008) *Leadership: the challenge for the information profession*, Facet.

Smith, G. S. (2002) *Managerial Accounting for Libraries and other Not-for-Profit Organizations*, American Library Association.

Staines, G. M. (2016) *Go Get That Grant!: a practical guide for libraries and non-profit organizations*, 2nd edn, Rowman & Littlefield.

Wilsted, T. P. (2007) *Planning New and Remodeled Archival Facilities*, Society of American Archivists.

Writings related to specific types of archival institution

Bastian, J. A and Alexander, B. (2009) *Community Archives: the shaping of memory*, Facet.

Callison, C., Loriene, R. and LeCheminant, G. A. (2016) *Indigenous Notions of Ownership and Libraries, Archives and Museums*, De Gruyter Saur.

Council on Library and Information Resources (2008) *Beyond the Silos of the LAMs: collaboration among libraries, archives and museums*, OCLC Programs and Research.

Miller, C. (2008) *Managing Congressional Collections*, Society of American Archivists.

Pieris, A. (2016) *Indigenous Cultural Centers and Museums: an illustrated international survey*, Rowman & Littlefield.

Prom, C. J. and Swain, E. D. (eds) (2008) *College and University Archives: readings in theory and practice*, Society of American Archivists.

Slate, J. H. and Minchew, K. L. (2016) *Managing Local Government Archives*, Rowman & Littlefield.

Thomas, L. M. and Whittaker, B. M. (eds) (2016) *New Directions for Special Collections*, Libraries Unlimited.

*Wythe, D. ed. (2004) *Museum Archives: an introduction*, 2nd edn, Society of American Archivists.

Writings on the acquisition and appraisal of archives

Boles, F. (2005) *Selecting and Appraising Archives and Manuscripts*, Society of American Archivists.

Cox, R. (2004) *No Innocent Deposits: rethinking archival appraisal*, Scarecrow Press.

Craig, B. (2004) *Archival Appraisal: theory and practice*, K.G. Saur.

Matassa, F. (forthcoming 2017) *Valuing your Collection*, Facet (specifically related to monetary appraisal).

*Shallcross, M. J. and Prom, C. J. (eds) (2016) *Appraisal and Acquisition Strategies*, Society of American Archivists.

Society of American Archivists (2013) *A Guide to Deeds of Gift* (brochure).

Manuals and guides to archival arrangement and description

Brenndorfer, T. (2016) *RDA Essentials*, Facet.

Duff, W. and Pitti, D. V. (2001) *Encoded Archival Description on the Internet*, Haworth Information Press.

El-Sherbini, M. (forthcoming 2017) *RDA: strategies for implementation*, Facet.

Hider, P. (2012) *Information Resource Description*, Facet.

Procter, M. and Cook, M. (2000) *Manual of Archival Description*, Gower.

*Roe, K. D. (2005) *Arranging and Describing Archives and Manuscripts*, Society of American Archivists.

Van Hooland, S. and Verborgh, R. (2014) *Linked Data for Libraries, Archives and Museums*, Facet.

Writings on authority control

Gagnon-Arguin, L. (1989) *An Introduction to Authority Control for Archivists*, Bureau of Canadian Archivists.

Olson, H. A. (2002) *The Power to Name: locating the limits of subject representation in libraries*, Kluwer.

Planning Committee on Descriptive Standards (1992) *Subject Indexing for Archives: the report of the Subject Indexing Working Group*, Bureau of Canadian Archivists.

Standards for archival description, authority control and naming conventions

Australian Society of Archivists (2007) *Describing Archives in Context: a guide to the Australasian practice*.

Canadian Council of Archives (2008) *Rules for Archival Description (RAD)*.

International Council on Archives (2000) *General International Standard Archival Description (ISAD (G))*.

International Council on Archives (2004) *International Standard Archival Authority Record for Corporate Bodies, Persons, and Families (ISAAR(CPF))*.

International Council on Archives (2008) *International Standard for Describing Institutions with Archival Holdings (ISDIAH)*.

International Council on Archives (2011) *International Standard for Describing Functions (ISDF)*.

International Council on Archives (2016) *Records in Contexts: a conceptual model for archival description (RiC)* (draft).

ISO 5963:1995 *Methods for Examining Documents, Determining their Subjects, and Selecting Indexing Terms*, International Standards Organization.

ISO 999:1996 *Guidelines for the Content, Organization and Presentation of Indexes*, International Standards Organization.

ISO 639:2002 *Codes for the Representation of Names of Languages, Alpha-2 Code*, International Standards Organization.

ISO 8601:2004 *Representation of Dates and Times*, International Standards Organization.

ISO 3166:2013 *Codes for the Representation of Names of Countries and their Subdivisions*, International Standards Organization.

Library of Congress (2016) *MAchine-Readable Cataloguing (MARC)*.

National Geospatial-Intelligence Agency (2016) *GEOnet Names Server*.

Society of American Archivists (2011) *Encoded Archival Context (EAC)*.

Society of American Archivists (2013) *Describing Archives: a content standard (DACS)*.

Society of American Archivists (2015) *Encoded Archival Description (EAD)*.

The Getty Research Institute (2015) *Getty Thesaurus of Geographic Names Online*.

United Nations Educational, Scientific and Cultural Organization (2016) *UNESCO Thesaurus*.

Writings on archival reference service

Hernon, P., Altman, E. and Dugan, R. E. (2015) *Assessing Service Quality: satisfying the expectations of library customers*, Facet.

Hughes, L. (2011) *Evaluating and Measuring the Value, Use and Impact of Digital Collections*, Facet.

*Pugh, M. J. (2005) *Providing Reference Services for Archives and Manuscripts*, Society of American Archivists.

Works on archival outreach and public engagement, including the use of social media

*Anderson, P. (2007) *What is Web 2.0? Ideas, technologies and implications for education,*

JISC Technology and Standards Watch,
www.ictliteracy.info/rf.pdf/Web2.0_research.pdf.
Bradley, P. (2015) *Social Media for Creative Libraries*, Facet.
Matassa, F. (2014) *Exhibitions: a handbook for museums, libraries and archives*, Facet.
*Theimer, K. (ed.) (2011) *A Different Kind of Web: new connections between archives and our users*, Society of American Archivists.
Thomsett-Scott, B. C. (2013) *Marketing with Social Media*, Facet.

Glossary of terms

The following select terms are relevant to the discussion throughout this book. The definitions provided are my own, but as appropriate I have built on definitions presented in a range of glossaries used in Canada, the USA and internationally. This glossary is not comprehensive, and I rarely included non-archival interpretations of terms (such as 'conservation' in the environmental sense). In keeping with the tenor of this book I have avoided attempts at prescription and restriction, opting instead for a more flexible approach.

Readers interested in more information about archival terminology will want to consult such sources as Richard Pearce-Moses, *A Glossary of Archival and Records Terminology* (Society of American Archivists, 2005), http://www2. archivists.org/glossary, or the ICA's resource *Multilingual Archival Terminology*, www.ciscra.org/mat/. Another useful resource is the *Glossary of Records and Information Management Terms*, published by the Association of Records Managers and Administrators and available online to ARMA members at www.arma.org/r1/publications.

Access points

Standardized terms, such as personal, corporate or geographic names, which are selected for use as preferred terms, in order to help users find relevant information in resources such as archival materials.

Accession

1. The process of transferring legal and physical control of archives from the creating agency or donor to the archival institution. 2. The archival materials that have been transferred to the archival institution as one unit at one time.

Accession record

An administrative and descriptive tool created by the archivist in order to identify the scope and contents of archival material that has been brought into archival custody. The accession record includes information about the creator or donor, conditions on access and use, physical qualities of or concerns about the materials and details about the nature of the accession (donation, transfer, loan and so on). Accession registers serve as the 'first' finding aid, allowing archivists to identify every accession received by the repository and document the location of materials before detailed finding aids have been prepared.

Accrual

An accession of archives added to an archival unit with the same provenance that is already held by the same archival institution.

Acquisition

1. The act of seeking out, selecting and obtaining archival materials, through transfer, donation, loan or purchase. 2. The archival materials that are selected and obtained by the archival institution.

Agent

A person or group, or an entity created by a person or group, responsible for taking action or making decisions and accountable for the consequences of those actions or decisions.

Analogue record

A record created by capturing a continuous signal in or on the media itself. (The word comes from the idea that the copy is 'analogous' to or bears a relationship to the original sound or image.) Analogue records differ from digital in that digital signals are represented in discrete numbers, whereas analogue signals are physically attached to a base, such as the grooves (the signal) on a vinyl record (the base).

Appraisal

The act of assessing the worth of archives as documentary evidence or as information in order to confirm if the entire archival unit ought to be acquired (appraisal for acquisition) or to decide which portions of it ought to be preserved and which will not be kept (appraisal for selection). See also monetary appraisal.

Architectural record

A plan, drawing, blueprint, sketch, model, specifications, photographs or other textual, graphic or visual document created, referred to and used to support the design and construction of physical structures such as buildings or landscapes.

Archival value

The enduring worth of records based on the documentary evidence or information they contain. The assessment of archival value helps justify the decision to keep them in archival care.

Archives

1. Documentary materials created, received, used and kept by a person, family, organization, government or other public or private entity in the conduct of their daily work and life and preserved because they contain enduring value as evidence of and information about activities and events. 2. The agency or institution responsible for acquiring and preserving archival materials and making those items available for use. 3. The building or other repository housing archival collections. Other terms used may include manuscripts, papers, private papers, *fonds*, groups and archival records.

Archivist

The person responsible for acquiring, preserving and making available archival materials and other related resources on behalf of an archival facility; the archivist's duties may include appraisal, acquisition, accessioning, arrangement, description, preservation and conservation, reference and access, and institutional management and planning. The archivist may also have greater record-keeping responsibilities in an organization that manages records and archives as part of a continuum of care.

Arrangement

The act and result of intellectually and/or physically organizing records in accordance with archival principles such as provenance and original order, and, as appropriate, into levels of arrangement (such as *fonds* or group, sub-*fonds* or sub-group, series, file, item and piece), or by identifying and linking functions, agents and records. The goal of arrangement is to support the physical and intellectual security and control of archives, preserve and illuminate their content, context and structure and document the progress of their creation, use, management, disposition and care before and after their transfer to archival custody or control.

Artefact

A physical object created, adapted, shaped or otherwise produced by human workmanship.

Artificial collection

A body of archival, documentary or resource materials with different sources or provenance, deliberately brought together and organized to facilitate management or use. Some artificial collections may be subject oriented or related to geography or chronology; materials may also be accumulated according to type of material, such as postcards or stamps.

Audiovisual archives

Documentary materials with enduring evidential or informational value that are composed of sounds and graphics or images rather than text, such as films or videotapes. Materials that do not include sound, such as silent films, are usually considered audiovisual; purely pictorial images, such as photographs or drawings, are defined as visual archives.

Authenticity

The quality in documentary materials, such as records and archives, of being genuine and not corrupted or altered. The authenticity of records and archives are usually inferred from an analysis of the materials and an understanding of the actions associated with their creation, management and use, including an assessment of the physical characteristics, content, context and structure of the materials in question.

Authority control

The process of selecting and confirming particular terms or names to be used as access points when describing archives, such as personal or corporate names, geographic names, subjects, functions and forms. Authority control ensures that language is used consistently, supporting the retrieval and use of materials.

Authority list

A list of standardized terms, such as personal, corporate or geographic names, which are to be used as preferred terms to help researchers find relevant information when using resources such as archival materials.

Big data

Extremely large data sets that may be analysed using computer technologies to search for patterns, identify trends or find commonalities across different pieces of information.

Born-digital record

A record originally created and stored in electronic format.

Cartographic record

A graphic record that uses images, numbers or reliefs to represent linear surfaces or physical, cultural or other features of the earth or other bodies, such as moons or other planets.

Case files

Digital or paper series of records that document particular interactions between individuals and agencies, such as individual military service records, personnel files or accounts payable files.

Chain of custody

The clear progression of events involved with the life of records or archives, from their creation and use to their preservation in archival care. A strong chain of custody demonstrates clear ownership and provides evidence of how and where archives were managed over time. (Museums, art galleries, libraries and other cultural institutions interpret chain of custody differently; the archival concept is addressed here.)

Class

See series.

Conservation

The active protection of archival material, often by the use of physical and chemical treatments in order to resist further deterioration but without adversely affecting the integrity of the original.

Continuum

A record-keeping concept referring to a consistent and coherent process of records care throughout the life of records, from the design and development of record-keeping systems through the creation and preservation of records, to their retention and use as archives. The continuum is often compared with the life cycle, which approaches records and archives management in a more linear fashion. See also life cycle.

Copyright

The legal right of the creator or author of a work of authorship, such as a piece of writing, music, picture or photograph, to determine who may publish, copy and distribute that work. Copyright usually remains with the creator of a work for a predetermined time, after which the work moves into the public domain and can be freely used by other people. Copyright is also referred to by the broader term intellectual property rights.

Data

One or more elements of raw content, such as letters, numbers or symbols, that refer to or represent ideas, objects, events, concepts and things.

Deaccession

The act of removing archival or other resource materials permanently from the physical control and legal ownership of the archival institution.

Deacidification

The process of neutralizing the acid in archival materials, particularly textual documents and other largely paper-based items, by raising their pH value to a minimum of 7.0. The deacidification process is intended to help preserve archives and thereby extend their life.

Description

The act of establishing intellectual control over archives, by creating finding aids or other access tools, in order to identify the content, context and structure of archives; their origins and relationship to the creating agency or individual; and the actions taken by the archival institution as custodian and caretaker to receive, appraise and process the archives.

Descriptive inventory
A finding aid that describes the contents of individual archival units by describing the organization and activities of the agency that created the records as well as the physical extent, chronological scope and subject content of the records themselves. In addition to this information, an inventory may include lists of box or file titles or other descriptive information.

Digital object
An electronic item to be managed following archival principles and practices. Examples of digital objects might be a PDF document, a photograph in TIFF form or an e-mail. A digital object may contain many different elements. A digital copy of an annual report, for instance, might be defined as one digital object for the purposes of arrangement and description, but it might be composed of word-processed text, digital photographs, copies of PowerPoint slides or tables produced using Excel software, all of which are also 'digital objects' that need to be preserved with their authenticity intact, so that the whole report can be accessed and used accurately at any time in the future.

Digital preservation
The formal action of ensuring that digital objects remain accessible and usable over time. While analogue preservation usually seeks to preserve both the content and the original form of an archival item, digital preservation seeks to preserve the different component parts of a digital object so that the whole can be accessed and used accurately at any time in the future, even if the media on which the data are stored keep changing.

Digital record
A record that can be stored, transmitted or processed by a computer. The term can be equated with digital object, but a digital record may consist of several digital objects, and a digital object may be composed of many elements. A digital record may also be referred to as an electronic record.

Digitization
The process of transforming analogue archival materials, such as paper-based textual records, photographs, cassette or reel-to-reel sound or video recordings, into binary electronic (digital) form, to support preservation, storage and access. A documentary item that has been converted from hard copy or manual form to digital form may be referred to as a digitized

record or digitized archive. The terms digitalized and digitalization are also used in some societies.

Document

Information or data fixed in some medium, such as paper, film or digital bits and bytes.

Documentary evidence

A record that is deemed to be an objective representation of actual recollections, decisions, opinions or ideas and so provides confirmation or proof.

Donation

Archival material that is permanently transferred from one party to another, such as from the creator of the archives to an archival institution, without compensation.

Electronic record

A record that is maintained in a coded format and so can only be accessed using a computer system that converts the codes or numbers into text, images or sounds that can be processed by the human eye or ear. Also referred to as a digital record.

Emergency plan

A set of policies and procedures developed and tested by an organization to be used during an emergency or disaster to prevent or reduce damage to the organization, its people, its resources and, in the archival environment, its documentary holdings.

Ephemera

Miscellaneous documentary items, such as advertisements, posters, broadsides, postcards, business cards, brochures or tickets, created for a specific purpose and generally intended to be discarded after use.

Evidence

In a legal environment, information or proof admitted into judicial proceedings and relevant to a specific case to establish an alleged or disputed fact. See also documentary evidence.

Evidential value

In an archival environment, the value of records and archives as authentic, trustworthy information on decisions, actions, transactions and communications, either by the person or agency that created those materials or by persons or groups associated with those records or archives.

File

1. The act of placing records or archives into predetermined locations, physically in folders or virtually in computer systems, according to a chosen order (such as imposed by a formal classification scheme). 2. An organized assembly of documents within a series, brought together intellectually or physically according to a particular topic, activity or event, or even by form or name, in one or several folders. A file is usually the basic unit within a record series. A file can be found in any format, but the term folder is more commonly used in digital record-keeping environments. 3. In a computer environment, a logical assembly of data stored within a computer system, in which case the term file can be used to describe a wide range of data from a single document to an entire database.

File series

See series.

Finding aid

Any descriptive tool created by an archival institution or by the agency that created the records in question, that identifies the content, context and structure of archives, as well as their significance, scope, nature and/or purpose.

***Fonds* (group)**

The whole of body of documents, regardless of form or medium, created or accumulated by a particular individual, family, corporate body or other agency as part of life and work and retained because those materials have ongoing archival value as evidence of those functions and activities.

Function

The sum total of tasks or activities performed by an agent to accomplish a particular goal or objective. A function may be divided into subordinate functions if needed. Examples of functions might include environmental management, climate control or pollution monitoring. In arrangement and description, functions are associated with series of records and with the agents responsible for their creation and use.

Group
See *fonds* (group).

Guide
A type of finding aid that describes some or all of the holdings of one or more archival repositories. Guides may describe the entire holdings of an archival institution, or they may focus on particular subjects, times or places. Repository guides are created to provide a brief description of a large group of holdings, such as all the archives within an institution or all the acquisitions received in the last number of years. Thematic guides provide a brief description of holdings within one institution or across many institutions related to a particular subject, time, place or event.

Index
An organized list of words, names or terms that identifies and refers to relevant information in archival materials, which may be organized in a different order. Indexes may be created to identify subjects, places, names or other information found in a specific body of archives or across the holdings of an institution.

Information
Data, ideas, thoughts or memories, irrespective of form or medium.

Intellectual property rights
See copyright.

Intrinsic value
The worth of a unit of archival material that is associated with characteristics such as its physical qualities; its association with particular events or issues; its content, structure and context; or its original form and material nature. These qualities are inherent in the material itself, which means that materials with high intrinsic value are often kept in their original physical form whenever possible.

Inventory
See descriptive inventory.

Item

The basic physical unit within a file, such as an individual letter, report, photograph, audio cassette, film reel or scrapbook.

Life cycle

In a records and archives environment, the concept that a record follows a cycle from 'birth' to 'death' (or 'second life' in archival care): a record may be created, used for so long as it has continuing value and then disposed of by destruction or by transfer to an archival institution. The life cycle is often contrasted with the records continuum, which approaches records care in a more holistic fashion. See also continuum.

List

A type of finding aid containing a written series of discrete items, such as the names of files or boxes, name or place information, or lists identifying the contents or location of files or folders. See also descriptive inventory and location file.

Loan

Archival material that is temporarily transferred from one party to another, such as from the creator of the archives to an archival institution, usually without compensation. A loan may be time limited for the purpose of exhibits, reproduction, publications or reference.

Location file

An administrative finding aid that identifies where in the repository certain archival holdings have been stored, so that materials may be retrieved and replaced easily and consistently. This may take the form of a paper file, a list or entries into an administrative database.

Macro-appraisal

An appraisal theory that identifies the value of records based on the role of the record creators, placing priority on why the records were created (function), and where and how they were created (structure), rather than on their content.

Manuscripts

A term used to refer to non-official or personal archives, as opposed to public or corporate records. Other terms for the same concept include archives, papers, personal papers and private papers.

Metadata

A set of data that describes and provides information about other data. The date and time stamp on a Twitter message or the sender and recipient information in an e-mail are forms of metadata.

Monetary appraisal

The act of assessing archives (or other historical or informational resources) to determine their financial value on the open market.

Original order

The order and organization in which records were created, used, maintained and stored by the creator or office of origin. Original order is variously interpreted as the last remaining order of archives before their transfer into archival custody or the different orders in which archives were used and managed over time.

Orphaned works

In the context of copyright, those archival items where the identity of the person or agency holding copyright cannot be determined, or where the identity of the most likely right holder is known but that person or agency cannot be located.

Papers

Personal or private materials, as distinct from corporate or government records. Other terms for the same concept include manuscripts, personal papers and private papers.

Personal papers

See papers.

pH value

A measure of the level of acid in paper or other materials. The value is measured on a scale from 0 to 14. The neutral point is 7.0, while values above 7.0 are alkaline and values below 7.0 are acidic.

Piece

The single indivisible unit within an item, such as each sheet of paper comprising a 20-page letter or each photograph in a photograph album.

Plan

A graphic drawing or sketch of any surface showing the relative positions of various objects, such as the parts of a building, elements of a landscape or other physical features.

Post-custodialism

The concept that archives do not need to be in the physical custody of an archival institution to be managed and that the archivist can instead control the management of records that remain in the physical possession of record creators.

Preservation

The passive protection of archival material, in which no physical or chemical treatment is performed. Preservation is the total sum of processes and tasks performed in order to protect records and archives against damage or deterioration, including developing sound preservation policies, maintaining adequate environmental and storage conditions, housing records and archives in stable (inert or acid-free) storage containers and organizing, handling and managing archives in order to ensure they are protected from harm.

Private papers

See papers.

Processing

The act of physically sorting archives in order to apply chosen archival arrangements and prepare archives for storage and use. Steps involved in processing may include sorting, packing, labelling and shelving.

Provenance

The origin or source of something, or the person, agency or office of origin that created, acquired, used and retained a body of records in the course of their work or life. Provenance may also refer to the different creators, users and managers of archives who can be identified as having influenced the nature, scope and order of the materials during the course of their creation and management. The archival definition of provenance differs from archaeological concepts of provenience and library and museum usage of provenance.

Record

A piece of information that has been captured on some fixed medium and that has been created and is used to remember events or information or to provide accountability for decisions or actions.

Record keeping

The act of making and managing complete, authentic and reliable evidence of actions, transactions or decisions by creating and keeping records, data or other information sources with their evidential value intact. The term records management tends to be used to refer to a less holistic approach, with emphasis on the role of the records manager, not the agency responsible for the actions in the first instance, to undertake necessary actions to manage records. See also records management.

Records continuum

See continuum.

Records management

The act of systematically administering and controlling the creation, management, use and disposal of records in order to enhance efficiency, improve economy and produce authentic and reliable documentary evidence and information. Records management usually takes place in an organizational environment but may also be practised by individuals or families. The term record keeping, which implies a wider and more holistic approach to records care, is increasingly used in place of records management. See also record keeping.

Records series

See series. See also function.

Repository

The building or facility that houses archival materials. See also archives.

Repository guide

See guide.

Respect des fonds

An overarching concept, of which provenance and original order are parts, that means that in order to protect the integrity of archives, all archives from one particular creator or source (provenance) must be kept together as a unified whole, not separated into artificial groups or intermingled with archives from another source, and that all archives within that unified whole should be preserved in the order in which they were made and used (original order). See also provenance and original order.

Restoration

The repair or alteration of an item, either to return it to its original appearance or to improve its aesthetic qualities. Restoration is often undertaken when the look of an item is important and if there is no danger of altering the authenticity of the original.

Sampling

The selection of particular items from a body of archives in order to provide a representation of the whole body while not retaining every document.

Series

In a *fonds*-oriented approach to arrangement and description, aggregations of files or other records within a larger *fonds* or group that relate to the same processes or that are evidence of a common form, purpose or use. In some jurisdictions, terms such as 'file series', 'records series' or 'class' are also used to refer to the series. See also function.

Sound recordings

Documentary materials that are composed of sounds rather than graphics, images or text, such as music, spoken word or soundscapes (recordings of natural or human-made sounds). Materials that also include visual images as well as sounds are usually considered audiovisual.

Sub-*fonds* or sub-group

The archives of an administrative unit directly related to or, usually, subordinate to a larger creating agency, which is identified as the creator of a *fonds*; the creator of a sub-*fonds* or sub-group will likely have its own distinct record-keeping system and organizational structure.

Sub-series

A body of documents within a series that can be readily distinguished from the larger series by some common quality, such as filing arrangement, type, purpose, form or content.

Textual record

Documentary materials that are composed of written words or symbols only, rather than graphics, images or sounds. Materials that also include graphics or images may still be defined as textual if their primary purpose is to document or communicate words rather than images.

Thematic guide

See guide.

Thesaurus

A controlled vocabulary of keywords and terms showing relationships between different terms and indicating hierarchies among terms. Preferred and alternate terms are usually identified, to support the process of description and indexing.

Transfer

The administrative and physical movement of archives from the creating agency, usually an organization, government or corporate office, to an archival institution administered by the same creating agency, in order to preserve the materials for reference and research use and long-term preservation.

Trusted digital repository

A combination of people, policies, procedures and technologies that work together, ideally according to established standards and best practice requirements, to ensure that digital objects – any item to be preserved in digital form – can be captured and preserved with their authenticity as evidence protected and their content, context and structure intact, so that they may be available for ongoing use in future.

Visual archives

Documentary materials with enduring evidential or informational value that are composed of images rather than text, such as photographs, paintings, drawings or films. Materials that also include sound may be defined as audiovisual archives.

Vital records

1. Records needed to support recovery after a disaster or emergency, or records essential to protecting the assets of the organization or demonstrating its responsibilities, as well as protecting employees,

volunteers or the public. Also known as essential records. 2. Records that document significant life events, including births, marriages or deaths.

Weeding

The removal of obsolete or superseded individual documents from a file or series of records or archives.

Index